THOMAS MORE AND ERASMUS

THOMAS MORE
AND
ERASMUS

by

E. E. REYNOLDS

FORDHAM UNIVERSITY PRESS
NEW YORK

MADE AND PRINTED IN GREAT BRITAIN
NIHIL OBSTAT: IOANNES M. T. BARTON, S.T.D., L.S.S.; IMPRIMATUR: PATRITIUS CASEY,
VICARIUS GENERALIS; WESTMONASTERII: DIE 3 MAII 1965. THE "NIHIL OBSTAT" AND
"IMPRIMATUR" ARE A DECLARATION THAT A BOOK OR PAMPHLET IS CONSIDERED TO BE FREE
FROM DOCTRINAL OR MORAL ERROR. IT IS NOT IMPLIED THAT THOSE WHO HAVE GRANTED
THE "NIHIL OBSTAT" AND "IMPRIMATUR" AGREE WITH THE CONTENTS, OPINIONS OR
STATEMENTS EXPRESSED.

Contents

Contents

Illustrations

Preface

THIS BOOK is a study of the relations between Thomas More and Erasmus Roterodamus, a study of a friendship that quickly passed into legend. Some matters that would have to be considered at length in a biography of either of them, can only be touched upon in these pages. These two outstanding personalities cannot be treated in isolation. They were closely associated with other Christian Humanists, to use a label that is convenient provided we do not attempt a precise definition. The first part of the book therefore covers the same ground as Frederic Seebohm's *Oxford Reformers* (1867), a book so deservedly popular that it was reissued in Everyman's Library. The title was not well-chosen as it suggested the story of a circle of friends at Oxford who were consciously planning a reform of the Church. Perhaps the *London Humanists* would have been less misleading. Some of Seebohm's views can no longer be maintained, but the older ones of us look back with gratitude to a book that gave us so much pleasure.

It will be soon apparent that, apart from the works of Erasmus and More, my main debt is to the finished scholarship of *Opus Epistolarum Des. Erasmi Roterodami*, edited by P. S. & H. M. Allen (12 vols. 1906-1958). This contains the correspondence between More and Erasmus that is omitted from *The Correspondence of Sir Thomas More*, edited by Elizabeth F. Rogers (1947), a volume that contains the rest of his letters. My quotations from these volumes are so numerous that I have preferred not to pepper the pages with references since the reader who wishes to consult the full texts can easily trace them from the names and dates given. Other books to which I am indebted are mentioned in the footnotes. I would, however, like to recall an older book that has not been entirely superseded, R. B. Drummond's *Erasmus* (2 vols. 1873).

There is need for a full-scale critical biography of Erasmus. When it was suggested to P. S. Allen that he should write such a book, he replied that it could not be done until he had completed his edition of the letters. Unfortunately, he did not live to complete his life's work. The material awaits the biographer!

I have not added a bibliography. A list of titles and authors would have little value since more detailed information can so easily be obtained now from our public libraries. I hope that my footnotes will serve as a guide to the most helpful books.

My warmest thanks are due to my friend the Abbé Germain Marc'hadour of the Catholic University of Angers. His careful reading of my manuscript has saved me from a number of errors, and his own *L'Univers de Thomas More* (1963) has proved an invaluable and reliable guide to chronology and sources.

I regret that Mr Craig R. Thompson's translation of the *Colloquies of Erasmus* (University of Chicago, 1965) appeared too late for me to profit from its informative introduction and notes. Dare one hope that this enjoyable translation will be reprinted in a less expensive form so that it can reach a wider public?

CHAPTER I

Erasmus Roterodamus

THE FIRST MEETING between Thomas More and Erasmus became the matter of legend. In one form the story was that when Lord Chancellor More was once dining with the Lord Mayor of London, a stranger asked to see him. After some conversation, the stranger, who was Erasmus, declared, "Aut tu es Morus aut nullus". (You are More or no one.) To this More replied, "Et tu es Deus aud daemon aut meus Erasmus". (You are either God or the devil or my Erasmus.)[1] Another version describes how they met at a meal as strangers and got on to the subject of the Real Presence; this led to a similar exchange of declarations. "Aut tu es Morus aut Erasmus." "Aut tu es Erasmus aut diabolus." The Elizabethan authors of *The Booke of Sir Thomas More* set the meeting in More's house at Chelsea when he was Lord Chancellor. To test

"if great Erasmus can distinguish
Merit and outward ceremony",

More arranges for a servant to play the part of the Lord Chancellor when the Earl of Surrey brings Erasmus to be introduced. The servant bungles and the deception is uncovered. In the margin of the manuscript are the words, "et tu Erasmus aut Diabolus".

The circumstances of these folk-tales are wide of the truth. Erasmus and More first met in 1499, thirty years before More became Chancellor and twenty-five years before he left the City for Chelsea. Neither of them was well-known, still less famous, at the time of their meeting; More was then just over twenty years of age and Erasmus was his senior by about ten years. There may be a kernel of truth in these fantastic stories; perhaps

[1]It is in this form that the tradition is given in Cresacre More's biography, p. 92.

I

the first meeting was by chance. Their significance lies in their evidence of the place both men held in common repute and in the recognition that their meeting was an important event.

The year of Erasmus' birth is uncertain; scholars leave us to choose between 1466 and 1469. The uncertainty is partly the fault of Erasmus himself, and partly due to the contemporary indifference to such details; when a man announced his age, it was, as often as not, an approximation with a margin of a year or two on either side; he was never asked to produce a birth certificate, nor to fill in forms. Erasmus may not have been certain himself of the exact year of his birth, and he was careless in the use of dates. Nor does it matter very much whether he was born in 1466 or 1469; the earlier date is assumed in these pages; it is more important to note the period. Paul II was Pope and it was under his patronage that the printing press came to Rome. Charles the Bold was Duke of Burgundy, and the marriage of his daughter Mary to Maximilian, son of the Emperor Frederick III, in 1477 brought the Habsburgs to the Netherlands. Louis XI was King of France, and Edward IV, King of England. Lorenzo de' Medici was soon to dominate Florence and to gain the cognomen of The Magnificent. We can therefore see Erasmus at the parting of the way between medieval and modern times—to use terms that must not be used to imply a sudden break between one and the other.

Erasmus was born on 27 October, 1466, at Rotterdam,[2] not then an important town but a busy one. Holland (the Counties of N. and S. Holland of today) was at that period a backwater of political Europe. Its control had passed from the Bishops of Utrecht to the Dukes of Burgundy. The people were heavy-minded and, for the most part, uncultured. Erasmus was an illegitimate child, but the exact circumstances cannot now be discovered. His references to his parentage are not all of a piece. The most romantic version is the basis of Charles Reade's *The*

---

[2]"July, 1641. Rotterdam . . . the publique statue of the learned Erasmus, which of brasse and a goodly piece; so we pass'd us his house; or rather the mean cottage wherein he was borne, over which there are extant this distic in capital letters.

Ædibus tuis ortus, mundum decoravit, Erasmus,
Artibus ingenuis, Religione, Fide."
John Evelyn's *Diary*.

Cloister and the Hearth (1861). According to this the father of Erasmus was named Gerard and was one of the ten sons of Helias (or Elias). Gerard fell in love with Margaret the daughter of a physician, but before he could marry her, his brothers contrived to drive him out of Holland. He made his way to Rome and there gained a living as a copyist. News was sent to him that Margaret had died. He became a priest and returned to his native land only to learn that she was alive and had borne him a son—Erasmus. Against this must be put the fact that Erasmus had an elder brother, Peter, which rules out an affair of sudden passion. His father, Gerard, did become a priest; the moot point was whether he had been ordained before or after his liaison; if after, he was guilty of a grave sin. When Erasmus himself became a priest and sought benefices, it was necessary for him to get papal dispensation from the impediment of illegitimacy. No doubt he would have preferred to "let the dead bury their dead" since he himself was free from blame, but the exigences of canon law made that impossible; even so it may have been difficult to get the truth of a liaison that had occurred many years earlier.

The dispensation granted by Pope Leo X was addressed "Erasmo Rogerii Roterodamensis".[3] There was no uniform system of surnames in use in Holland at that time; the "Rogerus" may have been derived from a grandfather. By 1506 Erasmus had adopted the form "Desiderius Erasmus Roterodamus", the first name having been added in 1496. This adoption of Latin names was part of the contemporary academic style; thus the French scholar Jacques Lefèvre d'Etaples called himself Faber Stapulensis, and the German scholar John Hausschein used the name Œcolampadius.

It is not possible to determine how far the irregularity of his birth affected Erasmus' outlook on life;[4] it may account in part for his somewhat bitter references to his upbringing. It was a further misfortune that he lost both his parents before his future could be planned. He had his elementary schooling at Gouda, a

---

[3] In his *Lectures on Modern History*, Lord Acton spoke of 'Erasmus Roger', an appellation that must puzzle some readers.

[4] Illegitimacy was not an insuperable impediment; it may be noted that Cuthbert Tunstall was illegitimate.

small town twelve miles from Rotterdam. His father had a living near or at Gouda, which may have been his own birthplace. About 1475 the two brothers, Peter and Erasmus, were sent to school at Deventer, some eighty miles to the east of Rotterdam and just within the eastern portion of the Bishopric of Utrecht. The school attached to the Cathedral of St Lebuin was among the most famed in the country. That the father chose this school for his sons, and that the mother went with them, is evidence of strong family affection, but on this aspect of his childhood Erasmus was silent. At some period, it is not clear whether it was before the Deventer days or was an interruption of them, he was for a short time in the choir of Utrecht Cathedral. As their mother was at Deventer, it seems likely that the boys lived with her and not in the hostel or Fraterhouse of the Brethren of the Common Life, of whom more must be said presently. Not all the masters in the school were Brethren, but to one of them, John Synthen, Erasmus expressed his gratitude. During the last year or two he benefited from the influence of the headmaster, Alexander van Heek, who had himself been trained in a Frater-house and was a friend of Rudolf Husman (Agricola), one of the few Netherlanders who had studied in Italy. Erasmus remained at Deventer for some nine years; when he was eighteen, his mother died of the plague and his father called the two boys back to Gouda, and he himself died shortly after their return. Their guardians then sent them to the Brethren's school at 's-Hertogen-bosch (Bois-le-Duc) in North Brabant. There they lived in the Fraterhouse. They hoped to go to a university but their guardians kept them at school for two or three years in spite of their ages. Erasmus later blamed them for his loss of a university training and hinted that they had mismanaged his father's estate; perhaps so, but it is difficult to believe that a parish priest could have left much property; Gerard could certainly not have inherited much as he was one of ten brothers and his own chief property seems to have been some manuscripts he had brought back from Rome.

Erasmus had little good to say of his schooldays; this may have been because he was slow in his intellectual development for he was not an outstanding scholar at Deventer. This was not the fault of his schoolmasters though the regimen at 's-Hertogenbosch seems to have been severe. If he and his brother lived with their mother at Deventer, as seems likely, he escaped much of the hard life of a schoolboy of those days. By comparison, especially during adolescence, his last school must have seemed harsh. Yet he gained a thorough knowledge of Latin with the rudiments of Greek and there seems to have been little restriction on his reading, for it was in his schooldays that he laid the foundation of his wide knowledge of Latin literature. While he was at 's-Hertogenbosch his masters asked him to make a paraphrase of Lorenzo Valla's *Elegantiae*. Valla, who died in Rome in 1457, was a leading Italian humanist, but a doubtful Christian. This book was a guide to those who wished to revive the standards of Ciceronian Latin prose, and it had considerable influence. The fact that Erasmus was asked to undertake such a task is evidence that his masters were not so imperceptive as he held them to be. This intensive study of a key book in the revival of Latin studies was of considerable importance in his own development.

He blamed his schools, and later his monastery, for his poor health. There seems, however, to have been some constitutional weakness in his digestion. Yet his travels were to bring real physical hardships that do not seem to have harmed him and he lived to the age of seventy, a considerable age for those times. Perhaps his debility forced him to live temperately and so prolonged his life, but his complete absorption in his work may have been as potent a factor. A parallel may be drawn with Thomas Carlyle who grumbled about his stomach for eighty-five years.

The Brethren of the Common Life were not innovators in education if we have in mind methods of teaching. Erasmus complained that they still used medieval textbooks, yet they extended the range of reading for their pupils to include Cicero, Virgil and Horace. When all teaching was oral the textbook was not so important. The Brethren were innovators in a more important part of education, in the inculcation of the principles of right conduct and of the good life. To this Erasmus owed far more than he recognized. Unperceived by himself, he was permanently influenced by his association with the Brethren.

This calls for further consideration.

We must go back to Deventer in the second half of the fourteenth century. Gerard Groote (1340-1384), a native of the town, was trained in the schools of Paris and returned to his native land to a life of ease in the enjoyment of rich benefices, although it was not until 1380 that he was ordained deacon; he was not ordained priest. It was when he was close on thirty years of age that he experienced a conversion of life and for several years he retired to the Charterhouse at Arnhem, but his vocation was to live in the world and use his spiritual gifts for the enlightenment of ordinary folk. His preaching and his manner of life drew many to him. Among his followers was a priest, Florence Radewijns of Deventer, who was master of the Cathedral school. It was he who conceived the idea of bringing together like-minded priests and especially laymen to live together. Gerard Groote was at first doubtful as he feared conflict with the established Orders, but Florence was not thinking of a new Order. So the Brethren of the Common Life were established within the Church as a voluntary association, each group living in a Fraterhouse with possessions in common ownership. The members did not take irrevocable vows but promised to live together in poverty and continence and to devote their time to prayer, meditation and the study of the New Testament. They did not live out of the world; they supported themselves in part by copying manuscripts and they soon gained a reputation for the accuracy and fineness of their work. It was perhaps inevitable that they established schools. Among the earliest was that at 's-Hertogenbosch to which Erasmus and his brother went. Sometimes, instead of staffing the schools themselves, they became masters in other schools, as in the one attached to St Lebuin's at Deventer. Florence was also responsible for the first hostel, *domus pauperum*, for poorer pupils at Deventer; here the boys lived under the direction of the Brethren.

A second outcome of Gerard Groote's influence was as important. Some of his disciples had vocations for the monastic life. At first he was as doubtful of the wisdom of this as he had been of Florence's proposals, but he gave his consent towards the end of his life; he opposed the suggestion that they should enter one of the stricter Orders, such as the Cistercians or Carthusians, but advised them to become Canons Regular of St Augustine as they would then not be so completely cut off from the world. Two years after his death, these followers founded the monastery at Windesheim between Deventer and Zwolle. We cannot here trace the stages of their progress; their example not only led to the foundation of many independent priories (eighty-two by 1464) in the Netherlands and in the neighbouring parts of Germany, but to a revival of the true spirit of monasticism through the region.

These two groups, the Brethren of the Common Life and the Austin Canons of Windesheim, exerted a powerful influence on the religious life of the people. The characteristic of this *devotio moderna*, as it was termed, was the emphasis placed on personal sanctification through disciplined training in prayer and meditation and the study of the New Testament. We must not think of this as a movement outside the Church; it was within the Church and its adherents were devoted to the full liturgy. They did not give the importance usual at that time to popular practices such as pilgrimages and the veneration of relics, and they were unconcerned with the institutional side of the Church. They emphasized the good life. We have seen that the copying of manuscripts had a large part in the labours of the Brethren. They were not primarily scholars, but in their study of the Faith they went back to the early Fathers, particularly to St Jerome, so much so that they were sometimes spoken of as Hieronymians (Jeromians, as we might say). They turned away from the abstruse disputations of the schools and sought the sources. They were not mystics though Gerard Groote himself had found inspiration in the teaching of Blessed John Ruysbroek (1293-1381) at Groenendael.

The fine flower of the *devotio moderna* is the *Imitatio Christi* of Thomas à Kempis. He had been a pupil at Deventer about 1390 and had come under the influence of Florence; nine years later he entered the monastery of Agnetenberg of which his brother, one of the original members of Windesheim, was prior. There Thomas remained for more than seventy years until his death at an advanced age. He wrote many works but he is now known

B

chiefly for this one book which, to use Dr Johnson's expressive words, "the world has opened its arms to receive". At first it seems to be a catena of quotations from the Bible; so it is in form, but the whole has been welded together to become an inexhaustible source of spiritual discipline and encouragement. As one reads it, with Erasmus in mind, one is impressed again and again with the many similarities to his teaching. A few quotations will suffice to establish this claim.

"Let it therefore be our chiefest care to meditate upon the life of Jesus Christ." (I.1.)

"I had rather feel compunction than know its definition." (I.1.)

"Better surely is the humble countryman that serveth God than the proud philosopher who considereth the course of the heavens and neglecteth himself." (I.2.)

"O if they were as diligent in rooting out vices and implanting virtues as they are in debating questions, there would not be so much evil and scandal among the people, nor so much laxity in communities." (I.3.)

"Some carry their devotion in their books only, some in images, some in outward signs and figures." (III.3.)

"I [our Lord speaks] am he who in a moment lifteth up the humble mind to apprehend more of the reasons of everlasting truth than one that hath studied ten years in the schools." (III.43.)

"Many run to sundry places to visit the relics of saints and while listening to their deeds gaze with wonder upon the spacious buildings of their churches, look upon and kiss their sacred bones, wrapped in silks and gold. And lo! thou art thyself here present with me on the altar, my God." (IV.1.)

"It is a blessed simplicity that leaveth the difficult ways of questionings and goeth along by the plain sure path of God's commandments. Many have lost devotion when they search into things too high."' (IV.18.)

We shall see such themes developed in Erasmus' writings. The spirit of the *devotio moderna* found expression in his work. Nor is this surprising. He came directly or indirectly under the influence of the Brethren of the Common Life until he was twenty years of age, a determinative period of a man's life. The same influence was to continue, though more remotely, for another seven or eight years.

We have to rely on his own account for what followed the school at 's-Hertogenbosch. By 1497 only one of his guardians was active, the schoolmaster of Gouda. Erasmus contended that he and his brother were forced against their wills to become monks. This is difficult to believe; throughout his life Erasmus showed a sturdy spirit of independence and he resolutely took his own way. The two young men would have preferred to go to a university but we do not know if the funds were available. By this time Erasmus' love of scholarship had developed and there were few opportunities for its satisfaction outside a university or a monastery. The elder brother, Peter, gave way first of all and entered the monastery of Sion at Delft. For a few years the two brothers kept in touch but in later life they had few contacts since one remained in his monastery and the other was in the world. Erasmus was persuaded by an old school friend of Deventer days to enter the monastery of Steyn near Gouda. This was a Priory of Augustinian Canons though not of the Windesheim Congregation, but, no doubt, as a member of the same Order, it had been influenced for good by the example set them.

What mental equipment did Erasmus take with him to Steyn? His schools had given him a thorough knowledge of Latin and had encouraged wide reading; his concentrated study of Valla's *Elegantiae* had made him aware of the most advanced views on the use of Latin. He would also have shared the devotion of the Brethren to St Jerome. More important was the religious atmosphere in which he lived for so many years together with the ethical teaching he had received from men who had voluntarily accepted poverty and the discipline of community life; their example was such that at one time he had thought of becoming one of them. He was professed in 1488, and was ordained priest by the Bishop of Utrecht on 25 April 1492.

We know nothing of Erasmus as a priest, but we should not expect to know much. Of a parish priest we can say whether he is assiduous in carrying out his duties, but his inner life is not recorded. Erasmus never had a cure of souls. We must guard against assuming that silence on this aspect of his life implies that he took his obligations lightly. One assertion can be made that applies to his whole life as a Catholic. He retained the affections of William Warham, John Colet, Cuthbert Tunstall, John Fisher and Thomas More, to name some of his English friends. Is it conceivable that such men would have so regarded him, had he been a negligent priest, or had he been at variance with the teaching of the Church?

One thing can be said with certainty: Erasmus had no vocation for the monastic life, and the bitterness with which at times he criticized monks and friars may in part be attributed to his own failure to adapt himself to monastic discipline; there were more serious and well-founded reasons for his attacks on bad monks, but his experience put an edge on his remarks. There were elements in his personality that conflicted with the enclosed life. He was by nature a wanderer; in spite of the dangers and discomforts of travel in his day, he was constantly on the move. Sometimes, of course, circumstances made it necessary for him to go here or to go there, but as often it was to satisfy his craving for change of scene, or to see his friends. During the last forty years of his life, his longest period of settlement was at Basle from 1521 to 1529. Even when he did seem established for a time, as at Cambridge from 1509, or near Louvain from 1517, he would frequently go off to stay with friends. This restlessness was part of his nature. A second element may be noted. He loved meeting people. A long list could be made of his friendships with men in many countries. At all times, even in his last years when he was a sick man, he welcomed visitors, especially young students, and his doors were never closed to them. This interest in his fellow men is displayed in his *Colloquies*, where we meet a host of people of many ranks and occupations, all observed with a discerning eye. What is also noticeable is his complete lack of interest in women; he was a natural celibate.

The monastery at Steyn does not seem to have been unduly austere in its conduct; not that it was lax but some of the monks may have been easy-going and not all may have had true vocations. Erasmus seems to have had ample opportunity to follow his own studies in addition to the prescribed theological training. There was a fair library and it was there that he gained his knowledge of the works of St Jerome; he was so impressed by the letters that, he declared, "I have written every one of them down with my own fingers". He assiduously practised the writing of Latin both prose and verse and, with like-minded friends, he discussed the problems of rhetoric. The theological course would be on the established scholastic lines and he then acquired his strong dislike for the word-spinning and verbal subtleties that marked the declining stages of the system. He formed close friendships with one or two of his fellow Canons, especially with Servatius Roger[5] who, however, discouraged a relationship he thought was becoming too possessive. Perhaps he was mindful of the warning given by Thomas à Kempis against "inordinate affections". Servatius later became Prior of Steyn and there are a number of letters between him and Erasmus that show their continued friendship even when Servatius thought that Erasmus should return to Steyn.

After six years at Steyn, Erasmus became more restless. His greatest desire was to get to Italy to study Greek, but there were no funds available. Then release came towards the end of 1493 when the Bishop of Cambrai, Henry of Bergen, invited him to become his secretary; he owed this, probably, to his growing reputation as a Latinist. It was a further inducement that the Bishop was planning to go to Rome in the hope of becoming a Cardinal. The chance of getting to Italy soon faded and Erasmns found little satisfaction in accompanying the Bishop to his various residences and to the court at Brussels. While they were there, Erasmus was able to visit the Austin Canons at Groenendael of which Bl. John Ruysbroeck had been the first Prior. He there discovered the works of St Augustine and he became absorbed in reading them, but he did not find them as congenial as the writings of St Jerome. At Bergen he made a good friend in James Batt, the schoolmaster, and it was he, it seems, who suggested to Erasmus that, as he could not go to Italy, he should go to study

---

[5]Was Servatius Roger related to Erasmus? The lack of system in the use of surnames makes it impossible to be sure.

at Paris. The Bishop gave his consent and promised to support him financially, a promise that was kept only by fits and starts. So in 1495, probably in the early autumn, Erasmus reached Paris.

He went to the College of Montaigu which had been refounded by his countryman Jean Standonck (1443-1504), who had himself been a pupil of the Brethren at Gouda. This association no doubt explains Erasmus' choice of the Montaigu. Standonck was an extreme ascetic; he established a *domus pauperum* and enforced a strict regimen. If even half the complaints Erasmus made were well-founded, there must have been a lack of humaneness and common sense in the conduct of the place. Erasmus, however, recognized Standonck's merits. "In his youth", he wrote, "when he was very poor, he was very charitable, and that is much to be commended, and if he still supplied the necessities of young men by finding the means for them to continue their studies, he would not have had enough money to have spent lavishly, but he would have been praiseworthy." As for himself, Erasmus declared, "I brought nothing out of it but my body full of gross humours and my clothes full of lice". The "gross humours" he put down to the absence of meat from the diet and to the predominance of fish, a food to which he was antipathetic. His position was anomalous; he was thirty years of age and a priest, and he must have found the association with much younger men irksome, and the over-strict regulation of his life was a further irritant. He left the Montaigu in ill health in the spring of 1496 and returned to Bergen; the Bishop was kind but unhelpful. During a visit to Steyn his friends urged him to try Paris again. He took back with him some Latin poems of his fellow Canon, William Hermens, and these, with his own, were printed in a small volume. At this period Erasmus thought of himself as a poet,[6] but his Latin verses were no more than competent exercises.

On his return to Paris in the later summer of 1496, he took lodgings. He resumed his attendance at theological courses with the intention of taking his degree,[7] but the University at that period was almost untouched by the revived interest in classical

[6] A term that included at that period a writer of elevated prose.
[7] He is described as a B.D. of Paris in the records of Cambridge University. See below, p. 59.

learning that came from Italy; scholasticism still informed the teaching and Erasmus soon wearied of what seemed to him profitless speculations on unessentials. The fact was that he had not yet found a clear direction for his abilities; he was sure that he wanted to devote himself to learning, but to what purpose he was uncertain.

He gained some reputation from a eulogistic letter he contributed to a book by the ageing Robert Gaguin (1433-1501), the General of the Trinitarians, and the outstanding Latin scholar of his generation in France. Such published work was a useful introduction to learned circles, but it could not provide the necessary bread and butter.

Here it would be as well to say something of this problem of maintenance. Erasmus received occasional funds from the Bishop of Cambrai, but these were neither large nor to be relied upon. Where could a penniless student look for support? There was no family behind Erasmus; there is not a single reference to his nine married uncles who must have refused to recognize their brother's children. This in itself may have added to Erasmus' resentment of his treatment as an orphan. A student or scholar thrown on his own resources had to find a patron until he could get preferment in the Church or in a university or school. It seems that Erasmus had no liking for the business of teaching. By the time he reached Paris he was old enough to offer himself as a private tutor, but he wanted to avoid engagements that would eat into the time he could devote to learning. This complete dedication to scholarship shaped his course of conduct. So for many years he had to search for patrons. There was nothing derogatory at that period in such a relationship; indeed, it was accepted as an obligation for a nobleman or a bishop or a wealthy merchant to support scholars. We must not project back into the sixteenth century our present-day views when the State has become the patron of students. The writing of books was not in itself a source of income, but a printed book with a dedicatory epistle was a recognized way of approaching a potential patron. As we read his letters, we may get irritated at his constant appeals for money, but it should be noted that the replies were always kindly and in no way reproachful; his correspondents knew that a man dedicated to learning could not live on air. As his fame grew, so men of position thought it a privilege to make him gifts which often took the form of gold or silver cups. His own standard of living was simple; he liked plain food and a sound wine. He was unusual in his day for his fussiness about cleanliness, and his discomfort in Paris was largely due to its filth and stench. His needs were few: a room to work in with his books around him, and friends for conversation. Certainly he repaid a thousandfold any financial help he received.

On his return to Paris, he seems to have tried to live on his meagre resources but was at length compelled to take pupils. The first were Christian and Henry Northoff, the sons of a Lubeck merchant. It was for them that he composed his early *Colloquies*. These were intended to extend the boys' knowledge of Latin by collecting alternative phrases from which a choice could be made. For example:

> "Ways of greeting someone on returning from a journey—We are glad you have come home well. It is a pleasure that you have come home safely. We congratulate you on your happy return. We thank God you have returned home safe, etc."

These lists were interspersed with brief dialogues. Such were the beginnings of a literary form that Erasmus was to make his own.

Then came three young Englishmen as his pupils. Robert Fisher[8] (d. 1511) was to follow an ecclesiastical career. It was for him that Erasmus first wrote his *De Conscribendis Epistolae*, on the art of letter-writing. Of the second, Thomas Grey, not much is known. Erasmus had a special affection for him and they kept in touch in after years. Grey paid a visit to his old tutor in Basle in 1523. The third of these young men was to have a decisive influence on the course of Erasmus' life; this was William Blount, Lord Mountjoy, who had succeeded to the title in 1485 while still a boy. His guardians sent him to Paris in 1496 under the care of Richard Whitford who had, for this purpose, been given a five years' leave of absence from Queens' College, Cambridge,

---

[8]He has been described as a cousin or relative of Bishop John Fisher, but there is no clear evidence of this. After leaving Paris he studied for seven years in Italy.

of which he was a Fellow. He was to become a valued friend of Thomas More and Erasmus. Mountjoy was highly intelligent and his association with Erasmus was among the great satisfactions of his life. The intimacy between them did not come suddenly. Erasmus was still intent on getting to Italy. He paid another visit to Holland at the end of 1498 in the hope of gaining the support of the Bishop of Cambrai, but he showed little interest in the project. Meantime James Batt had entered the service of the Lady Anne of Veere at the castle of Tournehem near St Omer, and Erasmus turned to him for help in winning her as a patroness; his suggestions on ways and means of gaining her support jar on us today. Batt was only partly successful and the Lady Anne gave intermittent help for a few years, but not enough for the Italian journey. Erasmus returned to Paris in the spring of 1499, and it was then that his friendship with Mountjoy became firmly established. Erasmus continued to work hard at his writings and tutoring in the hope of scraping together enough money to get him to Italy, but it was a slow business, and it was probably with relief that he accepted Mountjoy's invitation to go with him to England in the summer of 1499.

CHAPTER II

Young More

THE FIRST DATE in the life of Thomas More that can be given with certainty is 12 February 1496 when he was admitted to Lincoln's Inn. He shares with Erasmus a doubt as to the year of his birth, but the choice is limited to 6 or 7 February 1477 or 1478, with the balance in favour of the latter. On this point Erasmus does not help us. In the account of More that he wrote for Ulrich von Hutten in July 1519 he said, "I knew him first when he was not more than twenty-three, and now he is a little over forty". That meeting was in the summer of 1499. "Not more than twenty-three" gives us 1476 or 1478; "a little over forty", if it means "between forty and forty-one", gives us 1479. In these pages we shall accept 1478 as the year of birth. When Edward IV died, More was five years old, and the Battle of Bosworth was fought when he was seven years old. He was thirty-one when Henry VII died, and was twelve years older than Henry VIII. It is as well to have these facts in mind; he is so closely associated in our thoughts with Henry VIII that we tend to overlook his experience of the period of adaptation and change during the twenty-four years of Henry VII's reign, an experience that must have affected his views of government and monarchy.

His father was John More, a lawyer, who was born about 1451; he passed his youth and early manhood during the period of civil commotion known as the Wars of the Roses, and his knowledge of all that that meant would be passed on to his son. He was the eldest son of William More,[1] citizen and baker of London, who died in 1467. John More's mother was Johanna Leycester, whose grandfather had been a Chancery clerk. It was

[1]See Margaret Hastings, *The Ancestry of Sir Thomas More*, London Guildhall Miscellany, July 1961.

probably from him that John More eventually inherited lands in
North Mimms, Hertfordshire, and these may have included the
manor of Gobions. His first wife was Agnes the daughter of
Thomas Graunger, an Alderman of London who was Sheriff in
1503. When Thomas More described himself in his epitaph as
"of no noble, but of honest stock" (to use William Rastell's
wording) he was describing the standing of a well-established
citizen family. His father's marriage took place in the parish of St
Giles, Cripplegate, on 24 April 1474. If that indicates the parish
where John More was then living, he must have moved to Milk
Street in Cripplegate Within where, according to the family
tradition, his eldest son was born. The first child was a daughter,
Jane (born 1475) who married Richard Staverton, later City
Attorney. Thomas, as we have noted, was born in 1478. A sister,
Agatha, was born in the following year, to be followed a year
later by John who does not seem to have married; he became a
skilled copyist and perhaps acted as his brother's secretary; there
is no record of his death.[2] Edward, born in 1481, may have died
young. Lastly came Elizabeth, born 1482, who married John
Rastell; their son, William, printed his uncle's works.

Thomas went to St Anthony's School, one of the leading
grammar schools of London. He was probably about seven years
old and would already know his A-B-C book. The headmaster,
Nicholas Holt, had a good reputation, and, judging from his later
scholarship, the boy must have had a thorough grounding in
Latin. After five or six years at St Anthony's, he entered the
household of Archbishop (later Cardinal) Morton to whom tribute
is paid in *Utopia*. We do not know who was tutor to the boys
attached to the household at that time; no doubt most of them were
scions of noble families. This association with boys of higher social
rank was not the least important part in Thomas More's early
training. The experience of living in the Lord Chancellor-
Archbishop's Palace at Lambeth, where the leading men of the
day would be entertained, was in itself an education in manners
quite apart from the good talk he would hear as he waited at
table. This meant that in later life Thomas More could move

[2]Erasmus referred to him in a letter dated 27 November 1511.

with ease among men of all grades of society. His quickness of intellect and sharpness of wit were shown not only in his studies and conversation but in his skill in improvisation in interludes performed in the hall of the Palace. We can glimpse what this meant in *Fulgens and Lucres* by Henry Medwall who was Chaplain at Lambeth some few years later; the lighter side of the interlude is provided by two boys. The Archbishop noted all this and remarked to one of his guests, "This child here waiting at table, whosoever shall live to see it, will prove a marvellous man". It was not therefore surprising that Morton arranged for the boy about 1492 to go to Oxford University. It is not known with certainty which College More entered. Balliol was Morton's own College, but the family tradition (according to his great-grandson Cresacre) was that More went to Canterbury College (now absorbed in Christ Church). Neither Roper nor Harpsfield named the College although the latter was an Oxford man. Canterbury College had been established from Christ Church, the Cathedral monastery of Canterbury, and was a Benedictine foundation for the study of theology. The Warden and Fellows were monks. The "poor scholars" were expected to spend five or six years there. Anthony a Wood (1632-1695) said that Cresacre More was wrong and that Thomas More went to St Mary's College (Austin Canons). There may be some confusion here. Erasmus, as we shall see, stayed at St Mary's and his later close connexion with More may have led to the belief that he also had been at St Mary's. Whether it was one or other of these two colleges, or another, to which the boy went, he recalled the experience as one of austerity as his father did not believe in pampering the young. Harpsfield tells us that More was at Oxford for "not fully two years", too short a period, one would think, to have a determinative effect on a boy of fourteen or fifteen, but it may be noted that, if he went to Canterbury College, he came under Benedictine influence.[4] Both Colleges were vigorous at that period, but

---

[3] For a brief period the monks shared the fellowships with secular priests; in 1365 the Warden was a secular—John Wycliffe. A later Warden was Edward Bocking who was condemned with the Nun of Kent.

[4] A further link may be seen in the fact that the Benedictines of Christ Church, Canterbury, admitted Sir Thomas and Lady More to their confraternity in April 1530.

Oxford had not yet been radically affected by the new interest in classical studies that came from Italy. The University was still a centre of scholasticism just as Paris was at that time. It had long been possible to learn the elements of Greek at Oxford, but its study was not regarded as essential; interest in the language was promoted when more scholars returned from Italy with the necessary knowledge and enthusiasm. It is doubtful if Thomas More learned any Greek at Oxford; it would be outside the range of studies laid down for a young student.

It should be unnecessary to confute again the notion of the young Oxford scholar being a member of a group intent on pursuing humanistic studies.[5] Thomas More was too young, even as age went in those days, for that kind of association with men who were his seniors in age and scholarship. John Colet, by ten years his senior, may have been known to him as the son of a prominent London citizen, but we cannot be sure of the dates of his Oxford years. It seems likely that he left to travel in France and Italy in 1492. Thomas Linacre had gone to Italy in 1487 with William de Selling, Prior of Christ Church and a former member of Canterbury College. William Latimer was a fellow of All Souls' and did not go to Italy until some years later but it seems unlikely that he would know the boy More. William Lily had left Oxford before More's arrival, probably in the company of William Grocyn who returned alone in 1491; here again there is no definite evidence that Grocyn, who was well over forty years of age, knew More at Oxford. Cuthbert Tunstall was a student at Balliol at that time but in later years neither referred to any acquaintanceship at Oxford. More, indeed, rarely mentioned his Oxford days. In a letter to the University in 1518, he recalled that "it was at your University that my education began". In his bantering talk with his family after his resignation from the Chancellorship, he spoke of the meagreness of Oxford fare. The impression one gets is that his Oxford days were an interlude rather than an important stage in his development.

Erasmus stated that John More "thought fit to check these

[5]The list of confraters of the English Hospice, Rome, reads like a roll-call of English Humanists: 1490, William Warham, Thomas Linacre, William Lily; 1493, John Colet; 1501, Richard Charnock; 1511, William Latimer, Richard Pace.

studies [at Oxford] by cutting off supplies, and that, indeed, More was almost disowned, because he seemed to be deserting his father's profession". What are we to make of this? It is easy to read too much into such a statement. Unless he proposed going into the Church, More's future would almost inevitably lie in the law. He was attracted to a life of learning, but, in those days, a father's wishes were imperative. As we shall see, when Thomas More had completed his legal training, he tested his vocation for the religious life. John More's own achievement had been notable. His father was a baker and his grandfather a brewer, both citizens, which argues men of some substance. The father died when John More was about sixteen years of age; by then he may have already begun his apprenticeship in the law. It was not an easy course for the son of a citizen-tradesman; the Church was a more certain way for advancement for those without social standing. His practice was probably mainly in the City where his family connexions would help him. It was not until he was fifty-two that he became a sergeant-at-law, that is when his son Thomas had already been called to the Bar. In effect, John More had raised the social status of the family and would naturally wish his son to continue in the same course. There are, however, one or two points about John More's career that are obscure. It would seem that he must have rendered some service to Edward IV. There are three indications of this. He was granted a coat of arms during the reign of that king. He was able to place his son in the household of Archbishop Morton. Thirdly, in his Will, dated 24 February 1527, he provided for Masses for the soul of Edward IV; this was more than forty years after the death of that king, and eighteen years after the death of Henry VII, who is not mentioned in the Will. All this suggests an association with Edward IV and Morton. This too would be a sign of rising social position and would strengthen the father's hope that his son would go further. Indeed, this proved more than he could have expected, for when John More died in 1530, he himself was a judge of the King's Bench Court and his son was Lord Chancellor. It is against this family and civic background that we must see the early life of Thomas More.

Civil law was not taught at Oxford; the Inns of Court in London provided the necessary training and, in effect, formed a third university. John More was content for his son to be at Oxford in response to the wish of the Archbishop until the boy would be old enough to begin his studies in the lawyer's university. Thomas More accepted this decision though perhaps with a regretful glance back at Oxford. The old Roman virtue of *pietas* was a strongly marked characteristic of his; we shall see this not only in his relations with his father, but with his own family and with his prince; he admitted their claims upon him, and he accepted the duties these imposed.

His legal training can be briefly summarized. He entered New Inn about 1494. This was one of the ten or more Inns of Chancery that provided preliminary training. Here comes our first assured date in his life; he was admitted to Lincoln's Inn on 12 February 1496. Training was partly by attendance at the Courts in Westminster Hall during term time, and partly by discussion of cases (moots) under the direction of Readers during the vacations. Little is known about how the Inns of Court were organized during the sixteenth century, but, from the scanty records that survive, the average time between admission and Call to the Bar seems to have been six to eight years. We may therefore conjecture that More was called about 1501.

When Erasmus arrived in England in the summer of 1499, Thomas More, ten years his junior, was at Lincoln's Inn with still a year to go before reaching the grade of utter-barrister (or barrister-at-law, as we should say). Mountjoy took Erasmus with him to stay at Bedwell, a manor in Hertfordshire, belonging to Sir William Say, with whose daughter Mountjoy was affianced.[6] Erasmus thoroughly enjoyed his first experience of English country life and boasted that he had become quite a sportsman. Later they moved to Sir William Say's house near Greenwich. Sir William knew the Mores sufficiently well for the father and son to become trustees of his property in 1515. Thomas More may have been at this Greenwich house when Mountjoy brought Erasmus to stay there. The opening sentence of the account

---

[6] They may have been married, but this is doubtful.

Erasmus wrote in 1523 of an incident in their early association suggests that they were already on familiar terms. "Thomas More", he wrote, "who, while I was staying in the country house of Mountjoy (*sic*), had paid me a visit, took me out for a walk for relaxation of mind to a neighbouring village." This was Eltham, Kent, and, to the surprise of Erasmus, the purpose of their visit was to pay their respects to the children of Henry VII at the royal palace. Prince Arthur was not there, but they were presented to his brother, Henry, Duke of York, who was then eight years of age. Mountjoy was there; he was studying, or was about to study, history with the young prince. John Skelton, the poet, would also be in attendance as he was the prince's schoolmaster. He was an accomplished Latinist and had some knowledge of Greek and indeed may have been at Oxford in More's time. Skelton is not usually numbered among the humanists; perhaps his later eccentric poetry and conduct may have relegated him to the background, but a reading, for instance, of *A Replication* (1527) reveals some of the marks of humanism.

Erasmus was put out at not being warned that he was going to meet the Duke of York as it was customary on such an occasion for a scholar or poet to present a set of complimentary verses; the Duke himself pointed this out. As soon as he could Erasmus afterwards composed his *De Laudibus Britanniae*, a conventional production that served its purpose. He praised "Stelkon", as he spelled the name, calling him "that incomparable light and ornament of British letters". Many years afterwards Skelton recalled the phrase in his *Garden of Laurel*.

Erasmus wrote to More a few months later:

"As I can scarcely get any letters, I have showered curses on the head of the letter-carrier, through whose laziness and treachery I imagine it must be that I have been disappointed of the most eagerly expected letters of my dear More. I neither want nor ought to suspect that you have failed on your part; nevertheless I expostulated with you vehemently in my last letter. Nor am I afraid that you are in the least offended by the liberty I took, for you are not ignorant of that Spartan method of fighting 'usque ad cutem'. Joking apart, I do entreat you, sweetest

Thomas, that you will make amends with interest for the suffering caused me by the too long lack of yourself and your letters. In short, I look forward, not to a letter, but a whole bundle of letters which would weigh down even an Egyptian porter. As for you, I am sure you will not care in what fashion I write to the best-natured of men, and one who, I am persuaded, has no little love for me. Farewell, dearest More."

More was not, in fact, a ready correspondent. In a letter to Robert Fisher that December, Erasmus wrote, "When did nature ever create a character more gentle, endearing and happy than that of Thomas More?"

Clearly Erasmus had been immediately fascinated by the young More. Yet there were considerable differences in their circumstances. Ten years separated them in ages, and to a young man of twenty this put Erasmus among his seniors, to which must be added the fact that Erasmus was a priest and an Austin Canon. Their backgrounds were also different. More belonged to an established family with the security that went with it, and an assured future in prospect. By contrast, Erasmus was illegitimate and had been ignored by his nearest relatives; he had taken monastic vows; his future, unless he returned to his monastery, depended on the uncertain support of patrons. Yet in spite of these differences, they at once formed a friendship that was to last as long as they both lived. The initial attraction may have been the younger man's facility in Latin and his wide reading, for Latin had to be the language of their conversation. There were, however, distinct similarities of character and personality. Two friends who knew them intimately bear witness to this. Richard Whitford declared that Erasmus and More might have been twins, so like one another were they in genius and character. William Latimer wrote to Erasmus, "As for More, you know yourself how quick and sharp he is, how ardent his mind, and with what energy he applies himself to any task that he undertakes; in short, how like he is to yourself." They shared a quick sense of humour and a lively appreciation of the ridiculous and both detested humbug and hyprocrisy.

CHAPTER III

John Colet

ERASMUS WENT TO OXFORD in the autumn of 1499. This visit was a turning point in his life. Not that he experienced a flash of enlightenment; his native caution made him wary of accepting new ideas until he had considered them thoroughly; nonetheless it was a determinative period. His conversations there revealed to him the limitations of his scholarship, and, at the same time, helped him to discover his life's work. Previously his love of scholarship and of books had lacked a clear objective. He was a man of letters, or poet, as he called himself. After Oxford he became a man with a mission.

The circumstances of his going to Oxford are not known. It may have been the natural desire of a scholar to meet other scholars in a famous university. There is no reason to think that he was in search of further instruction in Greek. Grocyn had just settled in London and no outstanding Greek scholar had yet taken his place at the University. As an Austin Canon, Erasmus stayed at his Order's College of St Mary's, and he soon made a friend of the Prior, Richard Charnock, a man of scholarly tastes but whose Italian experience was yet to come.[1] Erasmus praised him as "humanissimus". He in his turn was quickly captured by the personality and charm of his guest. It seems to have been Charnock who first spoke of Erasmus to John Colet who, since his return from Italy, four years earlier, had been lecturing at the University. Colet at once wrote to Erasmus offering his services. He mentioned that he had heard of Erasmus in Paris, and added:

"But the strongest recommendation to me of all is this: that the venerable Prior with whom you are staying, assured me yester-

[1] See above, p. 19, n. 5.

24

day how great in his judgment, was your worth, and how distinguished your goodness."

Erasmus replied in a letter depreciating his claims on Colet's friendship:

"You will find me a man of slender fortune, or rather of none; a stranger to ambition, but most eager for friendship; one whose acquaintance with good letters is but scanty; but his admiration most ardent; one who honours integrity in others but counts his own as none; yielding readily to all in learning, but to none in loyalty; a man of simple, open, frank disposition, ignorant alike of pretence and disguise; of a timid but upright spirit; a man of few words; in short, one from whom you must expect nothing but qualities of heart."

That self-portrait was not far from the truth, but he was certainly not "a man of few words", but it is not uncommon for a ready writer and talker to imagine himself to be barely articulate. Perhaps the most perceptive phrase was, "of a timid but upright spirit". This exchange of notes brought the two men together and so began another of those friendships that meant so much to Erasmus.

He and John Colet were about the same age. When Erasmus was leaving the Deventer school, Colet was in his first year at Oxford.[2] The details of his university career have to be inferred as the records do not exist for his period. He was there for twenty-one years with an interval for theological study abroad from 1492 to 1496. This long course of study was necessary for the degree of Doctor of Divinity which he took in 1504. He left England, to quote Erasmus, "like a merchant seeking goodly wares. He visited France and then Italy and while there devoted himself entirely to the study of the sacred writers."[3] Unfortunately very little can be added to this bare statement. He seems to have been at Orleans early in his tour, and to have spent three months in the Spring of 1493 in Rome. On his way home he stopped in Paris towards the end of 1495. Anything further is conjectural. It has been assumed

---

[2] The standard biography is still that by J. H. Lupton (1887). Our knowledge has been increased by Dr Sears Jayne in his important inquiry, *John Colet and Marsilio Ficino* (1963).
[3] See J. H. Lupton, *Lives of Vitrier and Colet*, by Erasmus (1883).

that he must have met Marsilio Facino in Florence, but the discovery of a draft letter from Colet to him sent from Oxford about April 1499 rules out personal contact. "If I can only look upon you and see you in person, I shall be truly blessed." On his return to Oxford, Colet began lecturing on St Paul's Epistle to the Romans. He broke off the course after the first five chapters. Apparently these early lectures followed established scholastic lines. He then turned to Genesis and here he showed that he had been studying Pico della Mirandola's *Heptaplus*, and Ficino's *Theologica Platonica*. Later came Ficino's *Epistolae*; Colet's copy of that book with his marginal notes is at All Souls' College. The volume also contains two letters from Ficino and the letter just mentioned to him from Colet. At the same time he was reading the *Hierarchies* of Dionysius.[4] The effect of these studies was to change Colet's methods of exegesis; emphasis was now put on the historical setting and on the grammatical meaning of the text.

When we read of a student of those times going to Italy, we assume that he wanted to perfect his knowledge of Greek and to extend his Latin studies. We think of Grocyn of the older generation, and of Linacre and Latimer of Colet's own day. But he does not fit into this pattern. He does not, in fact, answer to the accepted conception of a humanist. In writing Latin he did not show that command of the language one would expect, and, indeed, Erasmus almost apologized for Colet's Latin style. The fact that he did not learn Greek at that time is also significant. He was not in search of that kind of scholarship. Indeed his attitude to the classics was not typical of a humanist. In a comment on 1 Corinthians x, 21, "To drink the Lord's cup, and yet to drink the cup of evil spirits . . . is impossible for you", he added to his explanation of the verse, the remark, "Now if anyone should say, as is often said, that to read heathen authors is of assistance for the right understanding of Holy Writ, let them reflect whether the very fact of such reliance being placed upon them, does not make them a chief obstacle to such understanding". He seems to have concentrated on theological studies in Italy.

---

[4] Still believed to be genuine until Grocyn proved the pseudonymity in lectures at St Paul's in 1501, though Lorenzo Valla had done so earlier, but this was not widely known.

It has been pointed out that it was not until several years after his return to Oxford that Colet began the serious study of the works of Pico and Ficino. As a result his lectures took on a new character; he now wanted, as he said, "to bring out St Paul's true meaning". He was not essentially a scholar nor a pure theologian; he was a moralist and his proper place was the pulpit. This can be seen in the way in which he would interrupt his exposition in order to denounce the evils of the day. An example may be taken from his lectures on 1 Corinthians vi. On the words, "Are you prepared to go to law before a profane court?", he made some remarks on the litigious habits of the clergy. "These men", he declared, "must see what loss to religion, what diminution of authority, what neglect of Christ, what blaspheming of God, ensues from their disputes and litigations." Another instance comes in his exposition of Romans xiv, 17, "The kingdom of God is not a matter of eating and drinking this or that". Colet commented, "Now what Paul says in this passage may also be said with the greatest truth about money, possessions, tithes, oblations, and whatever else is of an earthly nature. . . . For the Church is not tithes and oblations, as men, for the most part of narrow and grovelling minds, are wont in their conversation rashly to assert. But, as St Paul says, the Church and the Kingdom of God is righteousness and peace and joy in the Holy Spirit."[5] This attitude of the moralist would have a familiar ring in the ears of Erasmus, the pupil of the Brethren of the Common Life.

Manuscripts, some in Colet's hand, have survived of a few of these lectures. They were given in Latin so Erasmus would understand them, but they were supplemented by their exchange of ideas in conversation which would also be in Latin. Fortunately Erasmus recorded three such talks or discussions. He wrote the first to his friend John Sixtin in November from Oxford. The occasion was a meal in one of the College Halls in which Colet, Charnock and Erasmus shared. It has been conjectured that this was at Magdalen and that the headmaster of the school, Thomas Wolsey, may have been present. The discussion turned on the

---

[5] See Chapter V of J. H. Lupton's *Dean Colet*; also Lupton's four volumes of translations from Colet.

question of why God accepted the sacrifice of Abel and refused that of Cain (Genesis iv, 2-8). Colet argued that Cain had offended God by showing distrust of divine providence in tilling the earth, whereas Abel had shown his trust by being a shepherd, so being content with what God would provide. It may be noted that this was the kind of conundrum that exercised the wits of school-men; Colet's explanation seems to us forced and even fanciful. Erasmus and another of the guests argued against Colet, but unfortunately Erasmus did not record their opinion; he was, however, surprised at the vehemence with which Colet defended his own interpretation. The discussion became rather warm and, to lower the temperature, Erasmus told them a legend of Cain which he declared he had found in an ancient manuscript; it was an impromptu invention of the kind that came easily to him.

"This Cain was a man of art and industry, and withal greedy and covetous. He had often heard from his parents how, in the garden from which they had been driven, the corn grew as tall as bushes unchoked by weeds. When he brooded over these things and saw how poor a crop the ground produced, he was tempted to resort to treachery. He went to the angel who was the guardian of Paradise, and plying him with crafty arts and tempting him with promises, he begged just a few grains from the luxuriant crops of Eden. A few grains were obtained and sown by Cain. After each good crop he sowed more until a large area was covered with the finest corn. When God saw this He was angry. 'I see', He said, 'how this fellow delights in labour; I will give him his fill.' So He sent locusts to eat up Cain's fields and then hailstorms. Cain tried to appease God by burnt offerings but the smoke would not rise towards heaven. From this he knew that God's anger was turned on him and he despaired."

Erasmus declared that he had never enjoyed an after-dinner discussion so much, and he wrote to Mountjoy, "I cannot tell you how delighted I am with your England. With two such friends as Colet and Charnock, I would not refuse to live even in Scythia."

He had treated this question of Cain and Abel as an exercise in dialectics and not as a vital problem. Thus in his account he wrote, "then I said, in order to play my part, the part of a poet that is . . .". He had not yet taken up a definite position, but the deep seriousness of Colet—who may have frowned at the legend of Cain—was having its effect on him; it was drawing him away from the scholar's position of detachment and forcing him to reconsider his responsibility as a priest. He never lost this lighter touch in handling such questions and his ready wit sometimes misled his readers, yet underneath it all was an earnestness of purpose such as Colet himself expressed in his more solemn manner. Erasmus may have noted that Colet's vehemence was apt to provoke his listeners.

A second conversation, this time with Colet alone, turned on Our Lord's Agony in the Garden: "if it pleases thee, take away this chalice from before me". Erasmus argued that, for the moment, Our Lord's human nature had come uppermost, but his divine nature quickly reasserted itself and brought the victory. Colet would have none of this; love casts out fear and it is therefore unthinkable that One who loved men as none other has done, would be fearful at the thought of the terrible death that awaited him. St Jerome's opinion, said Colet, was correct; it was the acute awareness of the sin of the Jews that brought this agony upon him. Erasmus was voicing the traditional interpretation and he was not prepared to accept Jerome's explanation, devoted as he was to him. The discussion was interrupted by the entrance of Prior Charnock. Colet broke off saying he was sure Erasmus would agree with him after more thought. On his return to his room in St Mary's, Erasmus studied the question more closely; then he wrote a long disquisition setting out the arguments on both sides, but continuing to maintain his own position. He ended, "How rash it is in me, a mere tyro, whom you call a rhetorician, to venture upon theological ground, to enter an arena that is not mine". Colet replied at much shorter length as he was too beset with other affairs to deal fully with the argument. "In the meantime", he wrote, "do patiently listen to me. And if, as the flints strike together, any spark of fire is given out, let us both eagerly catch at it. For it is the truth that we seek, not the upholding of an opinion; and, as argument clashes with argument, the truth will perchance flash out like fire from steel when struck by steel. I cannot agree with your statement (an erroneous one, I think, though you have many to keep you company) that the Holy Scriptures from their prolific nature, gave birth to many senses, at least in any one kind. Not that I should be slow to admit that they are prolific in the highest degree, admiring, as I especially do, their superabundant fertility and fulness; but I deem it to be of the essence of fertility that it should bring forth, not a number of things, but some one thing that is perfectly genuine."

Here we can see one aspect of Colet's thought that impressed Erasmus who, though instinctively distrusting the sterile dialectics of the later schoolmen, still used the current method of exegesis. Colet wanted something more direct with the emphasis placed on "some one thing that is perfectly genuine". Erasmus must also have been shaken by Colet's description of him as a rhetorician, that is, a man who argued for the sake of arguing or for the display of purely intellectual ability.

Colet, however, was to go further as was shown in a third conversation. This can best be given in Erasmus' own words:

"Among friends and scholars, however, he would express his sentiments with the utmost freedom. As to the Scotists, for instance, to whom the run of men ascribe a subtlety peculiarly their own, he said that he considered them dull and stupid and any thing but intelligent. For it was the sign of a poor and barren intellect, he would say, to be quibbling about words and opinions of others, carping first at one thing and then at another, and analysing everything in minute detail. Yet for some reason he was even harder on Aquinas than on Scotus. For when I was once praising Aquinas to him as a writer not to be despised among the moderns since he appeared to me to have studied both the Scriptures and the Early Fathers and had also a certain flavour in his writings, he checked himself more than once from replying, and did not show his dislike. But when, in another conversation, I was reiterating the same opinions more strongly, he looked hard at me as if watching whether I were saying this seriously or in irony. And on perceiving that I was serious in what I said, he broke out passionately, 'What, do you extol to me such a man as Aquinas? If he had not been very arrogant indeed, he would surely not so rashly and proudly have taken upon himself to define all things. And unless his spirit had been somewhat worldly, he would surely not have corrupted the whole teaching of Christ by mixing it with his profane philosophy.' Struck by his manner, I began a more careful study of this author's writings, and, to be brief, my estimate of him was undoubtedly modified."

Two points are worth noting. Some critics have implied that Erasmus had not studied Aquinas; from this passage we see that he had in fact done so and was not satisfied with just one reading. Secondly, Erasmus accepted no ready-made opinions from others; they must first pass through his own mind and be fully tested. He did not adopt Colet's views on Aquinas, which were certainly ill-founded, if not absurd. There are later references to the Angelic Doctor that show that Erasmus regarded him as a great teacher, "not second to anyone in his day", he wrote, "nor to my mind has any later theologian excelled him in thoroughness, in soundness of mind, and in solid erudition". That is a long way from Colet's outburst.

This reluctance to commit himself until he had thought things through comes out clearly in the long letter written to Colet when Erasmus had decided to leave Oxford and return to Paris. Colet was most anxious for him to stay and suggested that he should remain at the University either to expound some book of the Old Testament, or to lecture on a secular subject. Colet evidently had no doubts of his friend's qualifications for such work. Erasmus replied:

"I do not wonder that you should shoulder such a burden, but you are able to bear it, but I do wonder greatly that you should call me, a mere nobody, to be a partner is so noble a work. For you exhort me, indeed you almost reproachfully urge me, that, by expounding either the ancient Moses or the eloquent Isaiah, in the same way as you have expounded St Paul, I should try, as you say, to put life into the studies of this University, now chilled by these winter months. But I, who have learned to live in solitude, know well how imperfectly

I am equipped for such a task; nor do I lay claim to sufficient learning to justify my undertaking it. . . . With what face can I teach what I myself have not learned? How shall I kindle the chilled warmth of others while I am trembling and shivering myself? . . . Nor indeed did I come here to teach poetry and rhetoric for these ceased to attract me when they ceased to be necessary. I refuse the one task because it does not come up to my purpose, the other because I never intended to follow the profession of what are called secular studies. As to the other, you exhort me in vain, as I know myself to be too unfit for it. . . . Be it, indeed, far from me to oppose your glorious and sacred labours. On the contrary, I will promise, since I am not yet fitted to be a coadjutor, sedulously to encourage and further them. For the rest, whenever I feel that I have the requisite firmness and strength I will join you, and, by your side, in theological teaching, I will zealously engage, if not in successful at least in earnest labour. In the meantime, nothing would be more delightful to me than that we should go on as we have begun, whether daily by word of mouth, or by letter, discussing the meaning of Holy Scripture."

That extract repays careful reading. Perhaps to no other man did Erasmus speak so frankly about himself or so carefully appraise his own abilities as he did to Colet. He knew he had not yet the learning necessary for the kind of work Colet proposed. It must have been a temptation to accept the offer. It would have meant continued association with Colet and Charnock and other scholars; it would mean a livelihood; as an Austin Canon he could have lived at St Mary's. The alternative was the uncertain and hard life of a needy scholar. It was not an easy decision to make. Oxford had disturbed Erasmus. He had seen in Colet a priest dedicated to the one purpose of expounding the Scriptures and directed towards the amendment of life; he came to see that here was an objective for his own studies; poetry and rhetoric no longer held him. He must gain more knowledge before he could teach others. It does not seem that Colet suggested a study of the Greek text of the New Testament, but Erasmus saw that this was an essential for him as a basis for future work.

So he left Oxford towards the end of 1499, and after a few

weeks with his London friends he left the country on 27 January 1500. During his six months in England he had managed to gather £20 in gifts from his well-wishers. With such a sum he could look forward to supporting himself economically in Paris for some months. His hopes, however, were shattered when the customs officers at Dover confiscated £18 under a regulation against taking gold out of the country. Mountjoy and More had both told him he could do so; it was most unfortunate advice. When he landed on the other side of the Channel, Erasmus must have felt almost destitute; his carefully laid plan had been ruined. It is not surprising that for a time his admiration for England was overclouded, but he did not allow this to damage the friendships he valued so highly. So once more he faced an uncertain future.

CHAPTER IV

More's Vocation

WHEN ERASMUS LEFT ENGLAND at the beginning of 1500, Thomas More had still a year's residence at Lincoln's Inn before him. Cardinal Morton died in September 1500 and that enables us to assign some verses of More's to a date before then. An Oxford friend and a former companion in Morton's household, John Holt,[1] had become tutor at Lambeth in 1495. He wrote a short Latin grammar for his pupils, *Lac Puerorum*, and to this More added two sets of verses to encourage the boys. The first was headed "On the learned labours of Mr Holt, an epigram by the eloquent youth, Thomas More". The little book was, in a sense, a grateful tribute to their patron.

The first extant letter by More is also to John Holt. It can be dated with some assurance because in it he refers to the recent reception in London on 12 November 1501 of the Princess Catherine of Aragon for her marriage to Prince Arthur. More wrote, "I am living my life just as I desire; God grant my desires may be good". This suggests that he was enjoying his freedom after his years of legal training; he could now feel that, after carrying out his father's wishes, he could plan his own life. The letter adds, "I have put away my Latin books to take up the study of Greek". His instructor, he noted, was William Grocyn, but he also had the help of William Lily, now living in London after some years abroad in Rhodes and Italy. It has been pointed out that Colet, Linacre, Latimer, Lily and Erasmus were all at least ten years older than More. This suggests that he must have matured intellectually very early in contrast with Erasmus' slower development. Nowhere is there any hint that these older men regarded More as their junior.

[1] He may have been the son of More's old schoolmaster, Nicholas Holt.

After qualifying as an utter-barrister about 1501, More, as Roper tells us, "read for a good space a public lecture of St Augustine, *De Civitate Dei*, in the church of St Lawrence in the Old Jewry; whereunto resorted Dr Grocin, an excellent man, and all the chief learned of the City of London". He dealt with the historical and philosophical aspects of the book rather than the theological. Roper continues, "Then was he made Reader of Furnivall's Inn, so remaining for the space of three years and more". The position of Reader, or lecturer, carried the responsibility for the training of those preparing to enter Lincoln's Inn. Then comes in Roper's account an important passage. "After which time, he gave himself to devotion and prayer in the Charterhouse of London, religiously living there without vow, four years." That seems definite enough but it raises a problem in chronology. If we take the minimum period of three years for More's Readership at Furnivall's Inn, we reach the date 1504. Now it can be said with some confidence that he married either at the end of that year or very early in 1505. How then can we fit in the four years at the Charterhouse? Clearly he did not withdraw completely from the world; he must have frequented the Charterhouse whenever his other duties allowed. It should not be forgotten that there were many Holy Days in the year at that time, and these could be given to his devotions at the Charterhouse. He may have lodged in the guesthouse,[2] but Cresacre More was probably recording a family tradition when he wrote that Thomas More was "dwelling near the Charterhouse". Cresacre conflates with this Stapleton's statement that More "thought for a time of becoming a Franciscan". Stapleton does not mention the Charterhouse but added that More and his friend Lily considered becoming priests. Here is one of those confusions that cannot now be disentangled. The important fact is that Thomas More felt drawn towards the monastic life and tested his vocation as thoroughly as he could short of entering the novitiate.

Erasmus wrote, "At the same time [after his legal training] with

---

[2] See the plan in *Charterhouse*, by Dom David Knowles and W. F. Grimes (1954). Lincoln's Inn was about three-quarters of a mile from the Charterhouse.

all his strength he turned towards the religious life, by watching, fasting, prayer, and similar tests, preparing himself for the priesthood; more wisely than the many who rush blindly into that arduous calling without making trial of themselves. And he had almost embraced this ministry, but being unable to master the desire for a wife, he decided to be a faithful husband rather than an unfaithful priest." This plain statement has been twisted to mean that More was shocked at the laxity of the monks. Even at the worst period of the suppression, not a shadow of scandal fell upon any of the Charterhouses. "Never reformed, because never deformed." It may be noted that John Colet, a stern critic of morals, frequented the Charterhouse at Sheen and planned to pass his last days there.

To this period can be assigned much of More's verse-making. He had an urge to write, to put his ideas on paper, and his inventive powers were later to find greater scope, but, like Erasmus, he began with poetry; none of it is remarkable but it helps us to see his state of mind. The best of his poems was a "Lamentation of the death of Queen Elizabeth" in 1503. His love of fun led him to write "A Merry Jest how a Sergeant would play the Friar". To these must be added verses for some tapestries in his father's house and some contributed to a "Book of Fortune". He had a liking for the Chaucerian seven-line stanza. This is not the only indication that he knew his Chaucer for there are other references and echoes. It was not until he was in the Tower thirty years later that he again made English verses "for his pastime".

Roper alone tells us that Thomas More was a Member of Parliament at the beginning of 1504, but his constituency is not known. The Commons then met in the Chapter House of Westminster Abbey, one of the few remaining places in which we can picture him in contemporary surroundings. According to Roper, Thomas More, probably voicing the objections of the City merchants, opposed Henry VII's demands for exceptional grants. This is not improbable but there is no confirmation of the story.[3] A further incident involving Bishop Fox and his chaplain,

[3]Roper's statement must be treated with some reserve.

Richard Whitford, suggests that the King was so incensed that More fell under his displeasure. There are, however, no signs in the known facts of More's life in support of this, but, again, it is not impossible. This Parliament was dissolved on 30 March and was the last of the reign. By this time, More may have been already contemplating marriage.

Meanwhile Colet had left Oxford. For a time he lived with his parents at Stepney where he was vicar. In May 1504 he was appointed to a Prebend in St Paul's and in the following year became Dean. A letter from More dated 23 October 1504 reveals something of the close relations that had developed between them.[4] Erasmus recorded Colet's opinion of their young friend. "John Colet, a man of keen and exact judgment, often observes in intimate conversation that Britain has only one genius, though this island is so rich in men of ability." When More wrote this letter, Colet was absent from London, perhaps at his other country living at Dennington in Suffolk.

"As I was walking in the law-courts [Westminster Hall] the other day, not myself being very busy, I met your servant. I was delighted to see him both because I have always been fond of him and especially because I thought he would not be here without you. But when I heard from him not only that you had not returned but that you would not do so for some time, my joyful expectation was changed to unutterable dejection. No annoyance that I could suffer is to be compared with the loss of your companionship which means so much to me. I have come to rely on your prudent advice, to find my recreation in your pleasant company, to be stirred by your powerful sermons, to be edified by your life and example; in short, to be guided by even the slightest indications of your opinions. When I had the advantage of all these helps, I used to feel strengthened; now that I am deprived of them I seem to languish and grow feeble. By following your footsteps I had escaped almost from the very gates of hell, and now, driven by some secret but irresistible force, I am falling back again

[4] The letter is known from Stapleton's *Tres Thomae*; it may originally have been in English and what we have is Stapleton's translation. This applies to other letters for which we have only Stapleton's version.

into the gruesome darkness. . . . For city life helps no one to be good, but rather, when a man is straining every nerve to climb the difficult path of virtue, it tempts him with every kind of allurement and drags him down to its own level with its manifold deceits. Wherever you turn, what do you see around you? Pretended friends, and the sweet poison of smooth flatterers, fierce hatreds, quarrels, rivalries and contentions. Look again and you will see butchers, confectioners, fishmongers, carriers, cooks and poultrymen, all occupied in serving sensuality, the world and the world's lord, the devil. Houses block out from us a large measure of the light, and our view is bounded not by the round horizon but by the lofty roofs. I really cannot blame you if you are not yet tired of the country where you live among simple people, unversed in the deceits of the towns. Wherever you cast your eyes, the smiling face of the earth greets you, the sweet fresh air invigorates you, the sight of the heavens charms you. You see nothing but the generous gifts of nature and the hallowed traces of innocence. But yet I do not wish you to be so enamoured of these delights as to be unwilling to return to us as soon as possible. But if you are repelled by the unpleasantness of town life, then let me suggest that you should come to your country parish of Stepney. It needs your fatherly care, and you will enjoy there all the advantages of your present abode and be able to come from time to time for a day or two into the city as if to an inn where so much useful work awaits you. For, in the country, where men are for the most part innocent, or certainly not enslaved by gross vice, the services of any physician can be helpful. But, in the city, because of the great numbers that congregate there and because of their long-standing habits of vice, no physician can do much good unless he be of the highest skill. Certainly there come from time to time into the pulpit of St Paul's preachers who promise us health, but, although they speak very eloquently, their life is in such sharp contrast to their words that they do more harm than good. For they cannot bring men to believe that though they are themselves obviously in direst need of the physician's help, they are yet fit to be entrusted with the cure of other men's ailments. Thus when men see that their diseases are being prescribed for by physicians who are themselves covered with sores, they immediately

1a. ST THOMAS MORE: *Medallion by Raymond Joly* (1961)

1b. ERASMUS: *Medallion by Quentin Metsys* (1519)

2. ERASMUS

by Quentin Metsys (1517)

become indignant and refuse to accept their remedies. But if, as observers of human nature assert, he is the best physician in whom the patient has the greatest confidence, it is beyond all doubt that you are the one who can do most for the cure of all in the city. Their readiness to allow you to treat their wounds, their trust, their obedience, has been proved to you by past experience, and is, in any case, clear now by the eagerness and expectation with which all are looking forward to your coming. Come then, my dear Colet, for Stepney's sake which mourns your long absence as deeply as a child his mother's, for the sake of your native city which should be no less dear to you than are your parents; finally, though I cannot hope that this will be a powerful motive for your return, come for my sake who am entirely devoted to you and anxiously await your coming.

Meanwhile, I pass my time with Grocin, Linacre and our dear friend Lily. The first, as you know, is the sole director of my life during your absence; the second my master in study, and the third the beloved partner in all my concerns. Farewell, and, as I know you do, ever love me."

This somewhat stilted letter provides an insight into More's mind at the age of about twenty-five. The reference to "the very gates of hell" hints at some profound religious crisis in which the spiritual guidance of Colet had proved decisive. This was written at the time when More made his final choice between a life of contemplation in the cloister and a life in the world as a married man and active lawyer. The letter suggests what a searching experience this had been and how far More was still dependent on the direction of Colet. It reveals an element in More's personality that can be underestimated by those who put most stress on his humour and good nature. There were two tendencies in him. The one is shown in the attraction to a life devoted to religion; the second in his very human longing for family life. Somehow the two had to be reconciled. In this letter his dislike of all that the world means is uppermost and is exaggerated; it was not an attractive picture that he drew of the life around him. This was an attitude we can find also in Colet's sermons. We can see traces of it throughout More's life. His *Treatise on the Four Last Things*,

D

set aside as unfinished about 1521, is a grim meditation; it is not a comfortable piece of writing. When his beloved daughter Margaret was at death's door, he declared that had she died "he would never have meddled with worldly matters after". In his grounds at Chelsea—twenty years after this letter was written—he had a building apart to which he could withdraw for "devout prayers and exercises". Holbein never more truly showed his insight than when he painted his great portrait of Thomas More; here is no witty, companionable father and friend, but a man whose thoughts were centred on the profound truths of life. It seemed as if he almost welcomed imprisonment in the Tower; it became his monastery. "I assure thee, on my faith, if it had not been for my wife and you that be my children, I would not have failed long ere this to have closed myself in as strait a room, and a straiter too." To the Councillors he said, "I had fully determined with myself, neither to study nor meddle with any matter of this world, but that my whole study be upon the Passion of Christ and mine own passage out of this world". So we reach the calm serenity of his testament, *A Dialogue of Comfort*.

This consideration has taken us ahead of chronology but it concerns an essential factor in his life that must not be forgotten. We must return to the period of his qualification as a lawyer. About 1504 he translated a life of Pico della Mirandola (1463-1494) with some selections from his writings and some verses on themes of his suggestion. This was produced at the same period as the letter just quoted, and it may be that Colet drew his attention to the book. Cresacre More suggested that the translation was made when More was "determined to marry", since it provided him with "a pattern of life". This may be so, but it may equally well have been done while his mind was still uncertain since it is a study of a young scholar who, but for his sudden death, would have become a Dominican friar; in fact, he had faced the same choice as More himself was facing. It would have been appropriate that Colet, More's spiritual director, should have drawn his attention to this parallel case. The book is addressed to a friend, Joyce Leigh (Lee), who was about to take the veil, or had already done so, in the Convent of the Minoresses or Poor

Clares at Aldgate.[5] The young Lees and Mores had been play-fellows in childhood; there was a brother, Edward, of whom we shall hear something further. There is nothing particularly apposite to the married state in the book; had it been it would not have been an appropriate offering to a nun. Pico combined the best of Italian humanism with true piety, and though to us he may seem a dim figure, to Thomas More he was a near contemporary. Here was a young man who had devoted himself eagerly to learning in many fields yet could not find rest in his scholarship; just before his early death, he decided to renounce the world. A life that in some respects reflected More's own problem captured his attention and in Pico's high ideals he found a pattern and a stimulus, but he took a different path from that chosen by Pico.

We get a picture of a very busy man; his work as Reader and practising lawyer; his lectures on St Augustine; his Greek studies; his meetings with his scholar friends; his attendance at sermons at St Paul's; his early verse-making; his Parliamentary experience; his devotions at the Charterhouse, and his visits to Netherhall, the home of his future wife—all this could have left little if any leisure. Then came his marriage, perhaps a month after that letter to Colet.

When he was about sixteen, More had fallen in love with a girl named Elizabeth, but they were kept apart. Twenty-five years later, he met her again and wrote some verses on the occasion. "The years, always envious of young beauty, have robbed you of yourself, but have not robbed me of you." When he came to marry it was to a daughter of John Colt of Netherhall, near Roydon, on the Herts-Essex border, about twelve miles from Gobions, the country home of the Mores. John Colt's father had been Chancellor of the Exchequer to Edward IV and this suggests the link with John More. The two families were on friendly visiting terms. Netherhall manor was held of Cardinal Morton. There were eighteen children in the Colt family, eleven of them girls. Thomas More married the eldest, Jane, towards the end of 1504 or early in 1505. There were four children: Margaret (b. 1505), Elizabeth

[5]The Minories, near the Tower, perpetuates the name.

(b. 1506), Cecily (b. 1507), and John (b. 1509). Jane More died in 1511. When he came to compose an epitaph for the chapel he added to the parish church at Chelsea, More described her as his "dear little wife" (*uxorcula*); that is how he remembered her nearly twenty years later when he had her remains transferred to the new vault.

Erasmus must have come to know Jane More well when he was a guest at The Barge in Bucklersbury where the Mores set up their home. Of her he wrote:

> "He married a young girl of good family, who had been brought up with her sisters in their parents' home in the country: choosing her, yet undeveloped, that he might the more readily mould her to his tastes. He had her taught literature, and trained her in every kind of music; and she was just growing into a charming life's companion for him, when she died young."

Erasmus may have been referring to Thomas and Jane More in his *Colloquy* on *The Discontented Wife* (first published in 1523), when he gave this picture of a newly married couple:

> "I have the honour to be acquainted with a gentleman of noble family, learned and of singular address and dexterity. He married a young lady of seventeen years of age, that had been educated all along in the country in her father's house. He had a mind to have a raw inexperienced maid that the more easily he might form her manners to his own humour. He began to instruct her in literature and music and to use her by degrees to repeat the heads of sermons that she heard. Now these things being wholly new to the girl she soon grew weary of this kind of life and she absolutely refused to submit to what her husband required of her."

This tallies in several points with the account just quoted from Erasmus, but it would be a mistake to see an exact record as given in the *Colloquy*, where the author would give some play to his imagination. Our sympathies are surely with Jane More; her young husband was a bit heavy-handed, but it may be noted that she had a firmness of spirit that was part of her elder daughter's inheritance. The story goes on to say that the young couple paid a visit to her father in the country. The husband complained to his father-in-law of her obstinacy. He had a talk with his daughter and the difficulty was resolved.

In 1524 Erasmus added *The Exorcism* to his *Colloquies*. It is tempting to see here a recollection of a prank played by More before his marriage when he used to visit the Colts. John Colt is there called "Polus", which in Greek means "colt". No name is given that can be recognized as the equivalent of More but the son-in-law of Polus is described as "a wonderful merry droll", and, it is added, "he would leave the most urgent affair in the world if such a comedy were either to be seen or acted". In the earlier *Colloquy* (*The Discontented Wife*) Erasmus had described the father (John Colt, as may be assumed) as "so wonderful cunning a man, that he would act any part as well as any comedian", and, certainly, Polus in this *Colloquy* lives up to that description. Briefly, he decided to play a trick on an over-credulous priest; in this scheme, his son-in-law convincingly took the part of a ghost draped in a white sheet and carrying a partly-obscured light.

Erasmus was able to renew and strengthen his friendship with Thomas More and to meet his young wife when he returned to England at the beginning of 1505.

CHAPTER V

Erasmus Learns Greek

ERASMUS HAS LEFT US a word-portrait of Thomas More:

"In stature he is not tall nor noticeably short, but he is so well-proportioned that you could not wish him otherwise. His skin is fair and his complexion neither pale nor ruddy but warm. His hair is dark blond or a darkish brown, his beard thin; his eyes bluish-grey and flecked. His nature may be read by his expression —always pleasant, friendly and cheerful with a smiling look, more suited to merriment than to grave dignity, but far removed from silly buffoonery. His right shoulder looks a little higher than the left, particularly when he is walking. Nothing else is remarkable except that his hands are somewhat clumsy compared with the rest of him. From boyhood he has not bothered about his outward appearance. His voice is neither strong nor feeble, but easily audible, not soft or melodious but that of a clear speaker. He has no natural gift for singing though he delights in all kinds of music."

Against that it is interesting to place a description of Erasmus written in 1540 by Beatus Rhenanus who first met Erasmus in Paris in 1504 and was to work closely with him in later years at Basle. In writing this description, Rhenanus seems to have had Erasmus' account of More before him as a model.

"In stature Erasmus was not a tall man, nor noticeably short, his figure being compact and elegant. His complexion was fair, with hair that in his younger days had a touch of red; his eyes were bluish-grey and his expression was lively. His voice was not powerful, his language beautifully chosen, his dress respectable and sober. He was most constant in his friendships, not one was ever broken. His memory was most retentive; as a boy he knew the whole of Terence and Horace by heart. He was liberal to the poor, to whom, as he returned from Mass, and on other occasions, he used to give money by his servant. He was especially generous and kind to any young and promising students who asked his help. In society he was polite and genial, without any air of superiority."

It is unfortunate that there are no early portraits of the two friends. Both were fifty years of age when surviving portraits were painted. For More we have to rely on Holbein's great painting of 1527 and the preliminary drawings. Erasmus was painted by Quentin Metsys in 1517 and by Holbein in several paintings from 1523 to 1532. Dürer made a sketch in 1520 and an elaborate engraving in 1526. It must be admitted that it is not easy to reconcile the portraits by these three artists; were they not labelled, I doubt if we should identify those of Metsys and Dürer as of the same person painted by Holbein, but there is a fine medallion by Metsys of 1519 that does suggest the later Erasmus of Holbein.

When Erasmus landed at Boulogne in the last week of January 1500, he found it necessary to go to Tournehem to refill his purse. James Batt did not fail him and at the beginning of February Erasmus was back in Paris, not in the moderate comfort to which he had looked forward on leaving England, but aware that he had a hard struggle before him. He had not given up his dream of Italy, but it now seemed farther off than ever. He began his studies in Greek but was not satisfied with his first instructor; thereafter he seems to have worked on his own by the system of translating into Latin from the Greek and then back again. In order to support himself he compiled what was to prove his most popular book, *Adagiorum Collectanea*, usually referred to as his *Adages*. The idea had been talked over at Oxford, and Charnock had urged him to carry it out. Mountjoy added his encouragement. This first edition, published in Paris in June 1500, contained 818 quotations, each with a brief explanatory note. The volume was dedicated to Mountjoy. The 1500 edition was but a shadow of what the book was to become in the course of many later editions each containing additional quotations. The scope was extended to cover Greek literature, each adage with its Latin translation, thus providing a useful adjunct to the study of Greek. The comments were also expanded and, as we shall see, the later editions became vehicles for conveying Erasmus' opinions on a wide range of topics.

For each edition Erasmus would receive a fee from the printers; this would no doubt increase in amount as his reputation spread; in addition he was given a number of copies of the book. We know that he sent a hundred copies to Grocyn of the first edition because at the end of 1504 Erasmus asked Colet to find out what had happened to them. "No doubt, after such a long time, the books must be sold and the money must have come to somebody, and it is likely to be more use to me now than ever before."

He wrote to James Batt in April 1500, "I have been applying my whole mind to the study of Greek, and as soon as I receive any money, I shall first buy Greek authors, and then some clothes". The plague drove him from Paris to Orleans in September but he was able to return three months later; in May 1501 a further outbreak of plague in Paris sent him off to Holland. He did not return to Paris for three years, a period that proved most productive. He went first to his monastery at Steyn, and later to Tournehem to stay with James Batt and to remind the Lady Veere of his needs. Later he stayed with the Abbot of St Bertin's at St Omer and from there went on to Louvain. It was at St Omer that he first came to know Jean Vitrier, a Franciscan friar who had been a pupil of Gaguin in Paris. Erasmus was quick to recognize and praise goodness and sanctity; one may note, for instance, the esteem he had for Bishop John Fisher of Rochester. In Colet he found a dedicated priest whose life reflected his teaching. So now in this Franciscan friar he saw the single-minded Christian. Erasmus, as we shall see, had little that was good to say of friars; in that, it must be admitted, he was in tune with popular opinion. It was therefore all the more memorable to meet such a man as Jean Vitrier, who himself, according to Erasmus, found the daily routine of a friar's life irksome. "Yet at no time did he counsel anyone else to change this way of life, or attempt anything of the kind himself, being ready to bear all things sooner than be a stumbling block in anyone's way." Did Erasmus sense here a rebuke to his own rejection of a life he had found burdensome? If so, he showed no sign of it in the character sketch he made of his new friend, a sketch he combined with one of John Colet. The two had things in common. Erasmus found to his delight that Vitrier, though trained in the "subtleties of Scotus", was so devoted to the Epistles of St Paul that "no one could be more intimately acquainted with his own finger-nails than he was with St Paul's writing". His sermons were not formal discourses stiffened with quotations, "now from Scotus, Aquinas and Durandus, now from Canon Law Doctors, or again from the philosophers or the poets, so that people come to think they know everything. The sermon he would deliver would be full of Holy Scripture, nor would he quote anything else. What he said came from the heart. He was possessed, good soul, with a zealous desire to draw men to the pure wisdom of Christ." That last phrase, "the pure wisdom of Christ", was often used by Erasmus as the ideal knowledge all should strive to gain. Vitrier had to suffer some persecution from those who resented his call to holy living, and the Dominicans cited him for heresy; his opposition to the trade in indulgences under Alexander VI (Borgia) led to trouble with his bishop. Finally he was relegated as confessor to a small convent. "There, with character un-changed, still, as far as was allowed him, teaching, consoling, exhorting, he peacefully ended his days." We can see here the qualities of a priest that always commanded Erasmus' admiration and respect. It may be that the example of Vitrier was one that influenced Erasmus' own conduct of his life.

It was to Jean Vitrier that Erasmus submitted his first sub-stantial work, the *Enchiridion Militis Christiani* which was begun at Tournehem and completed at Louvain during the years 1501-3. It is difficult to find a satisfactory English form for the title. Erasmus gave two explanations in the book itself. In the first he describes it as "this little treatise called *Enchiridion*, that is to say, just a little dagger which you must have always at hand"; the second explanation reads, "a little treatise fit to be carried in a man's hand". The first English translation, reputed to be by William Tyndale, though not published until 1533, was entitled *The Manual of the Christian Knight*. In the edition of 1518,

Erasmus stated that "some time ago I made it for myself and for a certain unlearned friend of mine". To Colet he wrote in December 1504, "The *Enchiridion* I wrote to display neither genius nor eloquence, but simply this—to encounteract the vulgar error of those who think that religion consists in ceremonies, while they neglect what really pertains to piety. I have tried to teach as it were the art of piety in the same way that others have laid down the rules of military discipline." That is an inadequate summary of this little book in which throughout the emphasis is put on the religion of the spirit. It is not unrelated to the teaching of *The Imitation of Christ*. The abuse of ceremonies was a minor theme, but, neither in this, nor in censuring other abuses, was Erasmus content to denounce. Thus on ceremonies he wrote, "I in no wise rebuke or check the ceremonies of Christians and of devout simple persons, that is, in such things as are approved by the authority of the Church; for they are partly signs of piety and partly helpers thereunto. It is not meet they should be disdained of them which are perfect lest by their example the weak person should take harm." So too in condemning an inordinate esteem for relics of saints, he wrote, "You honour saints and rejoice to touch their relics, but you despise the chief relics which they left behind them—their examples of pure living. There is no honour more pleasant to Mary than if you copied her humility. No religion is more acceptable to saints or more appropriate than if you laboured to reproduce their virtues." And again, "Do you honour the bones of St Paul in the shrine but not the mind of St Paul in his writings?" Such topics, however, were not the main theme of the book. His purpose was to provide a guide to the good life as revealed in the Gospels and Epistles. He seems to have had two chapters of St Paul in mind—the fifth chapter of Galatians and the sixth chapter of Ephesians. "Take up all God's armour, then, so you will be able to stand your ground when the evil time comes." One of the characteristics of the book is the constant reference to St Paul; here one can see the influence of Vitrier and Colet. It is interesting to note that Erasmus did not share Colet's objection to classical authors. His opinion was, "It is profitable to taste the learning of the ancient authors if it be done with caution and judgment, and further, with speed after the manner of a man who intends only to pass through the country and not to dwell there, provided, and this is the essential point, that all is applied and referred to Christ. For so all shall be clean to them that are clean." Colet, however, would have agreed with the advice, "Of the philosophers my opinion is that you should study Plato because he and his followers come nearest the thought of the prophets and of the Gospels".

The *Enchiridion* was first printed in February 1504 at Antwerp in a volume of miscellaneous writings entitled *Lucubratiunculae aliquot*; this included an account of the discussion between Colet and Erasmus on the Agony in the Garden. The *Enchiridion* did not attract much attention at that time and it was not until it was separately printed in 1518 that it became a popular book and was translated into other languages. Erasmus sent a copy of the *Lucubratiunculae* to Colet in June 1504; by then Erasmus had returned to Paris. They had not corresponded for several years. "I cannot tell you, most excellent Colet", wrote Erasmus, "how I am devoting myself with all my powers to the Scriptures and how I loathe everything that calls me away from that study, or even retards me. But the unkindness of fortune, who constantly regards me with the same sour look, was to blame that I could not free myself from these trifles. With this intention, accordingly, I returned to France so that, should I be unable to finish them, I may somehow throw them aside." Erasmus was here referring to such bread-and-butter tasks as he could pick up, such as writing dedications, panegyrics, and the like. He continued, "Then I shall be free to devote myself with my whole heart to the Scriptures in which I mean to spend the rest of my life. Three years ago I attempted something on the Epistle to the Romans, but I found myself deficient in Greek. Accordingly, for about three years I have been wholly occupied in Greek." He appealed to Colet for financial aid and hinted that perhaps Mountjoy would also help him so that he need not spend so much time in earning ready money. He mentioned that he was working on a new edition of the *Adages* which was printed in Paris in 1505. The letter ended with greetings to John Sixtin and Richard Charnock.

Evidently Erasmus thought that Colet was still at Oxford although designated Dean of St Paul's.

Another work that Erasmus saw through the press at Paris was the first printing of Lorenzo Valla's *Annotations on the New Testament*. During his three years in the Low Countries, Erasmus had visited a number of monasteries and convents to search their libraries for manuscripts. In the convent of the Premonstratensian Canonesses at Louvain—a most unlikely place—he found the manuscript of Valla's *Annotations*. He was an Italian humanist of the first half of the fifteenth century; he was absorbed in pure scholarship and untroubled by religious convictions.[1] Erasmus was well aware of the risk he ran in printing anything by such a suspected author. His own attitude to learning was given in the *Enchiridion*. "Whoever takes upon himself to fight the whole host of vices must provide himself with two special weapons—prayer and knowledge, otherwise called learning. Prayer pure and perfect lifts your soul to heaven, a tower beyond the reach of your enemies. Learning or knowledge arms the mind with sound principles and opinions and keeps you ever in remembrance of virtue so that neither can be lacking to the other. These two cleave together like friends, the one always meeting the need of the other. The one makes intercession and prays. The other shows what is to be desired and for what you should pray." Erasmus defended Valla's notes on the ground that they added to our knowledge of the text of the New Testament. Valla had concentrated on grammar and meaning and on errors he had found in translations; he had not ventured on interpretation. Erasmus pointed out that St Jerome had not claimed that a translator was inspired since his accuracy depended on his knowledge of Greek and Hebrew. Once the text had been established by the scholar, the theologian could take over, confident that the words he interpreted were authentic.

It is difficult to assess the influence of Valla on Erasmus; it was not a question of religious faith but of scholarship. Valla demonstrated the importance of establishing an accurate text as the only sound basis for exegesis. In this way he may have helped to focus

[1]For Valla, see Pastor, *History of the Popes*, I, pp. 13-22.

Erasmus' hitherto nebulous desires to promote a more lucid interpretation of the Scriptures. Valla had died before the age of printing set in, so his work was not widely known. Erasmus recognized his debt when he said, only two years before his death, "I place Valla among those of whom posterity should always preserve the memory".

Erasmus had thus come to see the importance of having a reliable text of the New Testament in Greek. A second task he had long had in mind was a new edition of the works of St Jerome. He was eager to get on with both these projects, but he still hoped to get to Italy to perfect his knowledge of Greek. It may be as a result of his letter to Colet that he was invited, perhaps by Mountjoy as well, to pay another visit to England. Perhaps they sent him funds for the journey, or the money he received from the printers for the new edition of the *Adages* and for Valla's *Annotations* made it possible for him to revisit his friends in London.

CHAPTER VI

Erasmus in England, 1505-6

THERE IS no detailed record of Erasmus' movements during his second visit to England; he seems to have divided his time between Mountjoy, Colet, More and Grocyn. At Stepney he stayed at the house of Colet's parents. The mother, Dame Christian, seems to have taken to Erasmus for, as late as 1516, she often made, as her son wrote, "cheerful and pleasant mention" of their former guest. It was at Colet's suggestion that Erasmus made a new translation into Latin of the Greek New Testament. For this he lent him two manuscripts from the Chapter Library of St Paul's. Unfortunately it is not known how old these were as they perished in the Great Fire of 1666 when the valuable library was destroyed, the same fire in which Colet's monument perished.

Erasmus made some new friends. He came to know William Warham, Archbishop of Canterbury and Lord Chancellor, John Fisher, recently made Bishop of Rochester and Chancellor of Cambridge, Richard Fox, Bishop of Winchester, Thomas Ruthall, the King's secretary and soon to be Bishop of Durham, and, of the older generation, Christopher Urswick, who, after a successful career as a diplomatist, had withdrawn to his benefice of Hackney where he spent the last twenty years of his life in retirement from public affairs. Both Erasmus and More must have gained much from their conversations with Urswick for few men had a greater experience of state matters than this close friend of the Lady Margaret Beaufort and her son Henry VII.

Of these new friends Archbishop Warham and Bishop Fisher were to prove the most constant supporters of Erasmus. Fisher had few resources, but Warham was generous in his gifts to the scholar for many years. This association with an Archbishop and two Bishops made it possible that an English benefice might be offered to Erasmus. With this in mind, he saw the need for getting the canonical defect of his illegitimacy removed. By the influence of his friends, this was done by a papal brief issued by Pope Julius II in January 1506.

Towards the end of 1505, Erasmus wrote to his friend Servatius Roger of Steyn from "London, from the bishop's palace". Both Fisher and Fox had palaces at Lambeth, as well, of course, as the Archbishop, but it seems likely that Erasmus was staying with Fox as his friend Richard Whitford was the bishop's chaplain. In this letter Erasmus wrote, "I have been some months with Mountjoy who pressed me to return to England not without the encouragement of eminent scholars. For there are in London five or six Latin and Greek scholars of deepest learning such as not even Italy could now show." The "five or six" would not include Colet and Fisher as neither knew Greek. The names that come to mind are: Grocyn, Linacre, Lily, More, Latimer, and perhaps Tunstall who had just returned from his six years in Italy and may have met Erasmus for the first time. In the same letter Erasmus set down his own intentions for he was answering an inquiry from Servatius Roger who thought it was time he returned to Steyn. Erasmus wrote, "I am considering again how best to devote the rest of my days entirely to piety and to Christ. I know that my constitution is delicate and that my strength has been weakened by study and also by misfortune. I see no freedom from study. So I have determined, content with my mediocrity, especially now that I have learned as much Greek as I need, to apply myself to thoughts about death and the salvation of my soul. I ought to have done so before this and have made better use of precious years." It may seem strange to us that a man of forty should turn his thoughts to death, but men then died at an age we should now consider young; plague and pestilence were ever-present threats. The fact that his decision to rest content with the learning he had so far gained was a passing mood, does not detract from the sincerity of his purpose. It was about this time that More completed his version of Pico's life and works and composed, on themes drawn from Pico, as his own addition,

Twelve Weapons of Spiritual Battle. His verses reflect the same mood expressed by Erasmus.

Erasmus, as always, was hard at work while in London. As part of his search for a more thorough knowledge of Greek, he translated into Latin the *Hecuba* and *Iphigenia* of Euripides; these he presented to Warham in manuscript in January 1506. In the same month he offered to Bishop Fox a translation of Lucian's *Toxaris*. He shared his interest in Lucian with More. What was it that so attracted them? In the dedication to Christopher Urswick of a translation of Lucian's *Micyllos*, Erasmus wrote, "Such is the grace of his style, the felicity of his invention, the elegance of his wit, the sharpness of his satire, that no comedy, no satire, that was ever written, can be compared with his dialogues, either for the pleasure or for the instruction they afford". Of this particular dialogue he noted, "You have here a cock talking with a cobbler, his master, more ludicrously than any professional jester, and yet more wisely than the vulgar herd of divines and philosophers in their schools, who, with a noble disdain of more important matters, dispute about pompous nothings". So Erasmus could see in the contemporary world material for the pen of a Lucian, and his own genius could supply the wit and satire. More had the same turn of mind and the two friends could enjoy Lucian and then apply the same method of criticism to the abuses they saw around them.

More translated *Cynicus, Philopseudes,* and *Necyomantia.* He and Erasmus both translated *Tyrannicida* and then each wrote a rhetorical declamation on the theme. The problem was that in a country where tyrannicide was rewarded by the state, a man killed a tyrant's son, and the tyrant then, for grief, committed suicide. The question posed was, "Is the assassin entitled to the reward?" Both Erasmus and More argued that he was not so entitled. We may note that this kind of conundrum was typical of some of the logic-chopping of the times, and also that Erasmus and More were to show in their later writings a strong dislike of tyranny in all its forms. In a dedicatory letter to Richard Whitford of the declamation on the *Tyrannicida,* Erasmus paid tribute to their friend Thomas More:

3. PETER GILLES
by Quentin Metsys (1517)

4. JOHN COLET
Drawing by Hans Holbein, at Windsor Castle

"For several years, my dearest Richard, I have been entirely
occupied with Greek literature; but lately, in order to resume
my familiarity with Latin, I have begun to declaim in that
language. In so doing I have yielded to the influence of Thomas
More, whose eloquence, as you know, is such that he could
persuade even an enemy to do whatever he pleased, while my
affection for the man is so great that if he bade me dance or hang
myself, I should do so at once. He is writing on the same subject
and in such a way as to thresh out and sift every part of it. For
I do not think, unless the vehemence of my love leads me astray,
that Nature ever formed a mind more alert, ready, discerning
and penetrating, or in a word more completely furnished with
every kind of faculty. Add to this a power of expression equal
to his intellect, a singular cheerfulness of character and an
abundance of wit, but only of the good-humoured kind, and
you miss nothing that should be found in a perfect advocate.
I have therefore not undertaken this task with any idea of either
surpassing or matching such an artist, but only to break a lance
as it were in this tourney of wits with the sweetest of all my
friends, with whom I am always pleased to join in any employ-
ment grave or gay. I have done this all the more willingly
because I very much wish this kind of exercise to be used in
schools where it should be of the greatest value."

The method was, in fact, used by Thomas More when his own
children and their companions were old enough to form his
"school". The praise Erasmus lavished on his friend may seem
extravagant and we must make allowance for this enthusiasm;
it was however a noticeable trait in the character of Erasmus that
he always praised his friends in the warmest terms; he never
showed the least sign of envy of their merits, nor indeed of their
worldly success.

He arranged for these translations to be printed by Badius in
Paris with the title *Luciani Opuscula* . . . *ab Erasmo Roterodamo et
Thoma Moro*. It was published in November 1506 and was
reprinted at least thirteen times during More's lifetime; Erasmus
added translations of other dialogues in later editions, but More
did not increase his share.

As a preface to his part of the book, More wrote a letter to
E

Thomas Ruthall, the King's secretary. The writer raised the question of the value of such classical writings to a Christian, a problem, as we have seen, considered by Colet and Erasmus.[1] More favoured Erasmus' view.

"Why indeed should I care for the opinion of a pagan on matters which are among the chief mysteries of the Christian faith [e.g. the immortality of the soul]? The dialogue *Philopseudes* teaches us, on the one hand, not to put faith in the illusions of magic, and on the other to keep our minds clear of the superstition that creeps in under the guise of religion. We shall lead a happier life when we are less terrified by those dismal and superstitious lies which are often repeated with so much confidence and authority that even St Augustine himself, a man of highest intelligence, with the deepest hatred of a lie, was induced by some impostor to narrate as a true event which had happened in his own time that story about the two Spurini, one dying and the other returning to life, which, with only a change of name, had been ridiculed by Lucian in this very dialogue so many years before. No wonder then if ruder minds are affected by the fictions of those who think they have done a lasting service to Christ when they have invented a fable about some saint or a tragic description of hell which either reduces an old woman to tears or makes her blood run cold. There is scarcely any life of a martyr or virgin in which some falsehood of this kind has not been inserted; an act of piety no doubt considering the risk that truth would be insufficient unless propped up by lies! Thus they have not scrupled to stain with fiction that religion which was founded by truth herself and ought to consist of naked truth. They have failed to see that such fables are so far from aiding religion that nothing can be more injurious to it. It is obvious, as St Augustine himself has observed, that where there is any scent of a lie, the authority of truth is immediately weakened and destroyed. Hence a suspicion has more than once occurred to me that such stories have been largely invented by crafty knaves and heretics partly for the purpose of amusing themselves with the credulity of persons more simple than wise, and partly to diminish the true

[1]This letter should be taken into account in considering Roper's story of how More fell out of the King's favour. There is nothing in it to suggest that More was seeking the secretary's mediation.

Christian histories by associating them with fictitious fables, the feigned incidents being often so near to those contained in holy scripture that the allusion cannot be mistaken. Therefore while the histories commended to us by divinely inspired scripture ought to be accepted with undoubted faith, the others tested by the doctrine of Christ should either be received with caution or rejected if we would avoid both empty confidence and superstitious fear.''

It was about this time, that is 1506, that Thomas More paid a visit to Coventry to see his sister Elizabeth who, a few years earlier, had married John Rastell, at the time of More's visit coroner of Coventry. The Rastells moved to London about 1510. At Coventry More had an encounter with a friar; this he described in a letter written to a monk about 1520.[2] The friar had declared that whoever recited daily Our Lady's Psalter (one hundred and fifty Hail Marys) could never be damned. The parish priest in vain warned his people that they should not believe such nonsense.

"While this question was raging, it happened that I arrived at Coventry on a visit to my sister. I was scarcely off my horse when the question was put even to me, whether anyone could be damned who daily recited Our Lady's Psalter. I laughed at the foolish inquiry, but was at once warned that I was doing a dangerous thing since a most holy and learned friar had preached against those that did so. I dismissed the matter as no affair of mine. I was then invited to dinner; I accepted and went. In comes an old friar, dryasdust, severe and sour; a boy follows him with some books. I saw that I was in for an argument. We sat down, and, so as to lose no time, the question was at once put by our host. The friar answered just as he had preached. I said nothing as I do not like to meddle in annoying and fruitless disputes. At last they asked my opinion. As I was obliged to speak, I told them what I thought, briefly and moderately. Then the friar poured out a long prepared speech which might have made two sermons. His whole argument depended on certain miracles which he read from a *Mariale* and from other books of that kind. When he had at last finished, I quietly answered that he had said nothing in his whole discourse capable of convincing those who did not admit the truth of those miracles which they might deny without abjuring the Christian faith, and that even if they were absolutely proved, they had little to do with the question. For though you may find a king ready to pardon something in an enemy at the prayers of his mother, yet there is nowhere one so foolish as to promulgate a law encouraging the disobedience of his subjects by a promise of impunity provided they paid homage to his mother. Much was said on both sides, but I only succeeded in getting laughed at while he was smothered with praise. . . . I have not related this in order to impute crime to any body of religious, since the same ground produces herbs both wholesome and poisonous. Nor do I wish to find fault with the custom of those who salute Our Lady, than which nothing can be more beneficial, but because some trust so much in their devotions that they draw from them boldness to sin."

These extracts from letters and dedicatory epistles by Erasmus and More show how closely their thoughts converged. It was inevitable that Erasmus as the older man should exert influence over the younger man and in their talks in Bucklersbury, and while working on Lucian they must have discussed a wide range of subjects. More was receptive but it would be misleading to regard him as an echo of Erasmus; his own strong intelligence contributed its part to their discussions. He too was greatly disturbed by the tenuous hold true religion had on the people around him. Much could be blamed on unlearned priests and on those more intent on gaining benefices than on gaining souls. We see the signs of disillusionment in his letter to Colet. He could not fail to notice how easily simple folk could be gulled, and how devotional practices, that were good and profitable in themselves, could be debased into something akin to superstition. It is almost instinctive for a man of intellectual power and with a turn for wit to use ridicule and satire as a weapon against abuses. The work of Lucian chimed with the mood of the two translators; the same critical spirit could pass on to consider the contemporary state of religion. Erasmus, Colet and More were anxious to purge the Church of abuses; how best this could be done was not yet clear, nor did they draw up a programme of action. Fortunately there were as yet no signs of schism, nor of any heretical upheaval within the Church. The tragedy was that such sincere Catholics as these three friends were unable to make an effective protest; they were not alone in their anxiety, for it was shared by others in Italy and France. A decade was to pass before Martin Luther made his protest and so brought about the cataclysm.

Erasmus was at Cambridge at least once, possibly twice, during this period. He was entered at Queens' College as a pensioner of Henry VII sometime between August 1505 and April 1506. In the choice of Cambridge rather than Oxford we may see the influence of Bishop Richard Fox and of Bishop John Fisher who was then Master of Queens' and of Richard Whitford who was a Fellow. Dr John Caius, who became a student of Gonville College in 1529, recalled a tradition that Erasmus was present when Henry VII visited Cambridge for the Feast of St George in 1506. This seems possible as Erasmus, described as a B.D. of Paris, had applied for admission to the doctor's degree before Easter of that year. Presumably he planned to go into residence, but suddenly came the longed-for opportunity of getting to Italy. Henry VII's physician, Giovanni Boerio, was looking for someone to accompany his two sons to Italy; perhaps Mountjoy suggested the name of Erasmus and he was invited to make the journey. So early in June 1506, after a long and stormy crossing of the Channel, he landed in France with his two charges.

CHAPTER VII

Italian Interlude

ERASMUS SPENT a week or so in Paris in the summer of 1506 before setting out for Italy. He wrote to a number of friends in England expressing his gratitude for their kindnesses to him. To Colet he wrote:

"When I arrived once more in France, it is hard to say how mixed were my feelings. I cannot easily tell you which weighed most, my joy in visiting again the friends I had left in France, or my sadness in leaving those I had recently found in England. This I can truly say—there is no one country which has given me friends so numerous, so sincere, so learned, so obliging, so noble and so accomplished in every way as the City of London has done. Each has so vied with the other in affection and helpfulness that I cannot tell whom I prefer. I am obliged to love them all alike. The absence of these must needs be painful, but I take heart again in the recollection of the past, keeping them as continually in mind as if they were present, and hoping that it may so turn out that I may soon return to them. I trust you, with my other friends, to do your best for the sake of your love and interest for me to bring this about as soon as you can."

We need not concern ourselves with the details of Erasmus' three years in Italy.[1] A few matters call for notice. He reached Turin in August and spent two or three weeks there during which he qualified for the degree of Doctor of Divinity. He claimed that he did so purely on the advice of his friends who thought that a doctorate would give him a more secure standing in the academic world and also lead to preferment. Presumably he

[1]The Italian years are examined closely in Augustin Renaudet, *Érasme en l'Italie* (1954). Some of the scholar's conclusions in this and his other important Erasmian studies are open to question.

engaged in disputations and the University would take into account his theological studies at Steyn and Paris and his association with Oxford and Cambridge; even so it must have been a perfunctory business.

On 11 November 1506 he witnessed at Bologna the triumphant entry of Julius II at the head of his troops. The Pope had launched war against Perugia and Bologna and had rapidly conquered the two cities. This spectacle of the Pope exulting over his fallen enemies filled Erasmus with horror and the Papal triumph made a lasting impression on his mind. "The high priest Julius", he wrote, "wages war, conquers, triumphs, and in effect plays the part of Julius [Caesar]."[2]

Erasmus settled at Bologna with his charges in January 1507, and while there profited from the friendship of Paul Bombasio, the leading Greek scholar of the University. At the end of the year he was free of his engagement with the Boerio boys and went to Venice where, for nearly nine months, he worked closely with Aldus Manutius, the famous printer. Erasmus had written to him on 28 October from Bologna. He congratulated Aldus on his output of Greek and Latin classics and added that scholars were looking forward to the projected edition of Plato in Greek. He expressed his surprise that Aldus had not yet printed a Greek New Testament. This suggests that Erasmus himself had not finally decided to work on such an edition himself. He sent Aldus his translations of the *Hecuba* and *Iphigenia* and hoped that the printer would undertake new editions "in your types, particularly the smaller types, the most beautiful of all". Aldus had made the first italic type designed for use in pocket editions of the classics. One passage in the letter throws light on the manner in which authors and editors were remunerated in those days. "If you insist on my having one hundred or two hundred copies, though the god of gain does not usually favour me, and such a package would be awkward to transport, I shall not say 'no', if only you fix a horse as the price."

Aldus Manutius was himself a scholar and he was glad to wel-

---

[2]Scholars dispute Erasmus' authorship of the biting satire entitled *Julius exclusus a coelis* (1518); he never categorically denied his responsibility, but, 'Aut Erasmus, aut nullus'.

come Erasmus to Venice. The two plays were printed and then Erasmus revised and greatly enlarged his *Adages*; this new edition, containing 3,260 quotations, appeared in September 1508. Many of the additions were from the Greek and, in selecting these, Erasmus had the use of Aldus's own library and of manuscripts readily lent to him by Venetian scholars. He found the atmosphere of the printing-shop most congenial, and it was noticed that he could go on preparing his copy or correcting proofs quite oblivious of the clatter and bustle around him. He would become completely absorbed in his work; it was this power of concentration that enabled him to produce the vast amount of work for which he was responsible. It was in Venice that he gained valuable experience in the whole craft of printing.

He lodged with Aldus's father-in-law, Andrea Asolano, who provided bed and board for over thirty of the household and printing staff. Greek was the language used at mealtimes. For several months Erasmus shared a room with Jerome Aleander, a man of great gifts who later left the paths of scholarship for those of church preferment; he became one of Erasmus' most bitter critics. Years later Erasmus added to his *Colloquies* one entitled "Sordid Wealth" in which he gave an unfavourable portrait of Andrea and the over-frugal regimen he imposed on his lodgers. It was the kind of ungracious lapse of which Erasmus was occasionally guilty. He was, in fact, not temperamentally fitted for communal living; he discovered this at Steyn and it proved true in Venice. Andrea was a man of parts; when Aldus died in 1515, Andrea successfully carried on the business until his nephew Paul was old enough to assume responsibility. It was at Venice that Erasmus suffered for the first time from the stone, and this may have sharpened his criticism of the meals he so disliked. Nothing could be done in those days to cure the disease, and the victim had to endure the attacks of pain as best he could. He did not allow it to interfere with his labours. He believed that good wine, especially the heavy wine of Burgundy, was beneficial and this explains the fuss he made about maintaining a supply. One of his objections to living in England was the difficulty in getting the wine he wanted.

He left Venice in the autumn of 1508 on taking up the position
of tutor to Alexander Stewart, the illegitimate son of James IV
of Scotland. This youth of fifteen had been appointed Archbishop
of St Andrew's three years before going to Italy. They passed
the winter at Padua. During a visit to Ferrara, Erasmus met
Richard Pace who was later to be a colleague with Ruthall,
Tunstall and More at the time of the Field of Cloth of Gold in
1520. So another friend was added to the long list that Erasmus
was forming. With his pupil he went on to Siena and then to
Rome where he passed several months broken by a journey to
Naples. Alexander, who became greatly attached to Erasmus, left
Rome for Scotland in the middle of May 1509.[3] At parting he
gave Erasmus a seal-ring engraved with the head of the god
Terminus. To this Erasmus added the motto *Concedo nulli* and
used it as his seal. Years later his critics declared that the motto
was an expression of his self-admiration; he explained that the
motto referred to Terminus (the last boundary stone) and not to
himself and was meant as a constant reminder that death is the
terminus of life.

It seems that Erasmus could have established himself in Rome
as he won the regard of Cardinals and other members of the
papal curia. He was tempted to remain, but he was still looking
towards England and the friends he had made there. Unfortunately
not many of his letters of the Italian period have survived but it
would appear likely that he had hinted how much he would like
to return to London if it could be made practicable for him.
This was certainly part of the intention of the letter he had written
to Colet from Paris on his way to Italy. The death of Henry VII
on 21 April 1509 opened the way. Mountjoy wrote to Erasmus
from Greenwich on 27 May. It seemed to his generation that
with the young king a happier era had dawned. So he urged
Erasmus to come to England and take advantage of the new
opportunities. "The Archbishop of Canterbury [Warham] is not
only absorbed in your *Adages* but he promises you a benefice and
sends you five pounds for your journey." To this Mountjoy added
another five pounds. This letter was probably written by Andrea

[3]Alexander and his father were killed at Flodden in 1513.

Ammonio, an Italian Latinist, who had been sent to England as apostolic notary and papal collector. He soon became one of Mountjoy's circle and particularly the friend of Thomas More with whom he lodged for some time. Erasmus left Rome at the end of June 1509.

What had he gained from his three years in Italy? Not what he had hoped for in 1493 when he first dreamed of Italy; his great desire then was to study Greek under the Italian masters, but during the long postponement he had studied Greek and had gained a sound knowledge of the language, though, owing perhaps to the way in which he had learned it, mainly by self-tuition, his knowledge was never that of the finished scholar. Undoubtedly his association with Bombasio in Bologna meant an advance in his learning. His residence in Venice was the most fruitful period of his Italian years. The Greek manuscripts he was able to study when revising his *Adages* greatly extended his reading and to this he added manuscripts in the libraries in Rome. He travelled widely in Italy from Turin to Venice down to Rome and Naples. This gave him a new world of folk to observe; he, a northerner, was brought into touch with the warmer civilization of the south. There was, however, one limitation; he did not learn Italian, just as he had not troubled to learn English and French save for sufficient of the speaking language for daily purposes. This may have been part of his intellectual economy, as it may be termed. He concentrated his mental energy on the classics and would not waste it on unnecessary learning. In Rome he came to know a few of the influential members of the curia and saw something of the government of the Church; this was a gain to one who was deeply concerned with the condition of Christian life. The leading attraction in Rome, as elsewhere, was for him in its libraries. The antiquities made little appeal to him and he seems to have travelled up and down Italy without a keen awareness of its wealth of architecture and paintings. Michelangelo, Raphael and Bramante were all at work in Rome while he was there, but they went unmentioned. Indeed the same observation may be made of the humanists with whom we are here concerned; they showed little appreciation of the arts apart from portrait painting. Nor can we find in their letters and other writings any references to current literature apart from controversial works. It is true that it was not a creative period in literature but it was not quite barren.

While Erasmus was in Italy, Thomas More was making progress in his professional career. It was probably in the summer or autumn of 1508 that he paid his first visit to the continent, going to Paris and Louvain where one of his interests was the course of studies and methods used in the Universities. He seems to have met Lefèvre d'Étaples in Paris. It may have been at this period that he and his friend William Lily engaged in friendly rivalry in making translations from the Greek anthology.[4] The coronation of Henry VIII and Catherine of Aragon on 24 June 1509 produced one long Latin poem and four short ones from Thomas More. The presentation copy of these is now in the British Museum. The *Carmen Gratulatorium* welcomed the coming of a new age. The day should be marked with a pure white stone as the beginning of freedom. The references to the extortions of Henry VII are unequivocal. "Now no one hesitates to show the possessions he has hitherto hidden from sight. Now it is possible to enjoy any profit which escaped the sly, grasping hands of many thieves." Yet the merits of the dead King were not overlooked. "You, Sire, have the wisdom of your father, your mother's kindly strength, the intelligence of your paternal grand-mother [Lady Margaret Beaufort] and the noble heart of your mother's father [Edward IV]. What wonder then if England rejoices since she has such a King as never before?" Thomas More was here reflecting the mood of the whole country at the opening of the new reign.

John Colet's father, Sir Henry, died late in 1505, leaving his only surviving son a considerable fortune. We have very few details of the Dean's life at this time; he was doing much to make St Paul's a more active centre of true religion but it was uphill work trying to clear the accumulated bad usages. He was also planning to apply his inheritance to the foundation of a new school, of which more must be said later and of the help that Erasmus gave him.

[4]Their versions were published in 1518. On the difficulty of dating, see *The Latin Epigrams of Sir Thomas More*, ed. L. Bradner and C. A. Lynch (1953).

CHAPTER VIII

Moria

ERASMUS REACHED LONDON in August 1509 and he went to stay first with Thomas and Jane More in Bucklersbury; there were now four children including the baby, the son John.

It has been a long and wearisome journey from Rome to London, without, it seems, any companion other than his servant. He had ridden over two hundred and fifty miles by way of Bologna, the Splugen Pass, to Lake Constance. It was easier after that as he could travel much of the way by boat down the Rhine. He broke his journey at Louvain before making the Channel crossing of which he was always apprehensive. When he arrived at Bucklersbury, he was prostrated by an attack of the stone; he was waiting for the books he had collected in Italy. He has been wrongly called a valetudinarian; much as he grumbled about his illnesses, or the cold weather, or draughty or over-heated rooms, his brain and pen were always active, and he had now arrived in London with a brilliant idea bubbling in his head. It was to find expression in his little book variously known as *Moriae Encomium*, *Stultitiae Laus*, *Moria*, or in English, *The Praise of Folly*. It was dedicated to his host, Thomas More.

"In my late travels from Italy to England", wrote Erasmus, "that I might not trifle away my time in the rehearsal of old wives' fables, I thought it more to the point to employ my thoughts in reflecting upon some past studies, or calling to remembrance several of those highly learned, as well as sharp-witted friends I had left behind here, among whom you were represented as the chief; whose memory, while absent at this distance, I respect with no less complacency than usual while present to enjoy your more intimate conversation, which last gave me the greatest satisfaction I could possibly hope for.

Having therefore resolved to do something and thinking that time improper for anything serious, I thought good to divert myself by drawing up a panegyric on Folly. What maggot, you say, put this into your head? Why the first hint was your own surname More, which comes as near the literal sound of the word *moria* as you yourself are distant from the significance of it, and that in all men's judgments is very wide. In the next place, I supposed that this kind of sporting wit would be more especially accepted by you who are accustomed to this kind of jocose raillery (such as, if I am not mistaken, is neither dull nor impertinent) to be greatly pleased, and in your ordinary talk to prove yourself a Democritus junior; for truly, as you do from a singular vein of wit very much differ from the common herd of mankind, so, by an incredible affability and pliableness of temper, you have the art of suiting your temper to all kinds of company."

During that thousand-mile journey from Rome, Erasmus must have reviewed in his mind the impressions he had received from his many contacts with scholars and clerics during the past three years; for a decade before that, since leaving Steyn, he had lived in France and England as well as in Flanders and Brabant. He must have met a wide variety of men and women as he travelled from inn to inn. In a matter of fifteen years he had seen more of people and places than was usual for a man of his age. Out of this store of experience, he was able to draw material for the study of mankind and its humours. His *Colloquies* alone bear witness to the keenness of his observation.

It was almost inevitable that his commentary should take the classic form of a rhetorical declamation; the originality was in putting the words into the mouth of Folly herself. Perhaps "Folly" is no longer the appropriate word to use in English; it conveys to us the idea of near imbecility and stupidity, but Erasmus' Folly was the incarnation of light-heartedness, high spirits and fun. It would not be straining the meaning too far to say that his little book is a defence of a sense of humour and of sincerity.

We can easily imagine the delight with which More listened as his friend read to him each evening the result of his day's writing. Other friends would join them. Ammonio seems to have been living with the Mores at this time, but Colet, Lily, and perhaps Grocyn would drop in and share the fun. They might suggest a touch here or more emphasis there. More liked the play on his own name and he used *Moria* as the title of the book when he wrote about it. This atmosphere of fun-making must not be allowed to overshadow the underlying seriousness of purpose. *Moria* and *Utopia* have been described by one modern author as "mere youthful amusements".[1] This in face of the fact that Erasmus had passed his fortieth birthday and that when More wrote *Utopia* he was serving on an important embassy. It is of course true that neither ever lost his sense of the ridiculous, but this is not to suggest that their best-known books were frivolous diversions. Once their salad days had passed, they wrote with a definite purpose in mind. They were not out to write pure literature. All their mature work was an expression of their belief in the importance of Christian morals and the wisdom of Christ. It was part of their achievement to show that wit and humour, satire and irony, could all be used in the service of righteousness, and that dullness and goodness are not synonymous.

The first part of *Moria* is Folly's praise of herself and of her benign influence on men's lives. This section takes up half the book; it is amusing and light-hearted. She claims that "I appear always in my natural colours", and has nothing but scorn for those who put on a pretence of wit and folly; among these she includes "some modern orators" who "deem it a doughty exploit if they but interlard a Latin sentence with some Greek word". It was this passage and others in which Folly laughs at ponderous scholarship that prompted Pope Leo X to say "I am glad our Erasmus is in *Moria* himself". Folly proceeds to give her ancestry and to describe her training and her attendants. Then she boldly asserts that she is the source of all the joy in life and that all its benefits come from her. There is a pleasant picture of the foolishness of childhood matched by the foolishness of old age; "it is a great kindness on my part that old men grow foolish since it is hereby only that they are freed from such vexations as

[1]Louis Bouyer, *Erasmus and the Humanist Experiment (Autour d'Érasme)*, p. 102.

would torment them if they were more wise". Folly is the best preservative of youth and the most effective antidote against age. As a balance to the "stiffness and morose humour" of the grown man, Folly prescribes "taking a wife, a creature as harmless and silly yet so useful and convenient". Again it is Folly "that makes true friends and keeps them so" since men are "by nature so prone to frailties, so humoursome and cross-grained" that they could not bear one another unless Folly blinded them to one another's faults. Self-love is another quality that makes life tolerable, "for we should sink without rescue into misery and despair if we were not buoyed up and supported by self-love, which is but the elder sister of Folly and her constant friend and assistant. For what is or can be more silly than to be lovers or admirers of ourselves?" "To enlarge further, I may well presume to aver that there are no considerable exploits performed, no useful arts invented, but that I am the respective author and manager of; as first, what is more lofty and heroic than war? And yet, what is more foolish than for some petty, trivial affront, to take such a revenge as both sides shall be sure to be losers, and where the quarrel must be decided at the price of so many limbs and lives?" Here was a theme to which Erasmus was to return again and again. Folly also ridicules Plato's notion that "happy are those commonwealths where either philosophers are elected kings, or kings turn philosophers". She shows by examples from history that when affairs are directed by "some learned bookish governor" the result is disastrous. We shall see this topic taken up in *Utopia*, as well as the subject of war and peace. Folly laughs at those who sweat and toil to win "new titles and distinctive badges of honour". She claims to be wiser than wisdom, for who is most serviceable to the world, "the wise man who can proceed resolutely to no attempt, or the fool that goes hand over head, leaps before he looks, and so ventures through the most hazardous undertaking without any sense or prospect of danger? In undertaking any enterprise, the wise man runs to consult his books and dazes himself with poring upon musty authors while the dispatchful fool rushes blindly on and does the business while the other is thinking of it."

The tone of the book changes when Folly comes to review her retinue. It is now the direct voice of Erasmus rather than Erasmus speaking by the mouth of Folly. The transition is skilfully done, but a harsher note is sounded. It is this portion of the book that has always attracted most attention; this is a pity as it tends to obscure the underlying purpose. There would be little point here in examining each member of the procession as it passed before Folly and occasioned her biting comments: lawyers, philosophers, divines, schoolmen, monks, friars, preachers, kings, courtiers, bishops, cardinals and popes. They are marked by pride, ostentation, affectation, self-seeking and hypocrisy. Much of this diatribe falls rather flat in our ears, especially that directed at the clergy, though echoes of it may occasionally be heard. There is, of course, the historical value of a contemporary view of society; human frailties and vices have not been banished but they take new and more subtle forms from age to age. We cannot afford to point the finger of scorn at our ancestors. The work that Erasmus did in his own times has to be repeated in each generation but the incidence changes.

The short concluding portion of *Moria* demands more careful examination as it gives the intention of the whole work. Erasmus accused the theologians and priests of his own day of wresting scriptural texts in accordance with their own predilections and thus perverting the true meaning. Here is a bantering reference to himself:

"Nay, St Paul himself, that great doctor of the Gentiles, writing to his Corinthians readily owns the name saying, *If any man speak as a fool, I am more*, as if to have been less so had been a reproach and disgrace. But perhaps I may be censured for misinterpreting this text by some modern annotators, who like crows pecking at one another's eyes, find fault and correct all that went before them, pretend each other their own glosses to contain the only true and genuine explication, among whom my Erasmus (whom I cannot but mention with respect) may challenge the second place, if not the first."

He gives an example of perverse interpretation:

"I myself was lately at a divinity disputation, where I very often pay my attendance, where one of the opponents demanded a reason why it should be thought more proper to silence all heretics by sword and faggot rather than convert them by moderate and sober arguments. A certain cynical old blade, who bore the character of a divine, legible in the frowns and wrinkles of his face, not without a great deal of disdain, answered that it was the express injunction of St Paul himself in those directions to Titus—*A man that is an heretic after the first and second admonition, reject*—quoting it in Latin where the word *reject* is *devita*; all the auditory wondered at this citation, and deemed it in no way applicable to his purpose. He at last explained himself saying that *devita* signified *de vita tollendum hereticum*, a heretic must be slain. Some smiled at his ignorance, but others approved of it as an orthodox comment. And however some disliked that such violence should be done to so easy a text, our hair-splitting and irrefragable doctor went on in triumph."[2]

Erasmus then turned to those passages in the first Epistle to the Corinthians in which St Paul says, "We are fools for Christ's sake", and, "If any man among you seemeth to be wise in this world, let him become a fool that he may be wise, for the wisdom of this world is foolishness with God." (I, iii, 18.) So Folly is led to declare that "all the final happiness which Christians through so many rubs and briars of difficulties contend for is at last no better than a sort of folly and madness". The whole argument cannot be given here, but a final quotation will show the deep seriousness that underlies this little book that has the deceptive appearance of a scholar's diversion. Folly is speaking of truly pious souls.

"By the same rule they measure all the other offices and duties of life, in each of which, whatever is earthly and corporeal shall, if not wholly rejected, yet at least be put behind what faith makes *the substance of things not seen*. Thus in the sacraments and all other acts of religion, they make a difference between the outward appearance or body of them and the more inward soul or spirit. As for instance, in fasting, they think it very ineffectual

[2]This story was not in the 1511 edition but was added in the Basle edition of 1519. There is reason to believe that it records an incident in the Convocation at St Paul's in 1512 when John Colet preached a notable sermon. See below, p. 81.

F

to abstain from flesh, or debar themselves of a meal's meat (which yet is all the vulgar understand by his duty) unless they likewise restrain their passions, subdue their anger and mortify their pride; that the soul being thus disengaged from the entanglement of the body, may have a better relish to spiritual subjects and take a foretaste of heaven. Thus, say they, in the Holy Eucharist, though the outward form and ceremonies are not wholly to be despised, yet are these prejudicial, at least unprofitable, if as bare signs only they are not accompanied with the thing signified, which is the *body and blood of Christ*, whose death, till his second coming, we are hereby to represent by the vanquishing and burying of our vile affections that they may rise to newness of life, and be united first to each other, then all to Christ. These are the actions and meditations of the truly pious person, while the vulgar place all their religion in crowding close to the altar, in listening to the words of the priest, and in being very circumspect at the observance of each trifling ceremony. Nor is it in such cases only as we have here given as instances, but through his whole course of life that the pious man, without any regard to the baser materials of the body, spends himself wholely in a fixed intentness upon spiritual, invisible and eternal objects."

Some of the ideas informing the satire and irony of *Moria* will be found in the letters of Thomas More to Colet and Ruthall from which extracts have been given; in particular we may note his complaints to Colet of preachers whose lives gainsaid their words, and of quarrelsome lawyers and self-seeking tradesmen, and in the letter to Ruthall the denunciation of fabulous stories that had grown up around the lives of martyrs and saints.

We do not know how long Erasmus stayed with More in 1509, nor how much time he gave to revising and polishing his book, but he was in no hurry to get it published. There is, indeed, a gap in our knowledge of his whereabouts from late in 1509 until the spring of 1511; his correspondence fails us during this period; presumably he was staying with his English friends among whom Mountjoy, Colet and Grocyn were likely to have been his hosts. In March 1511 he was with Linacre and in the following month with More again. He was at Dover on 10

April waiting to cross the Channel; he then wrote to Ammonio asking him to get More to let Colet have some books left at the Barge. He was in Paris in May arranging for Gilles Gourmont to print *Moria*, though that may not have been the main purpose of his visit. His later story that, against his will, friends arranged for the printing, must be dismissed as a literary device.

The first edition appeared in 1511. There may have been an earlier edition but, if so, no copy is extant. The interval between writing and printing seems unduly long; perhaps Erasmus hesitated to publish lest it should harm his hope of getting preferment in England. The little book was frequently reprinted in Cologne, Strasbourg and Basle but without his supervision. A French translation appeared in 1520 and an Italian in 1539. Ten years later came the English translation by Sir Thomas Chaloner;[3] John Wilson's translation was published in 1669, but the most popular version was that by White Kennett (later Bishop) which came out in 1683 and was reprinted six times in the first half of the eighteenth century. The first Dutch translation was published in 1560. It will be noted that, except for the first French version, none of these was published during Erasmus' lifetime. He showed little interest in his works being put into the vernacular; they were addressed to the Latin-reading public, the scholars, clerics, lawyers, and the like. They chuckled over *Moria*, as the Pope himself did, though some shook their heads at the more daring sallies. At first there was little outspoken criticism, but the Louvain theologians scented doubtful doctrine and resented the implied censure of themselves and their learning. They persuaded a young colleague, Martin van Dorp (1485-1525), to criticise *Moria* and, at the same time, voice their objections to Erasmus' declared intention of editing the Greek text of the New Testament. Here we are concerned only with the attack on *Moria*. Dorp was well-known to Erasmus, and indeed had undertaken to see his *Opuscula* through the press; his letter was therefore worded in a friendly vein though perhaps his instigators may have wished for something more trenchant. Dorp complained of the flippant tone of

---

[3]In 1628, John Milton wrote, "There is in the hands of everyone that most clever *Praise of Folly*".

Moria with its mocking of sacred subjects; he suggested that a counterbalance should be provided by "The Praise of Wisdom". The letter containing these criticisms was in circulation in the autumn of 1514 but did not come into the hands of Erasmus until June 1515. He was not unduly disturbed and replied in a kindly manner. *Moria*, he pointed out, was intended to do the same kind of good as the *Enchiridion* which had just been published separately. Erasmus may have thought that this in itself, with its homiletic style, supplied the counterbalance to the *Moria* that Dorp wanted. He stressed what he had said in the dedicatory letter; he was not attacking persons, none of whom were named, nor institutions. "He who in his strictures points indifferently to all, seems not angry at any one man but at all vices. Therefore, if anyone complains that he himself is reflected upon, he does but betray his own guilt. . . . I have not only stifled the mentioning of any one person, but have so tempered my style as the careful reader will easily perceive I aimed at diversion rather than satire." The reply, which is in effect "if the cap fits . . .", did not satisfy Dorp and the Louvain theologians; but this second letter was more concerned with the projected Greek New Testament than with *Moria*. Erasmus' answer has been lost, but Thomas More then entered the lists and wrote a lengthy reply while he was at Bruges in the autumn of 1515.[4] Only a small portion is concerned with *Moria*. He pointed out that the book had delighted the most learned men, not the unlettered crowd, and it was decried only by one or two disgruntled theologians. Dorp, he noted, had previously praised the bitter satires of Gerard Geldenhauer which scurrilously attacked monks and friars. In comparison, Erasmus was mild. As for a "Praise of Wisdom", that would not appease these angry theologians for Erasmus would have to exclude them from the company of Wisdom having already included them in that of Folly.

We shall return to this Dorp-Erasmus-More correspondence.

[4]First published in More's *Lucubrationes*, Basle, 1563. More said that *Moria* had been available "for more than seven times in seven years". This goes back to 1508 which is impossible; it does, however, suggest an edition earlier than that of 1511. There is a translation in Rogers, *Selected Letters* (Yale, 1961).

CHAPTER IX

Colet's School

THE DEATH of Sir Henry Colet in the autumn of 1505 meant that, apart from provision for his widow, Dame Christian, and minor bequests, his great wealth came to his only son John. Lack of documentary evidence makes it impossible to follow in detail the steps that led him to use his inheritance for the founding of St Paul's School, "my Grammar School", as he called it. In his Statutes,[1] Colet stated that he had founded the school "in the churchyard of St Paul's at the east end, in the year of Our Lord, 1512". It seems, however, that the school had already been at work for two or three years before that date. The explanation may be that it was only after an experimental period that he decided that he had discovered the best way of organizing the school and so could in 1512 draw up the final Statutes and place the school under the trusteeship of the Mercers' Company to "have all the cure and charge, rule and governance". He himself was by patrimony a freeman of that Company to which Thomas More was admitted in 1509. The Statutes are full of practical details that must have been based on experience.

It may be that Colet had been nursing his scheme for some time; his appointment as Dean in 1505 would provide a special stimulus as he would notice the way in which the Cathedral or Song-school was conducted; what he saw did not please him and, instead of reforming the old school, he determined to establish a new one that would not be under the control of the Cathedral Chapter. Colet was able to discuss his plans with Erasmus who was in England from January 1505 to June 1506. The only letter from Erasmus to Colet during the Italian years (Paris, June 1506) makes no mention of a school, but while he was in Italy Erasmus

[1]See, J. H. Lupton, *Life of Dean Colet* (1887). Appendix A.

75

was thinking out his *Copia* (*De duplici copia verborum ac rerem*), a book designed to give the young scholar a wide choice of words and ideas without encouraging verbosity or extravagance. When the book was finished, Colet at once showed his interest. This was in 1511. In a letter to Colet asking for financial help, Erasmus wrote from Cambridge,

> "I don't wonder that you, busy as you are with so many affairs, should have forgotten your promise, but when we were in your garden talking about *Copia*, I proposed to dedicate some juvenile work to our youthful prince, and you asked me to dedicate the new work to your new school. I answered with a smile that your new school was somewhat poverty-stricken and what I needed was someone who would pay ready cash. Then you smiled and said, with some hesitation, that you could not give as much as I needed, but would gladly give fifteen angels.[2] When you eagerly repeated this, I asked you if you thought that was enough. You declared that you would willingly pay that. Then I said I would gladly take it. This reminder will perhaps bring the matter to your memory."

Erasmus had the instincts of an educator though, apparently, without any liking for the actual task of teaching. A considerable part of his output was designed for use in schools and by students. *Adages*, *Copia* and *Colloquies* are the outstanding examples of this kind; he also produced many editions of classical texts for the use of learners. These books had a great sale, much of which did not benefit him financially, and they continued to be used long after his death. A whole progeny of adaptations and imitations showed how attractive and effective his methods proved to be. The extent of Erasmus' influence on teaching and teaching methods was considerable. Colet made good use of his friend's skill. A Latin grammar was a primary need, for the established books, often ridiculed by Erasmus and More, had long proved sterile and more likely to discourage a boy than to capture his interest. Colet invited Linacre to write a new grammar but what he produced was far above the heads of young pupils. It was later published as *Progymnasmata grammatices vulgaria* with prefatory

[2] The angel was worth 7s. 6d. in contemporary values.

poems by Thomas More and William Lily; this was published by More's brother-in-law, John Rastell, in 1525. Colet rightly considered that the book was not suited to his purpose, an opinion that offended Linacre, but Erasmus told Colet not to be too worried. "Though it is in the nature of man", he wrote, "to be as fond of their writings as parents are of their children, still I have the best reason for believing that he entertains the most friendly feelings towards you, and that he is not much annoyed at the rejection of his grammar." Colet himself wrote a short Accidence preceded by the articles of admission to the school and a summary of the elements of the Christian faith.[3] To this William Lily added a Syntax which Erasmus revised, and it is quite possible that More had a hand in it as the four friends were so closely in touch. This book had a remarkable history; in 1540 it was remodelled and became the national Latin grammar, eventually developing into the famous Eton grammar.[4] It is not surprising that Colet chose Lily as the first High Master of the new school and he seems to have worked with a nucleus of scholars for a year or so before Colet drew up his final Statutes. Among these early pupils was John Clement, of whose origins nothing is known. It may have been through Lily that Clement became a protégé of Thomas More and later tutor to his children. Another early pupil was Thomas Lupset. Both Clement and Lupset became lecturers in Greek at Wolsey's new college at Oxford, Corpus Christi.

It proved difficult to find a good under-master, or sur-master, to Lily. In this Colet sought the aid of Erasmus at Cambridge. He sent Colet a discourse on "The Method of Study" (*De Ratione Studii*) which included an account of the qualifications needed for a good schoolmaster. No one could possibly satisfy such high requirements, which included a mastery of Latin and Greek, both language and literature, as well as a grasp of other branches of knowledge. "I want a teacher", wrote Erasmus, "to have traversed the whole range of knowledge, that it may spare each of his scholars doing it. A diligent and thoroughly competent

---

[3] See Appendix B of Lupton, *op. cit.*
[4] On the history of these grammars see C. G. Allen, *Library*, Jan. 1954.

master might give boys a fair proficiency in both Latin and Greek in a shorter time and with less labour than the common run of pedagogues take to teach their nonsense."

To this Colet replied in September, 1511:

"I have read your *De Studiis* hastily but as yet I have been too busy to read it carefully. Glancing through it, not only do I approve everything but also greatly admire your genius, skill, learning, fulness and eloquence. I have often longed that the boys of my school should be taught in the way in which you say they should be. And often also have I longed that I could get such teachers as you have so well described. When I came to that point at the end of your letter where you say that you could educate boys up to a fair proficiency in both languages in fewer years than it takes these pedagogues to teach their nonsense, O Erasmus, how I longed that I could make you the master of my school! I have indeed some hope that you will give us a helping hand in teaching our teachers."

Erasmus wrote a month later describing his efforts to find a schoolmaster among the scholars at Cambridge.

"When I spoke of the under-master to some of the Masters of Arts, one of them, a man of some reputation, replied with a sneer, 'Who would endure to spend his life in a school among boys who could possibly manage to live anywhere else?' I answered quietly that I thought it a very honourable office to instruct youth in sound morals and useful learning and that Christ had not despised the tender years of children, and that no period of life so well repaid kindness or yielded more abundant fruit, youth being the seed-time on which the State depends for its future growth. I added that truly pious men would be of the opinion that in no other way could they serve God better than by bringing children to Christ. 'Whoever wishes to serve Christ', said he, turning up his nose in derision, 'let him enter a monastery and take religious vows.' I answered that Paul made true religion consist in works of charity, and that charity consists in doing all the good we can to our neighbours. He treated my remark with disdain, as if it only showed my ignorance. 'Lo', said he, 'we have left all; in this perfection consists.' 'He has not left all', I answered, 'who, when he has it in his power to do good to a great many, refuses the office because it is considered too humble.' And so to prevent a dispute, I left him."

Colet appointed as sur-master a Cambridge scholar with the admirable name of John Rightwise. As he was a student at King's College during Erasmus' residence at Cambridge, he had, no doubt, been recommended to Colet by Erasmus. On Lily's death in 1522, Rightwise became High Master and it was under him that the St Paul's boys became known for their performances of his interludes.[5]

Colet's Statutes deserve a closer study than would be in place here. One or two points may be noted. He gave as his purpose "to increase knowledge and worshipping God and Our Lord Jesus Christ and good Christian life and manners". We may place with this Erasmus' statement in the *Enchiridion*: "the chief care of Christian men ought to be applied to this point that their children straightaway from the cradle may receive and suck under the hands of them which are learned, opinions and persuasions meet and worthy of Christ". And we can add Thomas More's opinion: "Though I prefer learning joined with virtue to all the treasures of kings, yet renown for learning when it is not united with the good life, is nothing else than manifest and notorious infamy."[6] Here we have clear expressions of their common purpose by these three friends; their learning and their encouragement of learning were directed to the promotion of Christian living. Colet's school was dedicated to the Child Jesus and over the High Master's chair was a picture of the Child in an attitude of teaching with the inscription, "Hear ye him".

Erasmus composed a prayer for the school, a prayer that is still used there.

"We pray thee, Jesus Christ, who as a boy twelve years old, seated in the Temple, taught the teachers themselves, to whom the voice of the Father, sent from heaven, granted authority to teach all men, saying, 'This is my beloved son in whom I

---

[5]They presented *The Tragedy of Dido out of Virgil* before Henry VIII at Greenwich in 1527. The Elizabethan "Children of St Paul's" were of the Cathedral Song-school.
[6]See below, p. 134, for the continuation of this extract.

am well pleased: hear him'; who art the perfection of all the eternal wisdom of the Father, deign to illuminate our minds so that we learn thoroughly the lessons of virtuous literature, and that we may use them to thy glory, who liveth and reigneth, with the Father and the Holy Ghost, ever one God, world without end."

One provision of the Statutes revealed Colet's attitude to classical authors.

"As touching in this school what shall be taught by the masters and learned by the scholars, it passeth my wit to devise and determine in particular, but in general to speak and sum what to say my mind, I would they were taught all way in good literature both Latin and Greek and good authors such as have the very Roman eloquence joined with wisdom especially Christian authors that wrote their wisdom with clear and chaste Latin other in verse or in prose."

It will be noted that the opening sentence does not lay down a hard and fast rule, and it is followed by suggestions rather than injunctions. He recommended the *Institutum Christiani hominis* "which that learned Erasmus made at my request and the book called *Copia* of the same Erasmus". Other authors he suggested were such Christian poets as Sedulius, Juvencus, and Baptista Mantuanus (Shakespeare's "good old Mantuan"). He did not, however, forbid the reading of Cicero, Sallust, Virgil and Terence, but he did condemn later "Latin adulterate . . . which more rather may be called blotterature than literature". Colet was trying to solve a dilemma; he wanted his pupils to learn Latin of the classical period but he did not want them to be attracted by Roman paganism.

Erasmus' ideas on education were more fully developed in his *De Pueris statim ac liberaliter instituendis* (1529). In it he stressed the importance of the qualifications and character of the teacher who should be patient and sympathetic and not resort to flogging to drive in learning, but should devise pleasurable methods with an element of play and competition in them. The important thing was to rouse the real interest of the pupil so that he would learn willingly.[7]

The new school was not allowed to go uncriticized. A letter from Colet to Erasmus, which can probably be dated early in 1512, gives us a glimpse of the opposition.

"A certain bishop [Fitzjames of London?] who is held to be one of the wiser sort, has been blaspheming our school before a large concourse of people, declaring that I have erected a worthless thing, yea, a bad thing—yea, more (to give his own words) a temple of idolatry, which, indeed, I fancy he called it because the poets are to be taught there. At this, Erasmus, I am not angry, but laugh heartily."

Stapleton has preserved a fragment of a letter from More to Colet of this period. He wrote:

"I am not surprised that your excellent school is arousing envy. For as the Greeks came forth from the Trojan horse and destroyed barbarous Troy, so scholars are seen to come forth from your school to show up and overthrow the ignorance of others."

It was not only his school that was arousing opposition to Colet. His sermons and lectures in St Paul's Cathedral attracted great numbers, among whom would be Thomas More; "to be stirred up by your powerful sermons", as he had written. Three sermons preached on public occasions are important: the Convocation sermon of February 1512, a sermon before the King on Good Friday, 1513, and one in Westminster Abbey in November 1515 when Wolsey received the Cardinal's hat.

The Convocation sermon was the most notable of the three. Assembled in the Cathedral would be Archbishop Warham, Bishop John Fisher and other bishops of the province as well as abbots and the representatives of the clergy. Among them was Thomas Wolsey, Dean of Lincoln, with his feet now firmly placed on the ladder he was to climb rapidly. The text was Romans xii, 2. "Be you not conformed to this world, but be ye

[7]See W. H. Woodward, *Desiderius Erasmus concerning the Aim and Method of Education* (1904).

reformed in the newness of your understanding, that ye may prove what is the good will of God, well pleasing and perfect". Colet divided his sermon into two portions: the first on conformation to this world, and the second on the reformation of the Church. Under the first heading he pointed to the great evils existing among the clergy: pride in their own dignities, "carnal concupiscence", in banquetting and hunting, "procurers and finders of lusts", and covetousness in seeking more and richer benefices. Such evils meant that the priesthood was dishonoured and despised; "holy dignity in the Church is confused"; the laity follow this bad example. Such priests are hypocrites and "see nothing but earthly things". The preacher ended this part of his sermon with the words, "We are also nowadays grieved of heretics, men mad of marvellous foolishness. But the heresies of them are not so pestilent and pernicious unto us and the people as the evil and wicked life of priests."

He then turned to consider the manner in which reform could be best effected.

"This reformation and restoring of the Church's estate must need begin of you our fathers, and so follow in us your priests and in all the clergy. You are our heads, you are an example of living unto us. Unto you we look as unto marks of our direction. In you and in your life we desire to read, as in lively books, how and after what fashion we may live. Wherefore, if you will ponder and look unto our motes, first take away the blocks out of your eyes. It is an old proverb, 'Physician, heal thyself'."

He pointed out that there was no need to make new regulations; all that was required had already been laid down in the Councils of the Church. Then he noted particular injunctions that should be enforced. Let only worthy men be ordained; let promotion come by merit; let simony be abolished; let priests reside in their parishes and bishops in their dioceses; let monks observe their rule, and let the wealth of the Church be spent, not in buildings and pomp and feasting "but in things profitable and necessary to the Church". "Truly ye are gathered often time together, but, by your failure to speak the truth, yet I see not what fruit cometh of your assembling."

The sermon was printed in English and a separate Latin translation (probably by Colet) was also published.[8] A copy went to Erasmus.

The text of the sermon preached before the King on Good Friday, 1513, has not come down to us in its complete text; we owe our knowledge of it to Erasmus. War with France was imminent and it was expected that war with Scotland would follow, as it did. It was one of those wars of prestige for which there was no adequate excuse save Henry VIII's vision of himself as a warrior king. Colet was well aware of the situation when he mounted the pulpit in the Chapel Royal.

"He preached wonderfully", wrote Erasmus, "on the victory of Christ, exhorting all Christians to fight and conquer under the banner of Him their proper King. He showed that when wicked men, out of hatred and ambition, fought with and destroyed one another, they fought under the banner, not of Christ but of the Devil. He showed further how hard a thing it is to die a Christian death in battle; how few undertake a war except in hatred and ambition; how hardly possible it is for those who really have that brotherly love without which 'no one can see the Lord' to thrust their swords into their brothers' blood; he urged in conclusion, that instead of imitating the example of Caesars and Alexanders, the Christian ought rather to follow the example of Christ his Prince."

Colet's ill-wishers expected that such outspoken opinions on the eve of war would incur the King's wrath, but Henry's conduct was ever unpredictable, as many found to their cost. He sent for Colet and they talked together as they walked in the garden of the Friars Observant at Greenwich. The King felt that such a sermon undermined the morale of the soldiers by suggesting that war was not lawful for Christians. Colet, Erasmus and More strongly condemned warlike policies and wars themselves, but they did not take what we should call the extreme pacifist view to which Erasmus came the nearest. Even in *Utopia* war was considered a possibility and mercenaries were employed by the Utopians. The

[8]Printed in Appendix C in J. H. Lupton's *Life of Dean Colet*. The English version was reprinted at Cambridge in 1661; to it were added Erasmus' account of Colet, and More's letter of 1504.

King was satisfied with Colet's explanation, whatever it was, though it is not recorded. Erasmus added:

"on returning to the palace, the King had a wine-cup brought him and pledged Colet in it before he would let him depart. Then embracing him most courteously and promising all that could be expected from the most gracious of sovereigns, he let him go. And as the throng of courtiers was now standing round, eager to hear the result of the conference, the King, in the hearing of all, said, 'Let every man have his own doctor and everyone follow his liking, but this is the doctor for me'."

A later version of the incident[9] added that Colet then preached a second sermon to meet the King's wishes, but Erasmus gave no hint of this.

Colet got into trouble with Bishop Fitzjames of London in the summer of 1513 for his interpretation of the Scriptures and for his attacks on the clergy. He was cited before Archbishop Warham, who dismissed the charges, but Fitzjames suspended Colet from preaching for three months.

The third sermon that calls for notice was preached in Westminster Abbey in November 1515 when both Parliament and the Convocation were in session. The occasion was the official reception of the Cardinal's hat conferred on Wolsey by Leo XI. Wolsey had come a long way since Colet had preached to Convocation three years earlier. He organized a magnificent spectacle in his own triumph. To quote the account written by George Cavendish,

"Then was great and speedy provision and preparation made in Westminster Abbey for the confirmation of his high dignity; the which was executed by all the bishops and abbots nigh or about London, in rich mitres and copes, and other costly ornaments; which was done in so solemn wise as I have not seen the like unless it had been at the coronation of a mighty prince or king."

Who invited Colet to preach the sermon? The Abbot of Westminster, John Islip, who did so much to enrich the Abbey buildings, had the final say in the choice of preachers, but he may have

[9]It is given in Archbishop Parker's *De Antiquitate Ecclesiae* (1572).

accepted a suggestion from Wolsey. If the new Cardinal did make the choice, it was a strange one for he must have recalled the Convocation sermon with its strictures on those who sought "fat benefices and high promotions". The full text of this sermon has not been preserved but a summary is given in an official record at the College of Arms.[10] Colet first paid tribute to Wolsey's qualifications for his honour. Here it may be remarked that Colet, More and Erasmus all praised Wolsey's administration in those early years, but this ostentatious display in the Abbey was all too significant of the megalomania that so gripped him that the concern for justice that marked his first phase was speedily forgotten in his pursuit of his personal aggrandizement. After this eulogy, Colet uttered a warning of the dangers of the new dignity Wolsey had received.

"Let no one in so proud a position, made most illustrious by the dignity of such an honour, be puffed up by its greatness. But remember that Our Saviour in his own person said to his disciples, 'He who is least among you shall be greatest in the kingdom of heaven'. And again, 'He who exalts himself shall be humbled, and he who humbles himself shall be exalted'."

Wolsey was deaf to this warning against pride and ambition as he had been earlier to Colet's condemnation of covetousness among the clergy. As a modern historian has remarked, Wolsey showed no sign of humility when the ceremony was concluded.

"As the Archbishop of Canterbury [Warham] passed down the nave of Westminster Abbey, it was noted that no cross was borne before him; and none was ever borne again before him in Wolsey's presence. Wolsey had two, one as Cardinal, one as Archbishop [of York] wherever he went. Warham had not even one in his own province when it was illumined by Wolsey's superior lustre."[11]

Before the end of the year Warham surrendered the great seal and Cardinal Wolsey became Lord Chancellor of England. Early in 1516, More wrote to Erasmus,

[10]See R. Fiddes, *Life of Cardinal Wolsey* (1724), pp. 251-3.
[11]A. F. Pollard, *Wolsey*, p. 57.

"The Archbishop of Canterbury has finally been relieved of the office of Chancellor, a burden, which, as you know, he had tried extremely hard to shake off for several years; at long last he has attained his heart's desire, a life of privacy, and is having wonderful leisure amid his books with his memories of duties well done."

Wolsey was not a scholar nor a patron of scholars unless they brought grist to his mill. His foundations at Ipswich and Oxford were, in their way, a tribute to learning, but they were meant more as a tribute to the founder. Erasmus had some reason to think that Wolsey would help him, as he could so easily have done; there were polite exchanges that Erasmus interpreted as meaning more than they did; he was promised preferment that never came. When Wolsey found that Erasmus had no political weight, even as a Councillor of Charles V, he left him out of his calculations.

CHAPTER X

Erasmus at Cambridge

THE EDUCATIONAL BOOKS by Erasmus mentioned in the last chapter formed part of the work he did at Cambridge between August 1511 and February 1514. This has taken us ahead chronologically. After seeing *Moria* through the press in Paris, he returned to London about the middle of June 1511. We do not know what plans he had in mind, but England had captured his affection, though he thought poorly of its amenities; the attraction, apart from the possibility of patronage, was the group of humanists in London. During his stay in Cambridge he made the seventy-mile journey to London and back several times; he was always sure of a welcome in a number of households. There was Thomas More in Bucklersbury, John Colet at St Paul's or Stepney, Grocyn at St Lawrence Jewry, and Mountjoy in Knightrider Street. More and Grocyn were his favoured hosts. He wrote in November 1511 from Cambridge to Roger Wentford, the headmaster of St Anthony's School, "I cannot see how I can live with anyone there [London] except Grocin, and certainly there is nobody with whom I am more glad to be, but I am ashamed of the expense to him, especially as there is no return I can make, and he is so kind that he will not accept any payment". He was avoiding Mountjoy's house as he could not stomach "Mr Watchdog", or "Cerberus", as he called someone, perhaps the steward in charge during Mountjoy's frequent absences. More's hospitality was for a period in abeyance. His wife Jane had died in the summer of 1511, but a few months later he married again. The inevitable period of adjustment was not favourable to guests; Ammonio had left as he found Mistress Alice More difficult, and, at first, Erasmus may have felt unwelcome. Neither of them could have been an easy guest; unfortunately we lack her comments on them.

Erasmus himself fell seriously ill of the sweating-sickness while in London; Jane More may have been carried off by the same epidemic. He was sufficiently recovered to make the journey to Cambridge in the middle of August. One of the Fellows of Queens' College, Henry Bullock, whom he had known for several years, arranged for a carrier to bring the scholar's books and for a horse to carry the scholar. A good horse was a necessity in those times, especially for anyone who loved moving about as Erasmus did, and there are many references in his letters to this need.

The invitation to Cambridge came from Bishop John Fisher, the Chancellor of the University.[1] Although he was not himself a Greek scholar he was anxious that the language should be taught at the University. He was fortunate in persuading Erasmus to lecture on the subject; it may not have been easy to win him for Erasmus was chary of tying himself down to permanent engagements, but the knowledge that there were Greek manuscripts at Cambridge may have been the deciding factor. He was a member of Queens' College of which Fisher had been Master in 1505; his residence in the College was broken by his visits to London, by occasional periods when he lodged with Garrett Godfrey, a bookbinder, and by visits to the Gonnell family at Landbeach.[2] William Gonnell was a schoolmaster and copyist, and later, at Erasmus' recommendation, became a tutor in More's household. These absences were partly due to his restlessness, though at least one of his visits to Landbeach was in flight from the plague. His dislike of collegiate life may also have driven him away at times. This does not imply that he was at loggerheads with the Fellows at Queens'; some he certainly found dull,[3] but with several he made life-long friends. He just did not like that kind of life.

The position was not a lucrative one. He wrote to Colet soon after reaching Cambridge, "I see before me the footprints of Christian poverty". We do not know how much he received as lecturer; at most perhaps £20. He later gave divinity lectures

[1]This was an annual appointment; in 1514 Fisher became Chancellor for life, a unique distinction at that time.

[2]See *Erasmus at Cambridge* (Toronto, 1964), with letters translated by D. F. S. Thomson, and an informative Introduction by H. C. Porter, to which I am indebted.

[3]See above, p. 78.

and if this meant that he was Lady Margaret Professor, as is usually supposed, he would get another £13. There were difficulties about finding his salary for in 1512 the University appealed to Lord Mountjoy for a subsidy to meet the "immensum stipendium", surely a rhetorical exaggeration. He does not appear to have had many pupils but they were pioneers of the line of distinguished Greek scholars that Cambridge was to produce in the coming generation.

The majority of Erasmus' extant letters from Cambridge were to Ammonio; perhaps the fact that they were both foreigners as well as friends of More made them feel at liberty to voice their feelings with little restraint. Certainly the letters to Ammonio are among the most familiar Erasmus wrote; the day had not yet come when any letter by Erasmus would find its way into print. He found plenty to grumble about—the lack of warmth, the draughts, the dirt, the beer, the roguery of carriers who tapped the casks of Greek wine (malmsey) with which Ammonio kept him supplied. These complaints must not be taken too seriously; indeed we get the impression, perhaps an illusion, that the more Erasmus grumbled, the more he was enjoying life. There was, however, one serious trouble that recurred in Cambridge; he was again attacked by the gravel or stone, a complaint from which he was to suffer for the rest of his life. He announced the onset to Warham in January 1514. The Archbishop replied:

> "What business have you with stones? You have not I suppose any great buildings on hand. Therefore as stones are no affair of yours, pray free yourself as soon as you can from such a superfluous load and spend what money is needed to have those stones carried away."

This reminds us of how generous Warham was to Erasmus. The Archbishop had made him Rector of Aldington in Kent in March 1512, but Erasmus had resigned this in exchange for a pension of £20, which was subject to tax deductions.[4]

Erasmus had also applied to Fisher for financial help at the end of 1511. The Bishop replied:

[4] In the *Valor Ecclesiasticus* of 1535, the sum of £15 1s. 2d. "to be allowed one yearly pension unto master Erasmus for the term of his life".

"Greeting to you, Erasmus. I beg you, don't be too offended that I did not write when I sent to you recently. The messenger was in a hurry to leave town and I met him just as I was going out. So, as I was unable to write, I gave him the small gift you asked for; it was not, however, from the fund you assume to be at my disposal and to be of some size. Believe me, Erasmus, whatever may be said, I have no funds that I can use at my sole discretion. The use of that money is restricted, and cannot be varied just as we wish. I feel that you are so needed in our University that I will not let you be in want as long as there is anything to spare out of my own modest resources."

Probably Erasmus thought that a grant could be made to him out of the funds bequeathed by the Lady Margaret.

In the following year Fisher was appointed to attend the Fifth Lateran Council in Rome and he asked Erasmus to go with him, but "I received notice of this too late to have time to arrange my own affairs". And in another letter, "Had I been advised a little sooner, I would have gone with him". It was a disappointment for he would have liked to go to Rome again; he was always anxious to get news of Italy from Ammonio; but this nostalgia may have meant simply that wherever he was, he wanted to be somewhere else. Actually, Fisher did not attend the Council although he made preparations for doing so. The Council lasted from May 1512 to March 1517 and Fisher again hoped to take part in 1514. It is not known why he did not go. Erasmus wrote several letters to friends in Rome to introduce Fisher. In one he wrote, "Unless I am sadly mistaken, he is the one man at this time who is incomparable for uprightness of life, for learning, and for greatness of soul". They were of about the same age, but one detects in Erasmus' letters to Fisher a tone of respect, even veneration, that is absent from his letters to other friends.[5]

During his Cambridge years Erasmus did some fruitful work. The educational books already described were lesser productions compared with his two great projects; the recension of the Greek text of the New Testament, and his edition of St Jerome. He used four Greek manuscripts of the New Testament that were to

[5] See my *Saint John Fisher*, pp. 41 and 53.

be found in Cambridge libraries. For Jerome he could consult eight manuscript volumes, and in after years Robert Aldridge recalled how they worked at the collation of these. A later helper was the young Thomas Lupset who had been in John Colet's household. On 11 July 1513 Erasmus wrote to Colet, "I have finished collating the New Testament, and am now going to begin on St Jerome". But this was not all. He was adding to his *Adages*, and was also making translations into Latin from St Basil, Plutarch and Lucian.

A letter dated 9 May (1512?) to Ammonio gave the news that Erasmus was going on a pilgrimage. "I have taken a solemn vow for the good outcome of the Church's affairs; I am going to pay a visit to Our Lady of Walsingham, and I will there hang up a votive offering of a Greek poem." It may have been in that summer, or perhaps the following year, that he also made a pilgrimage to Canterbury with John Colet. These provided him with the material for his *Colloquy*, *A Religious Pilgrimage*, published in 1526. He gave the name of one of his Walsingham companions, Robert Aldrich. He disguised that of John Colet as Gratianus Pullus.[6]

Readers may be startled at the contrast between the bitterness of the attack on relics in this *Colloquy* and the fact that Erasmus himself went on a pilgrimage in fulfilment of a vow, and a doubt may arise as to his sincerity. This, however, is to misunderstand Erasmus and to confuse two distinct ideas. We know that in his early days at Paris he had made a vow in time of sickness. His ex-votive offerings were given in full belief in the power of prayer; they were not made with his tongue in his cheek.[7] But belief in prayer does not rule out scepticism as to the authenticity of relics, nor dislike of the exploitation of simple folk by the unscrupulous guardians. Indeed, the strength of faith in prayer increases sensitiveness to any form of superstition. The prayer he offered at Walsingham reads:

"Hail Mary, blessed mother of Jesus, the only woman to be the

---

[6]In his *Modus orandi Deum* (1524) Erasmus mentioned that he and Colet had visited the shrine of St Thomas of Canterbury.

[7]Seebohm was surely wrong in saying that this votive offering was "a joke played upon the ignorant Canons". (Everyman ed., p. 171.)

Virgin Mother of a God. Men bring you various gifts, some gold, some silver, while some like to offer precious stones. In return they may ask for health, or for riches, or for a life as long as Nestor's, or that their pregnant wives may make them proud fathers. This worshipper, however, comes with piety but in poverty, and just brings you some verses, for he has nothing else to offer in place of this meanest of gifts. But he asks for the greatest reward: a heart that honours God, and is free from all blemishes."

Walsingham and Canterbury were the two most famous shrines in England; Henry VIII and Queen Catherine had made pilgrimages to both. Walsingham, founded in 1061, was a Priory of Erasmus' own order, the Augustinian Canons. His hasty impression, for it could not be more, was that there was little to criticize.

"Are they men of good lives?"

"Not much amiss. They are richer in piety than in revenue." His brief encounter deceived him for the Bishop's visitation in 1514 revealed "a truly deplorable condition of things".[8] Erasmus was scornful of the number of doubtful relics displayed.

"And they tell the same stories about Our Lord's Cross that is shewn up and down, both publicly and privately, in so many places, that if all the fragments were gathered together, they would seem to be sufficient loading for a good large ship; and yet Our Lord carried the whole Cross upon his shoulders."

That was one side of Erasmus and the one that captured popular attention; the other side was too often overlooked.

"But we shall be pure if we venerate the Virgin as we ought."

"How would she have us venerate her?"

"You will perform most acceptable service to her if you imitate her."

"That's soon said, but not so easily performed."

"It is hard, indeed, but then it is very well worth the pains."

When Erasmus turned from Walsingham to Canterbury, there was a significant change of tone in the *Colloquy*. In the first part

---

[8] D. Knowles, *Religious Orders in England*, III, p. 75.

he was writing as the leader; in the second he gave place to Colet, and we may be sure that, such was his respect for Colet, he did not exaggerate the Dean's aversion to what he thought were unworthy practices. He put it to the guardian of the jewels and precious ornaments that if St Thomas were alive he would sell them all for the relief of the poor. Erasmus averred that, but for their letter of introduction from the Archbishop, they would have been turned out. In the *Colloquy* he seized the chance to pay a tribute to Warham.

"If you knew the man, you would take him for humanity itself. He was a man of that learning, of that candour of manners, of that piety of life, that there was nothing wanting in him to make him a most accomplished Prelate."

In 1538 the shrine of St Thomas of Canterbury was despoiled, but the jewels were not sold to help the poor; they went into the Royal Treasury.

It was during these Cambridge years that Erasmus became concerned with the defence of Johann Reuchlin (1455-1522), the leading European Hebraist of his day. A fanatical convert Jew, Johann Pfefferkorn, urged that all books in Hebrew should be destroyed, and he gained the support of the Dominicans. Reuchlin at once objected in the name of scholarship, and a fierce controversy broke out. The dispute dragged on for some years and was eventually referred to Rome. Erasmus leapt into a dispute that had resolved itself into one between the supporters of scholasticism and those of the new learning. Once more, in his view, the barbarians were trying to suppress sound learning. In defence of Reuchlin, he wrote many letters to influential patrons and to his friends to enlist their support. Colet, Fisher and More were brought into the affair. Fisher was greatly attracted by Reuchlin's work in Hebrew, and, according to Erasmus, even thought of arranging a meeting with the great scholar. In a letter to Martin Dorp, written in 1515, More wrote,

"I know the type of men who would not tolerate Reuchlin with any fairness. What a man! Extremely learned, prudent and honest, while his rivals, utterly ignorant, stupid and worthless liars, attacked him with such monstrous injustice that, had he taken to them with his fists, it would have seemed right to excuse him."

The friends of Reuchlin published in 1514 a volume of letters from his supporters, *Clarorum Virorum Epistolae ad Reuchlinum*; this seems to have suggested to Crotus Rubenus (who became Rector of Erfurt University in 1520) the compilation of *Epistolae Obscurorum Virorum*,[9] published in 1515. It was a satirical attack in dog-Latin on the scholastics for their "obscurantism", to use a term that the title of the book created. It was written in the broadest and sometimes grossest farce. A second part appeared in 1517; for this Ulrich von Hutten (1488-1523), the impoverished scion of a knightly family of Franconia, was responsible. He was something of a scholar but rather unstable in temperament. Erasmus strongly objected to this volume; his name was dragged into it, and he was saddled with the authorship of *Julius Exclusus*. He maintained that he himself was solely concerned with the defence of good learning and not with the opinions of Reuchlin on other matters. As he wrote in the 1519 Preface to the *Colloquies*, "I am not an Erasmist, nor am I a Reuchlinist". He would join no party or faction.

This affair covered several years and it has taken us away from Cambridge. Erasmus was in London for varying periods at least five times during 1512 and 1513. How often he stayed with More is not known, but there was always a room for him in Bucklersbury; the initially awkward period at the beginning of More's second marriage had passed and Erasmus came to respect Alice More. About this time Thomas More was writing his *Richard III* in English with a parallel version in Latin; Erasmus may have read the latter though he makes no direct mention of it; there may be an indirect reference in his letter to Hutten where he wrote of More "making experiments in every kind". *Richard III* was not only an experiment, it was a notable innovation as there was no tradition of vernacular historical writing of this kind with its dramatic narrative. For his purpose, More had excellent material at hand. As a boy he had lived through the

[9]Translated and edited by F. G. Stokes (1909).

reign of Richard III and he could recall stories told by Cardinal Morton; he could also draw upon the recollections of his father (a firm supporter of Edward IV) and of other contemporaries such as Archbishop Warham, Bishop Fitzjames, Sir John Cutte and Christopher Urswick. More did not complete the history; he had hinted that he might continue it through the reign of Henry VII. It has been suggested that he stopped because he was getting too near his own times and would find it embarrassing to refer to living people.[10] The book does not closely concern us here. Historians have questioned some of More's statements, but his view of Richard III was the popularly accepted one; it was adopted and perpetuated by Shakespeare, and no amount of research seems able to destroy it.[11] *Richard III* should be regarded not so much as an historical inquiry as a dramatic evocation.

Erasmus left Cambridge for good in February 1514 and, as far as is known, spent the next six months in or near London, staying part of the time with Ammonio but making a round of visits to his friends and paying his respects to the King and the Queen and to Bishop Wolsey, the rising man. It may have been that England's war with France and Scotland made him feel that the country was too disturbed for his peace of mind, but it is more probable that the need to get a printer at work was his decisive reason for leaving. No English printer at that time had Greek types; the first to use them was John Siberch, who came to Cambridge from Cologne in 1520. He annoyed Erasmus by publishing an unauthorized edition of *Libellus de Conscribendis Epistolis*. It was dedicated by the printer to John Fisher who was asked to gain Erasmus' favour as "you are all-powerful with" him. Siberch had been brought to Cambridge by Henry Bullock and Richard Croke. It has sometimes been said that Erasmus was responsible for Siberch's migration from Cologne, but there is no evidence for this.[12]

He crossed the Channel early in July and went to stay at

---

[10]See A. F. Pollard, *The Making of Sir Thomas More's "Richard III"*, in *Historical Essays in Honour of James Tait* (1933); also the edition, edited by R. S. Sylvester, in the Yale Edition (1964).

[11]See P. M. Kendall, *Richard III* (1956) for balanced discussion. E. M. W. Tillyard, *Shakespeare's History Plays* (1944), has some interesting pages on More's book.

[12]See E. P. Goldschmidt, *The First Cambridge Printer* (1955).

Hammes, near Calais, where Mountjoy was lieutenant, or governor. There a letter from Servatius Roger, Prior of Steyn, caught up with Erasmus. The letter is not extant but it was evidently a renewed request that the wandering scholar should return to his monastery. It called for a tactful reply, for Erasmus had no intention of going back. His letter, dated 8 July 1514, is of some length. In it he reviewed his past life; he pointed out that he had not freely chosen the monastic life.[13]

> "I have always regarded this one thing as harder than the rest, that I have been forced into a mode of life for which I was totally unfit both in body and mind; in mind, because I abhorred routine and loved liberty; in body because my constitution could not endure such labours."

Then he got on to one of his favourite themes.

> "We make Christian piety depend on place, dress, style of living, and on certain little rituals. We think a man lost who changes his white habit for a black, or his cowl for a cap, or occasionally moves from place to place. I should dare to say that Christian piety has suffered great damage from these so-called religious practices."

He must have felt that this was special pleading, so he passed on to mention all the important people who had favoured him in France, Italy and England—the Pope, the Cardinals, the King and Queen of England, the Archbishop of Canterbury. Oxford and Cambridge are also brought into the review. This part, one feels, is a bit overdrawn, but, no doubt, Erasmus knew his man.

Then comes a list of his publications and scholarly labours and an account of what he had been doing at Cambridge; a far better justification, one would have thought, than a catalogue of notabilities. A long passage is devoted to the question of his monastic habit, and he tells, what is surely rather a tall story, of how he was attacked in Bologna for wearing it, though the Bolognese must have been accustomed to regulars in all kinds of garb. So he reaches his conclusion:

---

[13]Barbara Flower's translation from the London edition of Huizinga's *Erasmus* (1952) is used here.

"As to your promising me your help in finding me a place where I can live with an excellent income, I cannot conjecture what this can be, unless perhaps you intend to place me among some community of nuns, to serve women—I who have never been willing to serve kings nor archbishops. I want no pay; I have no desire for riches, if only I have enough money to provide for my health and my literary leisure."

The final greeting reads, "Farewell, once my sweetest companion, now my revered father".

A clever letter; perhaps too clever, but a most revealing document.

By the middle of August, Erasmus was in Basle, and for the first time met Johann Froben.

CHAPTER XI

Novum Instrumentum

ERASMUS' RECENSION of the New Testament in Greek was originally entitled *Novum Instrumentum*; he was recalling that St Jerome had applied the term "instrumentum" to each of the Testaments. The word may here be translated "tool", for Erasmus believed that he was supplying the Christian scholar with the essential means for learning the wisdom of Christ.

In the preceding chapters a number of references have been made to his growing interest in the Greek text of the New Testament, but it cannot be said with certainty when it was he definitely decided to produce it himself. The need for such a text had been in his mind for perhaps a decade, and the influence of Valla and Colet had pointed in that direction. We have seen how in October 1507 he had written to Aldus Manutius from Bologna to express his surprise that the printer had not yet undertaken a New Testament in Greek. He may have wished to make sure that such a project was not already in hand, or he may have hoped that Aldus would ask him to undertake it. It was during his Cambridge years (1510-1514) that he seriously set to work. In his letter to Servatius Roger of July 1514, just after he had left England, he wrote: "I have corrected the New Testament from the Greek manuscripts and have annotated more than a thousand pages [of St Jerome] not without some benefit to theologians". He was then on his way to Basle, which he reached in August, and there he settled in Froben's printing office to supervise the production of the *Novum Instrumentum*. Printing began in January 1516 and the book was published in March. Concurrently he was at work on the printing of that long-cherished project of a new edition of the letters of St Jerome. The first volumes of this were published in April 1516 and the edition of nine folio volumes was completed by August.

The first edition of the *Novum Instrumentum* was printed in double columns, the Greek on the left and a new Latin translation on the right. A comparison of passages taken at random shows that the Latin version was not widely different from that of the Vulgate, but there were some variations that occasioned sharp criticism. In later editions he made more use of the translation he had made in England at Colet's suggestion some ten years previously;[1] this varied more from the Vulgate.

In a letter to Antony Pucci, the Papal Nuncio in Switzerland, dated 26 August 1518 from Basle, Erasmus gave an account of his method.

"Having first collated several copies made by Greek scribes, we followed that which appeared to be the most genuine, and having translated this into Latin, we placed our translation by the side of the Greek text so that the reader might readily compare the two, the translation being so made that it was our first care to preserve, as far as permissible, the integrity of the Latin tongue without injury to the simplicity of apostolic language. Our next care was to provide that any sentences that had before given trouble to the reader, either by ambiguity or obscurity of language or by faulty or unsuitable expression, should be explained and elucidated with as little deviation as possible from the words of the orginal and none from the sense; as to which we do not depend on any fancies of our own but seek it out of the writings of Origen, Basil, Chrysostom, Cyril, Jerome, Cyprian, Ambrose or Augustine. Some annotations were added (which we have now extended) wherein we inform the reader upon whose authority this or that rests, relying always upon the judgment of the old authors. We do not pull the Vulgate to pieces but we point out where it is defective, giving warning in any case of flagrant error on the part of the translator and explaining it where the version is involved or obscure."

This account calls for some comments. It should be kept in mind that the principles of textual criticism and of palaeography

[1]This translation did not include the Acts and the Apocalypse.

as accepted today were unknown in the sixteenth century. Erasmus' remark that "we followed that which appeared to be the most genuine" would make a modern scholar shudder as it suggests a purely subjective choice. For this edition he used the Cambridge manuscripts, and for later revisions consulted others. What he produced was unfortunately marred by bad proof-reading. Here may be noted an element in his personality that is sometimes overlooked. As soon as a manuscript was in the printer's hands, he became impatient to get the book published, and he often failed to give that meticulous care to accuracy that is the mark of the finished scholar, a care that can cause delay in publication; but of that there was never any risk with Erasmus. He loved to sit in the printing office and handle and correct the sheets as they came off the press, but he had not the patience to be a good proof-reader. "I had rather pour out than write", he himself admitted. His friends recognized this weakness. For instance, at the end of October 1516, Thomas More wrote to him, "Don't be in a hurry to publish a second edition. Out of friendship and concern for you, I beg and beseech you to lose no time in revising and correcting everything so as to leave the least possible opening for malicious criticism."

When Erasmus was revising the *Novum Instrumentum* for a new edition in July 1517 he was at Louvain and he had the invaluable help of Cuthbert Tunstall who happened to be on an embassy to Flanders at that time. Erasmus declared to Thomas More that Tunstall "is just like you", a curious judgment as their tempera-ments were not strikingly similar. When their joint labours were ended, Tunstall made Erasmus a gift of fifty crowns, and wrote, "You have opened the sources of Greek learning to our age and the splendour of your achievement has for ever thrown into the shade the work of earlier scholars as the rising sun blots out the stars". This may seem an extravagant tribute and we must make allowance for the whole-heartedness with which scholars of the day praised or damned one another. Imperfect as it was, this first printing of the Greek text was a landmark in biblical scholarship; it could not be ignored. Many editions were issued during Erasmus' lifetime, not all of which were seen through the press by him; with editorial emendation, it remained the working text long after his death. Indeed it was not fully superseded until the nineteenth century. It was not in fact the first recension to be made. The New Testament in the Complutensian (Alcalá) Polyglot edition, prepared under the direction of Cardinal Ximenes, was actually ready by 1514, but was not published until 1522. It was in four languages, Hebrew, Chaldee, Greek and Latin, and as it filled six volumes it was an expensive work and its usefulness was further limited by a printing of six hundred sets only. It could not therefore oust Erasmus' volume which was not expensive. It has been suggested that he hurried through the printing because he had heard of Cardinal Ximenes' preparations, but there is no evidence that he was aware of the project; as has been noted, the rushed printing was typical of his methods of working, and it may be that Froben was as eager to get the book to the fairs.

Even before the New Testament was published, Erasmus had to face criticism from those who had heard of his intention. Reference has already been made to the letter written by Martin Dorp in September 1514, an expostulation made at the request of the strongly conservative theologians of Louvain. Dorp questioned the wisdom of "correcting the text of the New Testament. . . . I am arguing now", he wrote, "with respect to the truthfulness and integrity of the Latin translation and I assert this of our Vulgate version. For it cannot be that the unanimous universal Church now for so many centuries has been mistaken, which has always used, and still both sanctions and uses, this version. . . . What if it be contended that the sense, as rendered by the Latin version, differs in truth from the Greek text? Then, indeed, goodbye to the Greek! I adhere to the Latin because I cannot bring my mind to believe that the Greek are more accurate than the Latin codices."

When a copy of this letter came into the hands of Erasmus about May 1515 (still a year before publication), he wrote a good-natured reply.

"You are unwilling that I should alter anything except where the Greek expresses the sense of the Vulgate more clearly, and you deny that in the Vulgate edition there are any mistakes. And you think it wrong that what has been approved by the sanction of so many ages and so many synods, should be unsettled by any means. I beseech you to consider, most learned Dorp, whether what you have written is true. How is it that Jerome, Augustine and Ambrose all cite texts which differ from the Vulgate? How is it that Jerome finds fault with and corrects many readings which we find in the Vulgate? What can you make of all this concurrent evidence—when the Greek versions differ from the Vulgate, when Jerome cites the text according to the Greek versions, when the oldest Latin versions do the same, when this reading suits the sense much better than that of the Vulgate—will you, treating all this with contempt, follow a version perhaps corrupted by some copyist?"

Dorp would not let the matter rest there; he wrote a second time (August 1515), re-emphasizing his main points but still writing in a friendly tone. Thomas More then took up the defence of Erasmus in a long letter to which reference has already been made in so far as Dorp criticized *Moria*.[2] He drew a distinction between theologians attacked by Erasmus and those whom he respected. The former were those who were content to go on repeating and refining their text-book knowledge, "who read nothing of the Fathers or of the Scriptures except in the sentences and the commentators on the Sentences". The theologians respected by Erasmus were those who studied the Scriptures and the works of St Jerome, St Augustine and the other Fathers, men who may never have written a line but who have not spent half a century quibbling about trifles. To illustrate the limitations of some so-called theologians whom Erasmus ridiculed, More gave an account of an incident that probably occurred at the table of his friend Antonio Bonvisi.

"I was once dining with an Italian merchant as learned as he was rich, indeed very rich. There was at table a monk who was a theologian and a notable disputant. . . . At the dinner nothing was said by anyone, however well weighed and carefully expressed, that this man did not, before the speaker had finished, seek to refute with a syllogism though the matter

[2] The letter is translated in *Selected Letters*, ed. E. F. Rogers (Yale, 1961), No. 4.

belonged neither to theology nor philosophy and was altogether foreign to his profession. But I am wrong: his profession was to dispute. . . . By degrees our host turned the conversation to theological subjects, such as usury, tithes, or confession to friars outside the penitent's parish. The merchant soon saw that the monk was not so well acquainted with his Bible as he was ready with his syllogisms, so he began to draw his arguments more from authority than from reasoning. He invented on the spur of the moment certain quotations in favour of his own side of the question, taking one from an Epistle of St Paul, another from St Peter, a third from the Gospel, and affecting to do this with the greatest exactness, naming the chapter, but so that if a book was divided into sixteen chapters, he would quote from the twentieth. What did our theologian do now? He had to dodge from side to side to escape these supposed texts. He managed it, however. He had no notion that the passages quoted were spurious, but he could not deny the authority of Scripture. 'Yes, sir,' he would say, 'your quotation is good, but I understand the text in this way.' And, when he was contradicted, he declared that he was speaking on the authority of Nicholas of Lyra."

That, More pointed out, was the kind of pseudo-theological discussion to which Erasmus so strongly objected. More also dealt with Dorp's contention that any doubt thrown on the integrity of the text of the Vulgate must undermine the authority of the Scriptures. He pointed out that exactly the same charge had been brought against St Jerome, and that there can be no end to improvements in the text until a perfect translation is made so that future generations can find nothing to correct. He pointed to similar valuable work on the text of the Scriptures in the five-version edition of the Psalms by Lefèvre d'Étaples and published in 1509.

It may seem to us that Dorp's objections were somewhat absurd, but we are the heirs of a long line of scholars who have devoted themselves to the textual criticism of the Scriptures; moreover, in recent years we have become accustomed to several new translations. To us it all seems so reasonable, but some of the contemporaries of More and Erasmus were deeply and sincerely

H

troubled at what seemed to them an almost sacrilegious tampering with Holy Writ. Fortunately, Erasmus did his work at a time when humanistic studies had created a favourable atmosphere, and the printing press was waiting for him. The *Novum Instrumentum* was published at the right moment and that fact largely explains its welcome. It is pleasant to record that Dorp withdrew his objections after the book had been published, and he did so publicly in a lecture at Louvain. To him Thomas More wrote in December 1516:

"Believe me, my dear Dorp, what you have done with such great humility, it is almost impossible to demand even from those whom the world nowadays considers as most humble. ... For that letter of mine was wordy rather than convincing, and when I compare it with your lecture, so eloquent, so full of cogent arguments, I feel quite ashamed, my dear Dorp, to see what little power my words could have had to win your consent, although your modesty or your courtesy leads you now to ascribe such power to them."

Thomas More was an enthusiastic agent for the *Novum Instrumentum* in England. He composed some Latin verses to the reader in which he pointed out how the inaccuracies of early translators and still more of copyists had been corrected; he declared that there was no greater nor more helpful work. In sending a copy to Wolsey, he added in verse a commendation and suggested that the Cardinal should cherish the author. The copy presented to Warham contained verses that rightly praised the Archbishop's generosity to Erasmus. "He provided the labour; you, good bishop, provided the support."

Tunstall's tribute has already been quoted; this carried the more weight since he himself was a Greek scholar and could appreciate the importance of the *Novum Instrumentum*, while at the same time having the learning to note its inaccuracies. Warham, Colet and Fisher were Greekless; their attention was attracted by the Latin translation and the notes. In June 1516, John Fisher wrote to Erasmus,

"You have put me greatly in your debt by the gift of your

Novum Instrumentum translated from the Greek. As soon as I received it and had seen some of the notes in which you extol your Canterbury Maecenas [Warham] with many compliments, I hurried to show him these passages. When he had read them, he promised he would do much for you and begged me, if I should write to you, to urge you to return. Indeed, I do not doubt if you do, he will be more generous than ever."

He persuaded Erasmus to spend ten days at Rochester that August to give him his first lessons in Greek. While Erasmus was there, Thomas More came down to see his two friends. Erasmus was again in England for a brief visit in April 1517 and on his way to Dover he once more stayed at Rochester. John Fisher wrote to him in June 1517:

"No sensible person could be offended at your [Latin] translation of the New Testament for the common benefit of everyone, since not only have you made many passages clear by your learning but you have indeed provided a full series of comments on the whole work; thus it is now possible for everyone to read and understand it with more gratification and pleasure.... I owe it to you, Erasmus, that I can to some extent understand where the Greek text does not quite agree with the Latin. Would that I could have had you as my tutor for a few months."

He went on to regret the number of misprints. He signed his letter, "Discipulus tuus, Io. Roffensis". This tribute was important to Erasmus for John Fisher was recognized as one of the leading theologians of the day. The letter is evidence that the bishop had made some progress in Greek; he was then forty-seven years of age. John Colet was a few years older, but he too decided that he must learn Greek and he was given his first lessons by his former pupil, John Clement. He acknowledged the receipt of a copy of the *Novum Instrumentum* in these terms:

"The copies of your new edition are both eagerly bought and everywhere read here. Many approve and admire your work; some also disapprove and carp at it, making the same objections as are found in Martin Dorp's letter to you. But these latter are the divines whom, in your *Moria* and elsewhere, you portray as truly as cleverly; men whose praise is blame, and whose blame is praise. For my part I love your work and welcome this new edition of yours but with conflicting feelings. For at one moment I am vexed at not having learned Greek, without a knowledge of which we are helpless; at another, I rejoice in the light you have poured from the sun of your intellect. Indeed, Erasmus, I marvel at your prolific powers, daily conceiving and bringing to birth such great works and producing them in such a finished state, especially as you have no resting-place and are not helped by any fixed stipends of any moment. We are looking forward to your St Jerome, a writer who owes much to you, I especially, who shall now, thanks to you, read him both corrected and explained. . . . Do not stop, Erasmus, but now that you have given us the New Testament, illustrate it also with your explanations and with commentaries of full length on the Gospels. Length with you is brevity. If you unlock the meaning, as none can do better than yourself, you will confer a great benefit on those who love the Scriptures, and will immortalize your name."

In this last suggestion we may perhaps see the germ of the *Paraphrases* that Erasmus wrote in later years. If mature scholars such as Fisher and Colet were brought to see the need for a knowledge of Greek by Erasmus' work, it may be safely conjectured that many others were influenced in the same way. This was one of the incidental effects of this important book.

The correspondence with Dorp had warned Erasmus of the kind of criticisms he could expect now that his work was in circulation. He prefaced the *Novum Instrumentum* with a "Paraclesis" followed by a suggestion to the student on the best method of studying the New Testament. Both these introductory parts were expanded in later editions and the second was published separately as *Ratio, sive Methodus verae Theologiae.*[3] Here it will be convenient to discuss these important writings in their final forms.

The key passage of the "Paraclesis" reads:

"The philosophy of Christ is to be learned from its few books

---

[3]The *Ratio* has been discussed in detail in Chapter XII of Louis Bouyer's *Erasmus and the Humanist Experiment* (1959).

with far less labour than the Aristotelian philosophy is to be extracted from its multitude of ponderous and conflicting commentaries. Nor is anxious preparatory learning needful to the Christian. Its means are simple and at hand to all. Only bring a pious and open heart, imbued above all things with a pure and simple faith. Only be teachable and you have already made much way in this philosophy. It supplies a spirit for the teacher, imparted to none more readily than to the simple-minded. Other philosophies, by the very difficulty of their precepts, are removed out of the range of most minds. No age, no sex, no condition of life is excluded from this. The sun itself is not more common and open to all than the teaching of Christ. For I utterly dissent from those who are unwilling that the Scriptures should be read by the unlearned translated into their vulgar tongue, as though Christ had taught such subtleties that they can scarcely be understood even by a few theologians, or as though the strength of the Christian religion consisted in men's ignorance of it. The mysteries of kings it may be safer to conceal, but Christ wished his mysteries to be published as openly as possible. I wish that even the weakest woman should read the Gospel and the epistles of Paul. And I wish these were translated into all languages so that they might be read and understood not only by Scots and Irishmen but also by Turks and Saracens. To make them understand is surely the first step. It may be that they [the Gospels] might be ridiculed by many, but some would take them to heart. I long that the husbandman should sing portions of them to himself as he follows the plough, that the weaver should hum them to the tune of his shuttle, that the traveller should beguile with their stories the tedium of his journey."

Erasmus then considered the tendency of theologians of his day to give more heed to the study of the arguments of the schoolmen than to the study of the Gospels. What is the authority of the commemtators in comparison with the words of Christ himself?

"If the footprints of Christ be anywhere shown to us, we kneel down and adore. Why do we not rather venerate the living and breathing picture of him in these books? If the vesture of Christ be exhibited, where will we not go to kiss it? Yet were his whole wardrobe exhibited, nothing could represent Christ more vividly and truly than these evangelical writings. Statues of wood and stone we decorate with gold and gems for the love of Christ. They only profess to give us the form of his body; these books present us with a living image of his most holy mind. Were we to have seen him with our own eyes, we should not have had so intimate a knowledge as they give of Christ, speaking, healing, dying, rising again, as it were, in our very presence."

Erasmus was here expressing again, with greater emphasis, views he had put foward in his *Enchiridion*.

The *Ratio* is an essential document for the understanding of Erasmus' mind. Perhaps it should be pointed out that it is not a treatise covering the whole range of Christian theology, so it is irrelevant to complain, as some of his critics have done, that he said nothing on this dogma or that. He kept strictly to his purpose, and the result is an excellent example of his powers of exposition, well organized and clearly expressed. His purpose was to lead men back to the sources of their Faith; he wanted to revitalize theology from the waters of the original spring.

He advised the student to "approach the New Testament, not with an unholy curiosity but with reverence; bearing in mind that his first and only aim and object should be that he may catch and be changed into the spirit of what he there learns. It is the food of the soul."

Then he described the intellectual equipment that was desirable.

"A fair knowledge of the three languages Latin, Greek and Hebrew, of course is the first thing. It would be well, too, were the student tolerably versed in other branches of learning and especially in knowledge of natural objects—animals, trees, precious stones—of the countries mentioned in the Scriptures, for if we are familiar with the country, we can in thought follow the history and picture it in our minds so that we seem not only to read it but to see it, and if we do this we shall not easily forget it."

Here he struck a new note. To us it seems obviously desirable that we should appreciate the historical and physical perspective as well as the verbal meaning and intention. Erasmus may have derived this suggestion from Colet. It was an unusual point to make in those days. The passage continues:

"The student should learn to quote Scripture, not second-hand, but from the fountain-head, and take care not to distort its meaning as some do, interpreting the 'Church' as the 'clergy', the 'laity' as the 'world', and the like. To get at the real meaning, it is not enough to take four or five isolated words; you must look where they come from, what was said, in what words, what preceded, what followed. And if you refer to the commentaries, choose out the best, such as Origen, Basil, Jerome, Ambrose, etc., and read even these with discrimination and judgment, for they were men ignorant of some things and mistaken in others. As to the Schoolmen, I had rather be a pious divine with Jerome than invincible with Scotus. Was ever a heretic converted by their subtleties? Let those who like follow the disputations of the schools; but let him who desires to be instructed in piety rather than in the art of disputation, first and above all, apply himself to those writings that flowed immediately from the fountain-head. That doctor is abundantly great who purely preaches Christ."

The true objective of the student was to come to know Jesus Christ and his wisdom from the Gospels and Epistles just as the Early Fathers did. As an indication of what this implied, the following passage may be given on "Christ becoming man for our sake".

"Next observe the whole course of his life, how he grew up to youth, always in favour with both God and man. . . . At twelve years of age, teaching and listening in the Temple, he first gave a glimpse of what he was. Then by his first miracle at the marriage feast, in private, he made himself known to the few. For it was not until after he had been baptized and commanded by the voice of his Father and the sign of the dove, not until after he had been tried and proved by the forty-days' fast and temptation of Satan, that he began the work of preaching. Mark his birth, education, preaching, death; you will find nothing but a perfect example of poverty and humility, yea, of innocence. The whole range of his doctrine, as it was consistent with itself, so it was consistent with his life, and also consistent with his nature. He taught innocence; he himself so lived that even suborned witnesses could not find anything that could plausibly be laid to his charge. He taught gentleness; he himself was led as a lamb to the slaughter. He taught poverty; we do not read that he possessed anything. He warned against pride and ambition; he himself washed the feet of his disciples. He taught that this was the way to true glory and immortality. He himself, by the ignominy of the cross, has obtained a name that is above all names; and whilst he sought no earthly kingdom, he earned the empire of both heaven and earth. When he rose from the dead, he taught what he had taught before—he taught that death is not to be feared by the good, and on that account he showed himself risen again. In the presence of the disciples he ascended into heaven that we might know whither we are to strive to follow. Lastly, that heavenly Spirit descended which by its inspiration made his apostles what Christ wished them to be. You may perhaps find in the books of Plato and Seneca what is not inconsistent with the teaching of Christ; you may find some things in the life of Socrates that are certainly consistent with the life of Christ; but this wide range, and all things belonging to it in harmonious agreement, you will find in Christ alone."

It would be difficult to find a clearer expression of what is meant by Christian Humanism than is given in this passage.

Erasmus again urged that the dead-weight of the over-curious speculations of the later Schoolmen, who often took their knowledge of the Scriptures at second-hand, must be lifted by this direct approach to the actual text of the New Testament. Ceremonies and special devotions are of value only when they are genuine aids to faith and not ends in themselves and carried out mechanically. Faith and Charity are asked of us by Christ. It is the interior life of the spirit that really matters—so wrote this former pupil of the Brethren of the Common Life.

There is much more in this remarkable declaration of aims and methods in which Erasmus summed up the contribution he had to make to the religious thought of his times. These brief extracts will at least indicate the nature of his "Theory and Method of True Theology".

It would be difficult to overstate the importance of this first printed edition of the Greek New Testament. Defective as it was, it opened a new era in biblical scholarship; much had yet to be learned, for instance of the relative importance of the codices, and for the next two centuries the advance, as we should think, was not impressive, but a beginning had been made. Erasmus had put the "tool" into the hands of his successors.

CHAPTER XII

Utopia

FEW YEARS have produced two such notable works as those published in 1516—the *Novum Instrumentum* of Erasmus and the *Utopia* of Thomas More. To these can be added the nine-volume edition of St Jerome by Erasmus, and his *Institutio Principis Christiani*; new editions were also published of *Luciani Opuscula* and of the *Enchiridion*. It was a great year for the two friends. While the works of Erasmus have been superseded or have lost current interest, *Utopia* remains provocative and stimulating.

On 12 May 1515 Thomas More, with John Clement in attendance, left London for Bruges on an embassy to Flanders. The Court of Common Council of London allowed him to appoint a deputy as Under-Sheriff during his absence; it had been at the request of the London merchants that More had been included in the embassy since the negotiations were mainly commercial and closely concerned City interests. The leader was Cuthbert Tunstall, chancellor to Archbishop Warham. He and More were about the same age and their new association strengthened an existing friendship. Fortunately we need not concern ourselves with the details of the negotiations; More had expected to be away for two or three months, but the affair dragged on month after month and it was not until late October that he at last got permission to return home. The business was tedious; there must have been many periods of delay when no business could be done while one side or the other waited for fresh instructions; the incidental outcome of these intervals of inaction was momentous.

Erasmus, who had been in London when More left, arrived in Bruges in June, but after a few days he went on to Antwerp. He had written from London to his old friend Peter Gilles, the Town Clerk of Antwerp.

"The two most learned men of all England are now at Bruges; Cuthbert Tunstall and Thomas More, to whom I inscribed *Moria*, both great friends of mine. If you should have the chance of offering them any civility, your services will be well bestowed."

More was in Antwerp in September and he soon found that Peter Gilles was a congenial spirit. Perhaps the notion of *Utopia* was already forming in More's mind and he probably discussed the idea with Gilles, for they shared the fun of it as their introductory letters show. This would explain the choice of Antwerp and Gilles' garden as the setting for the talk with the fictional Hythlodaye. When he left Flanders in October, More had with him the manuscript of what became the Second Book of *Utopia*; he may also have written the introductory pages of the First Book. Erasmus' account reads, "In *Utopia* his purpose was to show whence spring the evils of states. . . . He began with the Second Book, written at leisure, and then, when opportunity came, he added the First rapidly; this accounts for some unevenness in the [Latin] style."

There was a local tradition that More completed his *Utopia* at his father's country house of Gobions. It was recorded by Henry Peacham, the author of *The Compleat Gentleman* (1622).

"Merry John Heywood[1] wrote his Epigrams, as also Sir Thomas More his Utopia, in the parish wherein I was born (North Mimms in Hertfordshire, near to St Albans), where either of them dwelt and had fair possessions."

Peacham was wrong in saying that More had "possessions" in Hertfordshire; he would not have inherited Gobions until after the death of his step-mother.

Peter Gilles evidently thought that the whole book would be soon ready for the printer and he may have already arranged to get it printed. In his dedicatory letter to Gilles, More apologized for the delay. "I am almost ashamed, my dearest Peter," he wrote, "to send you this book about the commonwealth of Utopia after nearly a year when I am sure you expected it within six

[1] Merry John Heywood married More's niece, Joan Rastell.

weeks." He pleaded pressure of work, but there may have been another delaying factor: new problems called for treatment.

The First Book[2] opens with an account of the meeting with Hythlodaye; after six pages,[3] Peter Gilles interjected the suggestion that Hythlodaye should use his experience in the service of a prince. This was discussed for three pages, and then the subject was again changed and for eighteen pages Hythlodaye examined the problem, "Why do men become thieves?" This part brings in reminiscences of Cardinal Morton's household. The argument then returned to Peter Gilles' suggestion, and More and Hythlodaye exchanged views on the place of the philosopher in government; nine pages are taken up with this discussion, and in the remaining six pages Hythlodaye expounded his opinions on the evils of property, and answered criticisms from More and Gilles. So we are led to consider the polity of Utopia in the Second Book.

The argumentative part of the First Book has a vigour of its own that makes it the most readable portion of *Utopia*; there is an urgency, an immediacy, that is in striking contrast with the rest of the book. More was considering two very different problems: the first was the condition of England with rogues and thieves infesting society, while the second was a personal matter—should he enter the King's service? As we have seen, a considerable portion of the First Book was devoted to the question, "Why do men become thieves?". He tried to get to the causes of the trouble so that it could be cut off at the source. He, or Hythlodaye, offered the following explanations: penalties that were too severe to be deterrent; ex-soldiers (the futile French war ended in 1514), mutilated or able-bodied, were loose in the country; there were too many idle retainers in noble households; land was being enclosed and arable turned to pasture, thereby dispossessing whole families; the pursuit of riches and the spread of luxury and of gambling set bad examples to common folk. This deeply felt concern, so strongly expressed, was doubtless the outcome of

[2]The order of composition is discussed in J. H. Hexter, *More's "Utopia"* (1952), an acute commentary on some aspects of the book.

[3]These figures refer to the Everyman edition; they are given to show the proportions allotted to the several topics.

More's five years' experience as Under-Sheriff,[4] or magistrate as we should say, in his court at the Poultry Compter; there he would deal summarily with the rogues and vagabonds who were the bane of the City. More's attitude was unusual in his day; he wanted the penalty to fit the crime and he was anxious to get at the roots of the evils of society.

The personal problem of whether to take service under the King was much in his thoughts. It was inevitable that he should be called to such service for he had those abilities that the Tudors liked to use. He had shown these in a number of negotiations on behalf of the City Companies; he was an outstanding pleader and orator; his work as Under-Sheriff was appreciated, and he was *persona grata* with the Mayor and Aldermen, an important consideration when loans were needed by the Crown. Added to this was his success in the 1515 embassy. It would indeed have been surprising had he not been regarded favourably by the King and Wolsey. It was probably the latter who invited More to become a King's Counsel with a retaining fee of £100 a year. More wrote to Erasmus in February 1516,

> "On my return I had a yearly pension offered me by the King, which whether one looked to for profit or the honour of it, was not to be despised. This, however, I have hitherto refused, and shall, I think, continue to do so, because, if I took it, the place I now hold in the City, which I prefer to higher office, would either have to be given up, or retained, much to my regret, with some offence to the citizens, who, if they had any dispute with the government, as sometimes happens, about their privileges, would have less confidence in me as a paid pensioner of the King."

We may note his loyalty to his native City. As a King's Counsel he might be called upon to oppose the City in any dispute with the Crown. The financial problem for himself would also have to be taken into account. As he had found on his embassy, allowances were not generous, nor were they always paid promptly, and he had a family to support.

[4]When Erasmus wrote that More occupied "an office which has little work", he was misinformed. The Under-Sheriffs were the pack-horses of the City government, leaving the more decorative functions to the Sheriffs.

It so happened that Erasmus came to England late in July 1516 and stayed for about a month. Part of the period, perhaps most of it, was spent as More's guest. The two friends, sometimes perhaps with Colet and others of their circle, would discuss the Second Book of *Utopia* and the prospective First Book, just as they probably had discussed *Moria*. Only a few months earlier Erasmus had accepted the position of a Councillor to Charles, King of Spain, later the Emperor Charles V. It is true that in return for his pension, irregularly paid, Erasmus was not expected to undertake regular duties, but it gave him a status that warranted him in tendering advice, as he was to do, to Charles, and he had access to the Emperor. So the two friends would discuss the offer made to More. Erasmus opposed any such engagement and he always regretted that More eventually became a Councillor. In the discussion in *Utopia* on whether a philosopher should serve a prince, we can perhaps hear not only More arguing with himself but arguing with Erasmus.[5] Perhaps it was these talks that led More later to speak of "our *Utopia*", but this did not imply active collaboration: Erasmus could equally well have said "our *Moria*".

We know the outcome of More's deliberations. What was the compulsive reason that led him to give way? It has been persuasively argued[6] that the vigour of Wolsey's early administration of the law in favour of lesser-privileged people, and his apparent commitment to a peace policy from 1517, convinced Thomas More that he could render useful service and his own good relations with Wolsey may have strengthened his hopes. This is an attractive conjecture. Unfortunately he did not himself give his reasons even in writing to Erasmus. He was always reticent about his own affairs and became all but silent on state affairs. Another explanation seems to me as probable. Note has already been made of More's *pietas*, his clearly marked sense of duty to the community and to his prince, a sense that was reinforced when he made his great decision to live in the world rather than in the cloister. It should be noted that in between the publication of *Utopia* and the decision to enter the King's service, More had

[5]See above, p. 69.
[6]Hexter, *op. cit.*, pp. 138ff.

taken part in another embassy; he was at Calais from August to December 1517. Once again he had shown his skill as a negotiator and this may have made him more confident in his own powers. An invitation to enter the King's service in those times was only short of a command, though a refusal would not have led to consequences more serious than the loss of the King's goodwill; even that, however, was not to be lightly risked by one with a strong sense of public duty. So at length he gave way. Erasmus was far from happy at this decision; all Hythlodaye's arguments had been made in vain! In a letter to Tunstall, 24 April 1518, he wrote,

> "I should deplore the fortune of More in being enticed to Court if it were not that under such a King and with so many learned men for companions and colleagues, it may seem not a Court but a temple of the Muses. But meanwhile there is nothing brought us from Utopia to amuse us, and he, I am quite sure, would rather have his laugh than be borne aloft on a curule chair."

It was all the consolation Erasmus could find.

Perhaps More too wondered if he had made a mistake; he wrote to Bishop John Fisher, probably in 1518,

> "It was with the greatest unwillingness that I came to Court, as everyone knows, and as the King himself in a joke often throws up in my face. I am as uncomfortable there as a bad rider is in the saddle. . . . But the King has virtue and learning, and makes great progress in both with daily renewed zeal, so that the more I see of his Majesty advance in all the qualities that befit a good monarch, the less burdensome do I feel this life at Court."

Utopia is not a systematic exposition of a political philosophy and it is an unpromising task to try to deduce one from it. The reader must bear one or two points in mind, otherwise he will go astray in his interpretation.

The form is dramatic. The First Book is a dialogue and the Second a monologue or declamation. This makes it precarious to label any opinion as that of Thomas More himself. The reader will at once say that I have just ignored this very warning, but my contention is that the part of the First Book in which the nature of crime and the service of princes are discussed is of a different character from the rest of *Utopia*; it deals with immediate problems. Even so, it is unwise to say that all Hythlodaye's views correspond with those of More, or, when he is speaking himself, that he is revealing his own mind fully. The reader who ascribes to him every opinion expressed or implied in the Second Book will soon find himself in troubled waters as he reads of such topics as slavery, colonialism, mercenary warfare, the removal of children from their homes, euthanasia, courtship and divorce. The temptation is to select those opinions that fit into some scheme we ourselves devise and to ignore those that are awkward. Some commentators have yielded to this temptation with queer results. In spite of all that has been written about *Utopia* during the past seventy years, the view expressed by J. H. Lupton in 1895 still holds good. The Second Book, he wrote,

"is merely a series of essays, under some eight or nine headings, in which, under the thin disguise of a fictitious narrative, More gives utterance to his own views on various social, political, or religious questions. That these views are all alike seriously propounded, as held by himself, it would be preposterous to maintain. Such a notion would be to crystallize what More purposely left in a state of solution. . . . If the reader should complain that, on this showing, it is impossible to be sure what More really meant, the remark would have been equally true of much of his conversation, when it was often hard to make out whether he spoke in jest or in earnest. Socrates and More would have understood each other."[7]

The form of the book is not the only indication of the influence of More's delight in Lucian. We have to take into account the irony and the love of a joke and of leg-pulling, characteristics that became part of his legend. One example of this is given in his dedicatory letter to Peter Gilles in the first edition of 1516. This amusing letter gives a pleasant impression of Gilles, who so far entered the fun of the affair as to devise a Utopian alphabet. In his letter, More, in a matter-of-fact way, asked Gilles to get some

[7]Lupton's edition of *Utopia*, p. xli.

further information from Hythlodaye about the dimensions of the bridge at Amaurote and about the exact position of the island. Gilles kept up the joke in a letter to Busleiden (also in the first edition) in which he admits that when Hythlodaye was telling them of the geographic position of Utopia, he himself had a fit of coughing and so missed the details. In his letter More had explained why he wanted this information; "because there be with us a certain man, and especially one devout and godly man, a professor of divinity, who is exceedingly desirous to go to Utopia" as a missionary. When Ralph Robinson made his translation thirty-five years later he solemnly added at this point that the "professor of divinity" was "the late famous Vicar of Croydon, Rowland Philips".[8] The translator missed the joke, and he was not the last to do so.

A further obstacle to understanding is the application to *Utopia* of such terms as "communism" and "socialism". Both words are nineteenth-century inventions and each has now acquired a specific political connotation that would have been meaningless in Tudor England. The polity of Utopia is based on the common ownership of goods and the abolition of private property, but the use of slave or penal labour should not be ignored. To quote a notable passage:

"I can have no other notion of all other governments that I see or know, than that they are a conspiracy of the rich who on pretence of managing the public only pursue their private ends."

That is not what we know of communism in practice in our own day. Thomas More was not the precursor of Karl Marx.

Perhaps like "communism" the very word "Utopia" misleads us. To More it simply meant "Nowhere", "Nusquama", just a label, but, to quote the *O.E.D.*, it has come to mean "a state ideally perfect in respect of politics, laws, customs and conditions". This present-day usage leads us sometimes to think that every detail in Utopian life was part of More's conception of the

---

[8]More and Philips may have been acquainted in London as Philips was then rector of St Margaret Pattens in Eastcheap, but it is unlikely that he read *Utopia* in manuscript. Their most dramatic meeting was on 13 April 1534 at Lambeth.

J

ideal community. Erasmus' statement should not be forgotten: "his purpose was to show whence spring the evils of states", or, to put it another way, the book is critical of contemporary society and the emphasis is not so much on the polity and economy of Utopia as on the contrast with the existing state of affairs. We must read the criticism of society in the description of Utopia. Nor should we forget the final comment, "I cannot fully agree with everything he has related". It is, in fact, uncritical to take the book too seriously. As G. K. Chesterton remarked, More "was the founder of all Utopias, but he used Utopia as what it really is, a playground. His Utopia was partly a joke, but since his time, Utopians have seldom seen the joke."

The reader may ask why a book that is so enigmatic should prove perennially interesting. The answer is that it is bursting with ideas and is thus a stimulus to thought on matters that concern each of us, but what the reader thinks is not necessarily what More really thought. In writing of *Utopia* it is difficult to avoid such an expression as "More said"; here it should be understood as a convenient alternative to "in *Utopia* the view is expressed".

Erasmus left London in the middle of August 1516 for Rochester, where he spent ten days to give John Fisher his lessons in Greek. More went down to spend a day with them. The manuscript of *Utopia*, or *Nusquama*, as More still called it, was not quite completed but he was able to send it to Erasmus at the beginning of September. "I send you *Nusquama*, nowhere well written, with a prefatory letter to my dear Peter." A month later Erasmus wrote from Antwerp where he was the guest of Gilles, "Every care shall be taken about the Island. . . . Peter Gilles is simply in love with you; you are still always with us. He is wonderfully struck with your *Nusquama*." *Utopia* was published in December 1516. Lord Mountjoy at Tournai, of which he was lieutenant, wrote to Erasmus on 4 January 1517, to thank him for a copy, adding, "as I cannot enjoy the company of More himself, I shall at least find my dear More in *Utopia*".

The book was written in Latin as it was addressed to scholars and clerics; it was published abroad partly because English printers had not yet effectively entered the Continental market and partly because Erasmus with the help of Gilles could see the book through the press. The old idea that More feared the book might do him harm with Henry and Wolsey was nonsense; there was no secrecy and the book found a ready audience in England.

More had been anxious that, in the manner of the day, his book should have some introductory letters of recommendation from distinguished scholars. Perhaps he may have been somewhat diffident about a book that was of an unusual character. Two of the letters are of special interest as revealing how contemporaries interpreted *Utopia*. Jerome Busleiden was a wealthy scholar, both priest and state councillor, who founded the Trilingual College at Louvain. More had got to know him while in Flanders. His letter was included in the first edition. He commended the state of Utopia because

"in it all competition for ownership is taken away, and no one has any private property at all. For the rest, all men have things in common, with a view to the commonwealth itself; so that every matter, every action, however unimportant, whether public or private, instead of being directed to the greed of the many or the caprice of the few, has sole reference to the upholding of one uniform justice, equality and communion. When that is made the entire object of every action, there must needs be a clearance of all that serves as matter and fuel and feeder of intrigue, of luxury, envy and wrong; to which mankind are hurried on, even at times against their will, either by the possession of private property, or by burning thirst of gain, and that most pitiable of all things, ambition, to their own great and immeasurable loss."

A letter from the famous French scholar Guillaume Budé to Thomas Lupset[9] was added to the second (Paris) edition. Budé wrote:

"It holds with firm grip to three divine institutions, namely, the absolute equality, or if you prefer to call it so, the community of possessions, of all things good and bad among fellow-citizens; a settled and unwavering love of peace and quietness, and a

[9] In 1517 he was studying in Paris and saw through the press of Gilles de Gourmont the second (unauthorized) edition of *Utopia*.

contempt for gold and silver. Three things these, which over-turn, one may say, all fraud, all imposture, cheating, roguery and unprincipled deception. Would that Providence would cause these three principles of Utopian law to be fixed in the minds of all men! We should soon see pride, covetousness, insane competition and almost all other deadly weapons of our adversary the devil, fall powerless."

Two points should be stressed. Both writers emphasized the ethical, not the economic or political, aspect of the Utopian polity. This was certainly in keeping with More's mind; he had portrayed a non-Christian state where the classical virtues flourished. Secondly, both writers accepted the notion of com-munal property, an idea less startling then than now. Monastic life, however impaired, was a familiar and accepted association based on communal living. More had some experience of it in his Benedictine College at Oxford and at the London Charterhouse. To some extent his years of training in the law also made him familiar with communal meals and other customs. He may have learned from Erasmus about the Brethren of the Common Life and must have seen something of their work in Flanders. The attitude towards property was one that he shared with Colet, who, in a lecture on Romans, said:

"This law of corrupted nature is the same as that Law of Nations resorted to by nations all over the world; a law which brought *meum* and *tuum*—of property, that is to say, and deprivation; ideas clean contrary to a good and unsophisticated nature, for that would have a community in all things."

On this matter of communal living, Erasmus was silent. He had had too much of it! Few men would have been less fitted to live in Utopia, and, indeed, most of us would have found life in that over-regulated state dull and even repellent. Other ideas or opinions thrown out in *Utopia* can be found in *Moria* and also in a short treatise Erasmus wrote entitled *Institutio Principis Christiani* which was published in May 1516. He must surely have taken a copy for More when he went to England that August, and prob-ably a copy of the new edition of *Enchiridion*. The *Institutio*, or *Education of a Christian Prince*, was Erasmus' way of acknow-

ledging his appointment to the King of Spain's Council. It would
be a mistake to dismiss it as a conventional offering from a
scholar; even the most opportunist writing of Erasmus bears the
imprint of his mind. He wrote that a "prince should keep in
mind the same principle that people should remember in choosing
a prince, namely, the public good". So in *Utopia*, "a prince ought
to take more care of his people's happiness than of his own".
Erasmus continued, "As often as it comes into your mind that you
are a prince, call to mind also that you are a Christian prince. Do
not think that Christianity consists of ceremonies, that is, in
observing the ritual of the Church. The Christian is not he who is
baptized, or he who is consecrated, or he who is present at holy
rites; but he who is united to Christ in closest affection, and who
shows it by his holy actions. . . . There is no duty by the perform-
ance of which you can more secure the favour of God than by
making yourself a prince useful to the people." This is putting the
Utopian conception of a prince into a Christian setting. It would
have been fruitless to have advised the young king to do away
with private property, but Erasmus could go so far as to say,
"It ought to be provided that there be not too great an inequality
of wealth; not that I would have anyone deprived of his goods by
force, but that care should be taken lest the wealth of the community be limited to a few persons". His remedies included the
heavy taxation of luxuries and the light taxation of essentials.

The pursuit of a positive policy for peace was a subject on
which Erasmus and More both put marked emphasis, but the
treatment in the *Christian Prince* differs considerably from that in
Utopia and illustrates the danger of ignoring the irony in More's
work. Erasmus dealt with the problem in a direct manner. For
instance, "Because one prince offends another in some trifle, and
that a private matter, such as relationship by marriage, what is
this to the people as a whole? The good prince measures all
things by the advantage of the people, otherwise he would not
be a good prince. . . . But if some dissensions arise between
princes, why not rather resort to arbitrators? There are so many
bishops, abbots, scholars, serious magistrates, by whose judgment
such a matter might far more decently be composed than by so

much murder, pillage, and misery." It may be said that such advice sounds almost commonplace and is still too often ignored; but five hundred years have passed since the days of Erasmus and in his time such proposals were far from being part of man's political thinking; they have not lost their validity through age.

It has sometimes been argued that whereas More was a man of affairs, Erasmus lived in the scholar's ivory tower; this is to forget his constant journeyings and his intimate connexions with public men of several countries. When he pointed to dynastic rivalries as a cause of war, he showed how alive he was to the contemporary situation.

The section in *Utopia* dealing with war, "Of military affairs", begins with the statement that the Utopians "think there is nothing more inglorious than the glory of war". The reader may then become puzzled by the account of the warlike proceedings of the Utopians—their military training, their hiring of mercenaries, their subversive propaganda and their encouragement of treachery. All this is an ironical comment on contemporary policies; so too in the preceding section, the discussion on leagues and treaties is a criticism of the conduct of princes in More's own Europe. By the end of these sections, the reader is disgusted at such policies and practices, and that surely is what More intended.

A year after *Utopia* appeared, Erasmus published a short treatise that has been kept in print during this century. This was his *Querela Pacis*, the *Complaint of Peace*, in which Peace states her case as Folly had stated hers in *Moria*. The theme of peace and war comes time and time again in Erasmus' writings; it will be found in the *Colloquies* and the *Adages*. He had some knowledge of the devastation of war in his journeys from Flanders to Basle and down into Italy and he knew the dangers that threatened the traveller from bands of marauding soldiers. More had not seen such things. We cannot here summarize this forceful plea for peace, but one or two points may be noted. Erasmus declared that "there is no peace, even unjust, which is not preferable to the most just war", an adaptation of a saying by Cicero which had also been quoted by John Colet in one of his lectures. One passage from the *Complaint* is central to Erasmus' thinking on the subject:

"Formerly the Rhine separated France from Germany, but the Rhine cannot separate Christian from Christian. The Pyrenees put a frontier between the Gauls and the Spaniards, but these same mountains cannot divide mankind. The sea separates the English from the French, but it cannot break the bonds of the community of Christ."

We may recall John Colet's Good Friday sermon, as reported by Erasmus.

"They who through hatred or ambition were fighting and slaughtering one another by turns, were warring under the banner, not of Christ, but of the Devil. At the same time, he pointed out to them how hard a thing it was to die a Christian death; how few entered on a war unsullied by hatred or love of gain; how incompatible a thing it was that a man should have that brotherly love without which no one could see God, and yet bury his sword in his brother's heart."

Hythlodaye noted that Utopians

"judge that no man is to be esteemed our enemy that has never injured us, and that the partnership of human nature takes the place of a league. And that kindness and good-nature unite men more effectively and with greater strength than any agreements whatsoever, since thereby the engagements of men's hearts become stronger than the bond and obligation of words."

On the subject of crime and punishment, Erasmus was at one with More; greater attention should be given to the removal of the causes of crime and to its prevention; all possible alternatives should be tried before capital punishment is decreed. "Extreme justice is an extreme injury", said Hythlodaye, quoting Cicero's *Summum jus, summa injuria*, a maxim that Colet also commended. Idle people should be set to work or banished. The number of priests should be limited. The priests of Utopia "are men of eminent piety and therefore few in number". Unemployed ex-soldiers ("soldiers often prove brave robbers", said Hythlodaye) and parasitic nobles, "revellers, eager sportsmen", should not be allowed. "Among foolish pursuers of pleasure", the Utopians "reckon all that delight in hunting, fowling and gaming." There is an amusing description in *Moria* of those "who swear that the hideous blowing of horns and baying of dogs, gives more pleasure than anything else in the world".

Erasmus, Colet and More were united in their poor opinion of lawyers. In *Moria* we read of "the lawyer who is so silly as to be the proverbial ignoramus, and yet by such are difficulties resolved, all controversies determined, and all affairs managed so much to their own advantage that they get those estates to themselves which they are employed to recover for their clients". Colet spoke harshly of canon lawyers in his lectures. "One might suppose", he said, "they held their title and profession for no other purpose than this, namely like bloodsuckers, to render men bloodless and penniless by never-ending fines while they themselves are all swollen with thefts and robberies." As for the Utopians, "they have no lawyers among them, for they consider them as a sort of people whose profession it is to disguise matters and to argue legal points".

Other examples could be given to show how these three friends were thinking along the same lines. What discussions they must have had when Erasmus was in London! There is no reason to suppose that any one of them dominated the other two; three men of such quick intelligence and of such breadth of learning could exchange opinions and discuss differences on equal terms. The outcome is recorded in their works.

NOTE: No attempt has been made in this chapter to survey the whole field of Utopian ideas; many books have been written on *Utopia* to prove this or that theory; some stimulating, some amusing, some ridiculous. How More and Erasmus would have laughed could they have read some of them! The newcomer will find a useful guide in H. W. Donner's *Introduction to Utopia* (1945) with its many references to other books. J. H. Hexter's book on *Utopia* has been mentioned in the footnotes; it is refreshing. See also the Yale edition of *Utopia* (1964).

CHAPTER XIII

New Editions

ERASMUS HAD boldly dedicated the *Novum Instrumentum* to Pope Leo X, thereby hoping to forestall criticism. He wrote direct to the Pope in April 1517 to urge him to foster "first that truly Christian piety that has in many ways fallen into decay; secondly, the best kind of learning, hitherto partly neglected and partly corrupted, and, thirdly, the public and lasting concord of Christendom, the source and parent of piety and erudition". It was a formidable programme for the easy-going but shifty Medicean Pope, who, though a patron of learning and the arts like his father Lorenzo Il Magnifico, failed to see the trend of contemporary movements of thought or to realize how widely felt was the desire for reform within the Church. He could appreciate the learning of Erasmus without fully understanding his purpose. In August 1517 Erasmus wrote again, this time to ask for the Pope's favour. He wanted to get his clerical position regularized. Julius II had given him permission to wear ordinary clerical dress instead of that of an Augustinian monk, and, presumably, had lifted the impediment of illegitimacy, otherwise Erasmus could not have accepted the living of Aldington. As this dispensation was of limited scope and was not based, apparently, on a full disclosure of the facts, Erasmus now wanted to have it confirmed and, more importantly, to be freed from his monastic vows. Servatius Roger, the new Prior of Steyn, expected him to return to his monastery; we have seen how Erasmus dealt with his old friend's letter. The negotiations were arranged with the help of Ammonio who, as papal agent in England, was in a position to approach the right authorities. A letter was written to the papal chancery telling the story of the life of one Florentius;[1] under this

[1] It is interesting that he should have used the name of the effective founder of the Brethren of the Common Life.

guise Erasmus set down as much of his own history as seemed desirable. The letter was addressed to Lambertus Grunnius, otherwise unknown, who may have been a figment of Erasmus' imagination. Why he should have adopted this curiously round-about way of giving his personal story is hard to understand; perhaps he just enjoyed a little mystification, or was afraid that the letter might get into hostile hands. A formal letter was also sent to the Pope. The Bishop of Worcester, Silvestro Gigli, took the letters with him when he set out for the Lateran Council. After the appropriate delays, the Pope granted all that Erasmus desired. The brief was addressed "Dilecto filio Erasmo Rogerii Rotero-damensi clerico". Thus Erasmus was freed from his monastic vows.

Ammonio was commissioned to perform the official act and for this Erasmus hurried over to London from Antwerp so that he could formally receive the dispensation, on 7 April 1517. After a brief stay at Rochester with Bishop John Fisher, Erasmus left England for the last time at the end of the month. It had been his final parting with Ammonio who died of the sweating sickness in the following August. Both Erasmus and More were greatly distressed at the loss of Ammonio; he had lodged at the Barge for some time until Mistress Alice More got tired of him. It was the first break in the circle of humanist friends in London.

Erasmus was talking of settling down! He was now fifty years old, and, in contemporary reckoning, was entering his old age. Thoughts of England recurred but he had been disappointed. Henry VIII had not proved an active patron of learning and Wolsey, to quote Erasmus, "was discriminating in his friendliness and affability". Erasmus would recall that the historian Polydore Vergil had been imprisoned by Wolsey in 1515. Then there was the hatred of foreigners shown in the Ill May Day riots of 1517 when Thomas More had played a beneficial part long remembered in London legend. Erasmus also had a poor idea of English hygiene and he thought the recurrent waves of sweating stickness were evidence of a lack of fresh air and cleanliness; he was, for instance, horrified at the filth accumulated by rarely changed rushes on the floors.[2] These considerations were no doubt in his mind when he decided against a return to England. He had received several attractive invitations, notably a personal one from Francis of France, and there is no doubt that he would have been welcomed in Spain and Rome. He has been well called the last of the wandering scholars and to fix himself in one place was not in his nature. For some three years he used Louvain as his base but he was often away paying visits, especially to his friend Peter Gilles in Antwerp. The Louvain scholars were friendly as the earlier disagreement over the *Novum Instrumentum* had been resolved, but he had his detractors among the monks and friars. He might even have had a professorship in the University, but his instinct was to remain unattached and uncommitted.

Thomas More arrived in Calais at the beginning of September 1517 on another tiresome embassy, and was kept there, much to his annoyance, until December. There is no record that he and Erasmus met, though they probably did so, but they exchanged letters frequently. When More returned home in December, he carried with him portraits of Erasmus and Peter Gilles painted by Quentin Metsys. This friendly gift had been in preparation for some months. In May, soon after his short visit to England, Erasmus wrote from Antwerp:

"Peter Gilles and I are being painted in one picture which we intend to send you as a present before long. But it unluckily happened that on my return I found that Peter had been attacked by a serious illness, from which he has not even now recovered. I was myself fairly well, but somehow or other it occurred to my doctor to order me some pills for the purging of bile; and what he was fool enough to prescribe, I was fool enough to take. The portrait was already begun, but when I returned to the painter after taking the physic, he said it was not the same face; so the painting has been put off for some days till I can look more cheerful."

Shortly before leaving for Calais, More wrote:

[2]In 1524 he wrote a remarkable letter on the subject to his doctor friend John Francis, later physician to Wolsey. It shows how advanced were some of his notions on health. As we read, we are reminded of that garden-city Amaurot.

"The picture which represents your likeness with that of our Peter is expected greedily by me. I have no patience with an illness that delays my satisfaction for so long."

It was not until September that Erasmus was able to send the diptych to More at Calais.[3]

"I send the portraits so that we may in some way still be with you, if any chance should take us off. Peter pays half, and I half —not that we should, either of us, have been unwilling to pay the whole, but that the present may be common to both of us. . . . I am sorry you are shut up in Calais. If nothing else can be done, write frequently, though it be only a few words. Farewell, dearest of mortals."

Erasmus is shown in the portrait busy at work on his Paraphrase on St Paul's Epistle to the Romans, while Gilles holds in his hand a letter with More's handwriting cleverly imitated. More wrote to Gilles and enclosed some Latin verses in acknowledgment.

"My dear Peter," he wrote, "our Quentin has not only marvellously imitated all the objects he has depicted, but he has also shown his ability to be, if he turned his mind to it, a most skilful forger, having copied the address of my letter to you in such a way that I could not write it myself so like again. Therefore, unless he wants to keep the latter for any purpose of his own, or you for purposes of yours, please send it back to me; it will double the marvel if it is put by the side of the picture."

In his letter of thanks to Erasmus, More said:

"You cannot believe, my most dear Erasmus, how your eagerness to bind me still more closely to you, has heightened my love for you, though I thought nothing could be added to it. . . . It may be a proud thought, but most certainly I esteem your gift to mean that you would wish the memory of you to be renewed in my mind, not daily only, but every hour. You know me so well that I need not labour to prove to you that I am no greater boaster. Yet, to tell the truth, there is one craving

[3]See Plates 2 and 3.

for glory I cannot shake off, and it is wonderful how sweetly I am elated when the thought comes to me that I shall be commended to the most distant ages by the friendship, the letters, the books, the picture of Erasmus."

More added that he had taken advantage of two free days to visit Erasmus' friend the Abbot of St Bertin at St Omers. A fortnight later he wrote again; evidently it had again been suggested, probably by Wolsey, that More should enter the King's service. Once more Erasmus must have urged More to refuse:

"I approve of your plan", replied More, "in not wishing to be involved in the busy trifles of princes; and you show your love for me by desiring that I may be freed from such affairs in which, you well know, how unwillingly I am engaged."

He was not, however, to escape from "the busy trifles of princes", and on his return from Calais at the end of 1517, he gave his consent. The records are too scanty to give us a satisfactory account of his work as a councillor. He held judicial and financial offices, and he later accompanied the King and Queen in their progresses from royal manor to royal manor. Extant letters in his hand, mostly addressed to Wolsey, show that, for a time at least, he acted as the King's secretary. This was still a household appointment and it was not until the administrative reorganization under Thomas Cromwell that the King's secretary became, in effect, a minister of state. Fortunately we are not here concerned with More's career as a councillor, but it may be noted that for a decade his few private letters are silent on political affairs. He put into practice the opinion given to Hythlodaye, that it is the duty of a councillor to be content to give the best advice he can in the circumstances of the day, and not to act as if all men were perfect. So he reserved his views on public affairs for the King's ear, or for the council, and did not gossip.

One consolation Thomas More had in his attendance on the King was that among his colleagues were men of learning such as Richard Pace and John Clerk, both of whom had been at Italian Universities. In a letter of April 1518, Erasmus gave an account of how More had defended the teaching of Greek at

Oxford. Thanks to Bishop John Fisher and Erasmus' stay at
Cambridge, that University had gone ahead in Greek studies, and
St John's College, of which Fisher was the effective founder, was
trilingual. Oxford was still dominated by men who preferred the
old ways and regarded Greek with suspicion. The controversy
there became fierce. The students had entered the battle with
gusto and ranged themselves as Greeks and Trojans. Then a
university preacher denounced the obnoxious language from the
pulpit, calling its defenders "very devils" and the supporting
students "little devils". In his letter Erasmus gave an account of an
incident at Court that must have been sent to him by More or
Pace.

"A theologian who had to preach in the presence of the King,
began stupidly and impudently to attack Greek studies and the
new interpreters of Scripture. Pace looked at the King to see
how he took it. The King smiled. When the sermon was over,
the theologian was called. More was appointed to defend
Greek and the King himself was at the discussion. After
More, with much eloquence, had made a long defence
and the reply of the theologian was expected, instead of speaking, he suddenly went on his knees and asked pardon of the
King, affirming, however, in in his excuse, that while preaching
he had felt himself inspired to say what he did against Greek.
'The spirit that inspired you', said the King, 'was certainly not
that of Christ, but rather the spirit of Folly.' Then he asked
him if he had read any of the writings of Erasmus, since the
King perceived that he had been girding at me. He said he had
not. 'Then you clearly prove your folly', said the King, 'since
you condemn what you have not read.' 'Well, I have read one
thing called *Moria*', replied the theologian. 'May it please your
Highness', interposed Pace, 'his argument well befits the
book.' Meanwhile the theologian hits on an excuse for his
blunder. 'I am not altogether opposed to Greek', says he, 'since
it is derived from the Hebrew.' The King, astonished at the
man's folly, dismissed him and forbade him ever again to
preach at court."

Possibly at the suggestion of the King, Thomas More wrote a

letter to the University on the importance of Greek studies. One passage gives the main argument:

"Although no one denies that a man can be saved without a knowledge of Latin and Greek or of any literature at all, yet learning, yea even worldly learning, as he [the preacher] calls it, prepares the mind for virtue. Everyone knows that the attainment of this learning is almost the only reason why students flock to Oxford. But as for the rude and unlettered virtue, every honest woman can teach her children quite well at home. Moreover, it must be remembered that not all who come to you, come for the study of theology. The State needs men learned in the law. A knowledge, too, of human affairs, must be acquired, which is so useful even to a theologian that without it he may perhaps sing pleasantly to himself, but will certainly not sing agreeably to other people. And this knowledge can nowhere be drawn so abundantly as from the poets, orators and historians. There are even some who make the knowledge of things natural a road to heavenly contemplation and so pass from philosophy and the natural arts, which this man condemns under the general name of worldly literature, to theology, despoiling the women of Egypt to adorn a Queen. And as regards theology itself, which alone he seems to approve, if indeed he approves even that, I do not see how he can attain it without knowledge of the languages, either Hebrew, Greek or Latin, unless, indeed, the easy-going fellow thinks that sufficient books on the subject have been written in English. Or perhaps he thinks that the whole of theology is comprised within the limits of those questions on which such as he are always disputing, for the knowledge of which I confess that little enough Latin is wanted. But to confine theology, the august Queen of heaven, within such narrow limits would be not only iniquitous but impious. For does not theology also dwell in the Sacred Scriptures, and did it not thence make its way to the cells of all the ancient holy Fathers, I mean Augustine, Jerome, Ambrose, Cyprian, Chrysostom, Cyril, Gregory, and others of the same class, with whom the study of theology made its abode for more than a thousand years after the Passion of Christ before these trivial questions arose? And if any ignorant man boasts that he understands the works of those

Fathers without a thorough knowledge of the language in which each wrote, he will have to boast a long time before scholars will believe him."

In that passage the very accents of Erasmus can be heard.

More's long absences abroad and in attendance on the King were a special trial to him because they kept him away from his family at a period when his children most needed his guidance in their education. He had complete confidence in his wife, who, though not scholarly inclined herself, saw to it that the children carried out the instructions of their father and tutors. The latter were carefully chosen; John Clement was probably the first, but here we are concerned with another, William Gonnell whom, it will be recalled, Erasmus had come to know at Cambridge, so it was probably on his recommendation that Gonnell went to the More household. A letter from More to this tutor gives us an account of the principles to be followed. The date was probably the spring of 1518.

"Though I prefer learning joined with virtue to all the treasures of kings, yet renown for learning, when it is not united with the good life, is nothing else than splendid and notorious ignominy; this would be especially the case in a woman. Since erudition in a woman is a new thing and a reproach to the sloth of men, many will gladly assail it, and impute to literature what is really the fault of nature, thinking from the vices of the learned to get their own ignorance esteemed as a virtue. On the other hand if a woman (and this I desire and hope with you as their teacher for all my daughters) to eminent virtue should add an outwork of eevn moderate skill in literature, I think she will have more profit than if she obtained the riches of Croesus and the beauty of Helen. I do not say this because of the glory that will be hers, though glory follows virtue as a shadow follows a body, but because the reward of wisdom is too solid to be lost like riches or to decay like beauty, since it depends on the intimate consciousness of what is right, not on the talk of men, than which nothing is more foolish or mischievous."

The letter then urged the need

"to warn my children to avoid the precipices of pride and

haughtiness and to walk in the pleasant meadows of modesty; not to be dazzled at the sight of gold; not to lament that they do not possess what they erroneously admire in others; not to think more of themselves for gaudy trappings, nor less for the want of them; neither to deform the beauty that nature has given them by neglect, nor to try to heighten it by artifice; to put virtue in the first place, learning in the second; and in their studies to esteem most whatever may teach them piety towards God, charity to all, and Christian humility in themselves."

He advised Gonnell to introduce his pupils to the works of St Jerome and St Augustine.

"From them they will learn in particular what end they should propose to themselves in their studies and what is the fruit of their endeavours, namely the testimony of God and a good conscience. Thus peace and calm will abide in their hearts and they will be disturbed neither by a fulsome flattery nor by the stupidity of those illiterate men who despise learning."

More insisted that no distinction should be made between the training of his daughters and of his son.

"Nor do I think that the harvest will be affected whether it is a man or a woman who sows the field. They both have the same human nature, and the power of reasoning differentiates them from the beasts; both, therefore, are equally suited for those studies by which reason is cultivated, and is productive like a ploughed field on which the seed of good lessons has been sown."

This is an echo from *Utopia* where all received the same opportunities for learning; we can also hear the same warning against pride and ostentation.

The emphasis on moral principles will have been noted; we have seen the same priority given by John Colet in the statutes of his school and the cultivation of Virtue was the aim Erasmus set in his advocacy of the value of classical authors in reinforcing the Christian teaching. He, however, does not seem to have considered the education of girls, but when presented with the pro-

K

ductions of More's "school" in 1521 he wrote to Guillaume Budé,

"A year ago it occurred to More to send me a specimen of their progress in learning. He told them all to write to me, each without any help, nor did he suggest the subject nor make any corrections. When they offered their papers to their father for correction, he affected to be displeased with the bad hand-writing, and made them copy their letters out more neatly and accurately. When they had done so, he sealed the letters and sent them to me without changing a syllable. Believe me, my dear Budé, I never was more surprised; there was nothing whatever either silly or girlish in what they said, and the style was such that you could feel they were making daily progress."

He referred again to More's "school" in his *De Pueris . . . Instituendis* in 1529. "He, although deeply occupied in affairs of state, devoted his leisure to the instruction of his wife, his son and his daughters, both in the uprightness of life and in the liberal studies of Greek and Latin." Once again, "uprightness of life" is conjoined with "liberal studies".

Not much can be gleaned of the methods used by Thomas More and the tutors he selected. In some Latin verses he wrote to his "school" about 1519, he reminded them that he could not bear to see them weep but gave them cake and apples and pears, and that, on rare occasions, he used a birch of peacock's feathers. He encouraged the method of double-translation, that is, first from Latin into English and then back into Latin, and the same with Greek, and he set them subjects for declamation. Erasmus' ideas on education were similar to those put into practice by More. In a note on his *Colloquies*, Erasmus rebuked those who thought that such dialogues were too frivolous for instructional purposes. "The rules of grammar", he wrote, "are crabbed things to many persons. . . . It is important early to instil a taste for the best things into the minds of children, and I cannot see that anything is learned with greater success than what is learned by playing, and this is, in truth, a very harmless kind of fraud, to trick a person into his own profit." We have already remarked upon the interest he took in Colet's plans for his school. Here it will be appropriate to refer to the *Colloquy* of 1522, written after Colet's death, entitled *Pietas Puerilis*.[4] It ends with these lines,

"What Thales taught you that philosophy?"
"When I was a boy and very young, I happened to live in the house of that most honest of men, John Colet. Do you know him?"
"Know him? Ay, as well as I do you."
"He instructed me when young in these precepts."

Erasmus' educational work was largely directed towards supplying schools and students with the kind of material that would arouse their interest and so stimulate the learner to greater efforts. His *Colloquies* were the outstanding example of this purpose, but he also edited, or caused to be printed, a number of short texts. Thus in 1593 he edited the *Nux* (wrongly attributed to Ovid) and dedicated it to John More. "A nut", he wrote, "divides into four; share these with your three sisters. . . . There is no question of surpassing your father, but only of trying to equal him." At the same time he dedicated to Margaret Roper an edition of the *Hymn for the Epiphany* by Prudentius: "that the new-born Christ may bless your new-born son.[5] . . . Thank you for all your letters; even without a signature they would be recognized as from Thomas More's children." Two years later she translated into English a short commentary on the Lord's Prayer by Erasmus.

While More was engaged in argument with the Oxford scholars, and, at the same time, taking measures against the plague there, Erasmus was busy at Basle seeing the second edition of the *Novum Instrumentum* through the press. He now changed the title to *Novum Testamentum*. He had been forced to appeal to his friends for funds in order to get to Basle. On 5 March 1518, he wrote to Colet:

"I am obliged, in order to print the New Testament and some other books, to go either to Basle, or, more probably, to Venice, for I am deterred from Basle partly by the plague and partly by the death of Lachner whose financial aid was almost

[4]This dialogue is examined in detail in Louis Bouyer, *op. cit.*, ch. XIII.
[5]This son must have died young. Thomas, the eldest son to survive his parents, was born in 1534.

indispensable for the work. 'What', you will say, 'are you, an old man, in delicate health, going to undertake such a laborious journey? In these times too, than which none worse have been seen for six hundred years, while lawless robbery is everywhere!' But why do you say so? I was born to this fate; if I die, I die in a work which, unless I am mistaken, is not altogether a bad one. But if this last stroke of my work is accomplished according to my intention, and I should chance to return, I have made up my mind to spend the remainder of my life with you, in retirement from a world which is everywhere rotten. Ecclesiastical hypocrites rule in the courts of princes. The Court of Rome clearly has lost all sense of shame, for what could be more shameless than these continued indulgences? Now a war against the Turks is put forward as a pretext, when the real purpose is to drive the Spaniards from Naples. If these turmoils continue, the rule of the Turks would be easier to bear than that of these Christians."

He wrote also to Fisher and More in the same strain. With his letter to More he sent a copy of Luther's ninety-five theses, but without comment. The intention of retiring to England was a passing mood. He was bitterly disappointed with Leo X who was proving to be a political intriguer, and not a very astute one, rather than a reforming pope. Luther's Theses had been provoked by the unabashed traffic in indulgences by the Dominican friar, John Tetzel; the money raised was to go to the rebuilding of St Peter's in Rome, though, as everyone knew, a good percentage would stick to the fingers of the handlers. The new appeal was for a crusade against the Turks. Actually when Erasmus wrote the European situation was calm. A general peace had been achieved, largely because the conflicting princes were out of funds. Wolsey had played a part in this pacification. "English diplomats—Tunstall, West, Knight and More—seem to have been unanimous in persuading Wolsey that patience and peace would serve England better than passion and war."[6] Erasmus was convinced, as he wrote to More, that "the Pope and some princes are playing some fresh game under the pretext of a horrid war against the Turks". He had only too much justification for his suspicions.

It was at this pacification that the Emperor Maximilian remarked to his grandson, Charles of Spain, "You will deceive the French, and I, my boy, will deceive the English".

When Erasmus reached Basle in May 1518, he found much to occupy him. In addition to the *Novum Testamentum*, Froben printed new editions of the *Institutio Principis Christiani*, of the *Colloquiorum Formulae* (the *Colloquies*) and of the *Enchiridion*. Moreover Erasmus had arranged before going to Basle for the printing of More's *Epigrammata* and of the third edition of *Utopia*. Of these many works note must be taken of the new edition of the *Enchiridion*. It had first been published in February 1504 as part of Erasmus' *Lucubratiunculae aliquot*, and as such it had not attracted much attention. It was printed separately in June 1515 and at once began to gain in favour. For the 1518 edition Erasmus wrote an introductory epistle to Paul Volz, Abbot of the Benedictine monastery of Hugshofen in Alsace.[7] This letter is of considerable importance. Fourteen years had passed since the book's first appearance; this new edition gave him an opportunity to emphasize those themes that had gained greater urgency in his view and that were an essential part of his message to his generation.

We have seen how, in his letters just before he left for Basle, Erasmus had expressed his concern at the proposed crusade against the Turks. He thought it was all humbug, as it was. There had been peace with the Turks since 1503 and there were no signs of renewed attacks on Europe. This topic is prominent in the letter to Abbot Volz:

"The best way and most effectual to overcome and win the Turks should be they shall perceive that thing to shine in us which Christ taught and expressed in his living. If they shall perceive that we do not highly gape for their empires, do not desire their gold and goods, do not covet their possessions, but that we seek nothing else but their souls' health and the glory of God. This is that right and true and effectual divinity the which in time past subdued unto Christ arrogant and proud philosophers, and also mighty and invincible princes; if we

[7]Volz later accepted the doctrines of the reformers, in spite of which, Erasmus made him a legacy of 100 gold florins for the sake of old friendship. The quotations here are from Tyndale's translation.

thus do, then shall Christ ever be present and help us. For truly it is not meet nor convenient to declare ourselves Christians by this proof or token that we kill very many, but rather if we save very many; not if we send thousands of heathen people to hell, but if we make infidels faithful; not if we cruelly curse and excommunicate them, but if we with devout prayers and with all our hearts desire their health and pray unto God to send them better minds. If this be not our intent, it shall sooner come to pass that we shall degenerate them and turn into Turks ourselves than that we shall cause them to become Christians. And although the chance of war, which is ever doubtful and uncertain, shall fall so luckily to us that we had gotten the victory, so should it be brought to pass that the Pope's dominion and his Cardinals' might be enlarged, but not the kingdom of Christ."

He asked what the conquered Turks (those left alive) would think of our religion "when they shall see great doctors and teachers of religion so far disagreeing and of so sundry opinions among themselves that oftentimes they dispute and reason so long one with another, until they change colour and be pale, and revile one another, spitting each at other".

Erasmus put Christ in the centre round which human society revolves, and he pictured a series of circles. "Let Christ continue and abide, as he is indeed, a very centre or middle point unmoved, having certain circles going round about him; move not the mark out of his own place." The nearest circle, humanly speaking, is comprised of "priests, bishops, cardinals, popes and such to whom belongeth to follow the Lamb whithersoever he shall go; let them embrace and hold fast that most pure part, and so far forth as they may let them communicate and plenteously give the same unto their neighbours". These, the second circle, are the princes and governors in temporal authority. Erasmus here makes an interesting distinction by admitting that rulers are bound to make mistakes and even at times act selfishly and unjustly in the turmoil of human problems. Christ, he points out, did not concern himself with these purely practical situations; he refused to lay down the law "on such gross matters". It is the business of those of the first circle, the priests, to do all they can and "draw unto them those that be princes and have power and authority", and so keep them as near the centre as possible in "the business of the world". Princes and magistrates must be honoured when they do their office; and if sometimes they use their power for their own pleasure and profit, "yet peradventure it were best to suffer them, lest more hurt should spring therefrom". As More said to Hythlodaye, "If ill opinions cannot be quite rooted out, and you cannot cure some received vice according to your wishes, you must not therefore abandon the commonwealth".

The third circle round Christ "must all the common people be, as the most gross part of the world, but not yet so gross that they can pertain unto the mystical body of Christ". St Paul's words, "We, though many in number, form one body in Christ" (Rom. xii, 5), and his other statements on the same theme, were part of Erasmus' thinking. Thus in the *Enchiridion* we read, "Think this thing only, he is my brother in our Lord, co-heir in Christ, a member of the same body, redeemed with one blood, a fellow in the common faith, called unto the very same grace and felicity of the life to come, even as the apostle said, one body and one spirit as ye be called in one hope of your calling, one Lord, one faith, one baptism, one God and Father of all. . . . We all be members each one of another, members cleaving together to make a body. The head of the body is Christ; the head of Christ is God."

With these quotations may be placed one from John Colet's lectures on Romans on the same text:

"He would have all unite in one fellowship as members of one body, and each occupy his own place therein and acting according to his measure; not essaying more than his strength allows, nor failing in any way to do what his strength permits, but set all down in Christ and contribute as far as he can, the grace bestowed on him to the common good, ever mindful that he is a member of the body of Christ and called to live not to himself alone, but to the body; aye, even to die, if need be, for the safety of the body."[8]

[8]John Colet, *Enarratio in Epistolam S. Pauli ad Romanos*, ed. Lupton, p. 70.

Another parallel quotation comes from More's *Confutation*:

"The Catholic known Church is that mystical body, be it ever so sick, whereof the principal head is Christ. . . . It is enough that the body mystical of Christ, this Catholic Church, is that body that is animated, hath life spiritual, and is inspired with the Holy Spirit of God that maketh them of one faith in the House of God."[9]

So in his last days Thomas More could take his stand on the words "all Christendom is one corps".

The letter to Volz continues:

"And those which be in the third circle we ought to suffer in their infirmity, that as much as is possible we do call them unto those things which be more approved by Christ. For in the mystical body he that late was the foot may be the head. And like as princes if they be not all the best, must not with chiding be exasperated, lest, as St Augustine says, when they be moved they stir up more perilous tragedies, so the weak people, like as Christ suffered his apostles and nourished them, must be suffered, and after a fatherly manner cherished until they wax more aged and strong in Christ. For godliness also hath its infancy, it hath mean age, it hath full strength and perfect age. Yet all men after their degree must endeavour themselves to attain and come unto Christ."

It is a temptation to quote more at length from this close-packed letter, but it is essential reading for anyone who would understand the mind of Erasmus. Had I to select one, and only one, work of his that is most typical, I should not choose *The Praise of Folly* but this edition of the *Enchiridion* with the prefatory letter to Paul Volz.

[9]*English Works*, p. 527.

CHAPTER XIV

A Turning-point

THE THIRD EDITION of *Utopia* was printed by Froben at Basle and was published in March 1518; the volume included the *Epigrammata* of More and Erasmus. The original plan had been to produce a large volume that would include a number of pieces by Erasmus, such as *Querela Pacis*, with the Lucian translations by him and More, and also *Utopia* and the *Epigrammata*. By the time page 643 had been set up, Froben decided that the book was long enough to be issued as one volume in December 1517. *Utopia* and the *Epigrammata* appeared together as a separate volume in the following March, and was reprinted in December but without any corrections. Then a third edition, More's *Epigrammata* alone and corrected by him with some additions, was published in December 1520.

We have already discussed the earlier section in which More and Lily produced in friendly rivalry parallel Latin versions of Greek epigrams. Some of the other verses can be dated by internal evidence but others may have been composed at any time within the decade 1508 to 1518. Fourteen of More's epigrams are on kings and tyrants. Here are two:

> "To you, the king, who ravaged the world, they set up a statue of iron, far cheaper than bronze. This economy was the result of starvation, slaughter, the clash of arms, and destitution. These are the instruments by which your lust for wealth has brought ruin to all."

> "Among many kings there will be scarcely one, if there is in fact one, who is satisfied with one kingdom. Among many kings, there will be scarcely one, if in fact there is one, who rules a single kingdom well."[1]

[1] See *The Latin Epigrams of Thomas More*, trans. and ed. by L. Bradner and C. A. Lynch (1953). For criticism see H. A. Mason, *Humanism and Poetry in the Early Tudor Period* (1954), pp. 39-58.

The first may be compared with Erasmus' comment on the adage, *Scarabaeus aquilam querit*.

> "The eagle is the image of a king, for he is neither beautiful, nor musical, nor fit for good, but he is carnivorous, rapacious, a brigand, a destroyer, solitary, hated by all, a pest to all, who, though he can do more harm than anyone, wishes to do more harm than he can."

When the Peasants' War broke out in Germany in 1525, Erasmus added this rider: "The cruelty of kings is better than the universal confusion of anarchy". There is no need to point out the consonance of the second of More's epigrams with the teaching of Erasmus on war and peace. In his *Complaint of Peace* he urged that existing frontiers should be stabilized so that each king would be content with his own territory. How this desirable state of things was to be reached, Erasmus did not say.

Among the later verses in *Epigrammata* were several against Germain De Brie (Germanus Brixius), a French scholar who became a Canon of Notre Dame in Paris. These would not call for particular notice were they not part of a controversy that involved Erasmus as well as More and De Brie. The trouble began in 1513 when De Brie published some verses in praise of the French commander in a naval engagement. On 12 August 1512, during the war between France and England, an English ship, the *Regent*, grappled a French ship, *La Cordelière*; both were blown up when the magazine of *La Cordelière* caught fire. De Brie took the high patriotic line and lauded the courage of the French commander; More was annoyed and maintained the accuracy of the English version of the affair. It was a puerile argument since the facts could not be known, but we may note that More was not exempt from an attack of chauvinism. He wrote some pointed epigrams which, in the manner of the times, were circulated in manuscript. When the contents of the *Epigrammata* were being considered, More asked Erasmus not to include these against De Brie. There may have been a failure in communications, a not unusual happening in those days, or perhaps Froben decided to use these epigrams, so, in fact, they were included in the volume published in March 1518. De Brie was naturally annoyed and let it be known that he would reply. Erasmus tried to persuade him to refrain as he disliked seeing two of his friends at logger-heads, but *Antimorus* duly appeared in Paris in January 1520. It was a satirical poem with an appendix of the metrical and gram-matical errors De Brie had discovered in More's verses. More penned what Erasmus regarded as a "mordant" reply; he urged More not to print it as De Brie could do him no harm and it would be more dignified to keep silence. Before More received Erasmus' letter, Pynson had already published the letter, but as soon as Erasmus' protest reached him, More suppressed the edition. Among other points made by De Brie was that in his verses on the coronation of Henry VIII and Queen Catherine, More had disparaged Henry VII.[2] It was a valid criticism for More had declared that the new king "now gives to good men the honours and public offices that used to be sold to evil men". Even more pointed was the claim that, "Now it is possible to enjoy any profit which escaped the sly, grasping hands of many thieves", a reference to the over-ingenious exactions of Empson and Dudley, but also a reflection on their master Henry VII. Both More and Erasmus were disturbed at this accusation made by De Brie; perhaps they thought that Henry VIII might be offended at this criticism of his father. However, the King apparently was not upset. More frankly recognized that some of De Brie's criticisms of his verses were justified and he made some corrections in the final versions. He had ended his letter by wishing that he himself would have sound feet in his verses and that De Brie would have a sound head on his body.

There is, of course, nothing peculiar in sixteenth-century scholars losing their tempers and being schoolboyishly rude to each other; it happens in the twentieth century as well, save that the epithets flung are not quite so gross. The amusing aspect of the More-De Brie wrangle is that Erasmus, having tried to calm them down, within a short time, as we shall see, More did his best to calm down Erasmus in another flare-up.

Before we come to this episode, something should be said of a

[2]See above, p. 65.

long letter written by More in defence of Erasmus written to a monk; the story of the Coventry friar has already been extracted. It has been suggested[3] that John Batmanson, who died as Prior of the London Charterhouse in 1531, was the anonymous monk. He had been ordained in 1510, so at the time of his letter he was probably in his early thirties. More's letter was first published in a volume entitled *Epistolae Aliquot eruditorum* in 1520. The monk's letter is not extant but its contents can be inferred from More's reply. The writer was concerned lest More should be led astray through his attachment to Erasmus to adopt false doctrines and even to agree that the Early Fathers could have made mistakes. More's former connexion with the Charterhouse may have led Batmanson (accepting the identification) to pen his warning. He brought up again some of the well-worn criticisms of *Moria* and also referred to *Julius Exclusus* as the work of Erasmus. More did not categorically deny the last assumption; he contented himself by saying that he had heard conflicting opinions on the authorship. As to *Moria*, the criticisms originally made by Dorp had been fully answered. The monk had called in question a number of readings in the *Novum Instrumentum*, such as "sermo" for "verbum", which were the stock-in-trade of Erasmus' opponents. More defended the readings in some detail. He emphasized that the *Novum Instrumentum* had won the approval of the Pope and of such English scholars as Colet, Fisher, Warham, Tunstall, Pace and Grocyn. It was therefore temerarious for a "self-taught young fellow" to go against such weighty opinion. As to the Early Fathers,

"Do you deny that they ever made mistakes? I put it to you—when Augustine thought that Jerome had mistranslated a passage, and Jerome defended what he had done, was not one of the two mistaken? When Augustine asserted that the Septuagint is to be taken as an indubitably faithful translation, and Jerome denied it, was not one of the two mistaken?"

The monk had expressed his extreme resentment at the attacks made on monks and friars by Erasmus. More did not shirk this issue as the following passage shows.

[3]Dom David Knowles. *The Religious Orders in England*, III, Ap. I.

"Into what factions, into how many sects, are they divided! Then what tumults, what tragedies arise about little differences in the colour or mode of girding the monastic habit, or some matter of ceremony which, if not altogether despicable, is at all events not so important as to warrant the banishing of all charity. . . . They make more of things that appertain especially to the religious orders than of those very humble things that are in no way peculiar to them but shared by all Christian people, such as the common virtues—faith, hope, charity, the fear of God, humility, and others of the kind. . . . From reflections such as these you may learn the lesson that you should not grow proud of your own order, nothing could be more fatal, nor trust in private observances, and that you should place your your hopes rather in the Christian faith than in your own, and not trust in those things that you can do for yourself, but in those that you cannot do without God's help."

That reads almost like a quotation from Erasmus, but More was not content to leave the matter there; he expressed his deep esteem for the truly religious life of the cloister.

"I have no doubt that there is no good man to be found anywhere to whom all religious orders are not extremely dear and cherished. Not only have I ever loved them, but intensely venerated them; for I have been wont to honour the poorest person commended by his virtue more than one who is merely ennobled by his riches or illustrious by his birth. I desire, indeed, all men to honour you and your orders, and to regard you with the deepest charity, for your merits deserve it, and I know that by your prayers the misery of the world itself is somewhat diminished. If the assiduous prayer of the just man is of much value, what must be that of the unwearied prayers of so many thousands? Yet, on the other hand, I would wish that you should not with a false zeal be so partial to yourselves, that if anyone ventures to touch on what regards you, you should try, by your way of relating it, to give an evil turn to what he has said well, or that what he at least intended well, you should misinterpret and pervert."

The monk had complained (though why, it is hard to imagine) that Erasmus was too peripatetic; perhaps he was implying that

Erasmus lacked stability. This gave More an opening for a defence of this characteristic of which we have already made note. It provides a vivid picture of the wandering scholar.

"If one looks at his hard work, he sometimes does more work in one day than your people do in several months; if one judges the value of his work, he sometimes has done more for the whole Church in one month than you have in several years, unless you suppose that anybody's fasting and pious prayers have as deep and wide influence as his brilliant works, which are educating the entire world to the meaning of true holiness; or unless you suppose he is enjoying himself as he defies stormy seas and savage skies and all the scourges of land travel, provided it furthers the common cause. Possibly, it is not a pleasant experience to endure seasickness and the tortures of tossing waves and the threat of a deadly storm, and to stare at the ever-present menace of a shipwreck. Possibly, it is not a keen delight to plod along through dense forests and wild woodland, over rugged hilltops and steep mountains, along roads beset by bandits, or to be battered by the winds, spattered with mud, drenched by rains, weary of travelling, exhausted from hardships, and then to receive a shabby welcome and be refused the sort of food and bed you yourself are enjoying; and especially since all these many, many troubles, which would soon tire a healthy, sturdy young man, must be encountered and endured with a poor body that is growing old and has lost its strength from hard study and toil. . . . On these trips, which are the target of your criticisms, he spends his time only with those men approved for learning and goodness, and, as a result, his mind is ever nurturing some unborn idea, which eventually will be brought forth to the general profit of scholarship."[4]

This letter to a monk ends, "Farewell, and if you do not wish to be cloistered in vain, give yourself to the life of the spirit rather than to these squabbles".

It was soon Erasmus' turn to get angry and More's to urge restraint. Erasmus left Basle at the beginning of September 1518 and reached Louvain on the 21st. He had been far from well at Basle and the journey proved to be something of a nightmare as

[4] Translation from Rogers, *Selected Letters*, p. 138.

his sickness grew upon him. When he reached Louvain, he became critically ill; his doctors diagnosed the plague and deserted him. Rumour said that he was dead, and it was at this time that the Franciscans of Cologne declared that he died *sine lux, sine crux, sine Deus*. Though the doctors left him to his fate, his friends at Louvain, such as Dorp, came every day and "did much to make me well by their delightful company". When he recovered he wrote one of his most characteristic letters giving an account of his experiences; it was written to Beatus Rhenanus some time in October 1518. It is a lively narrative that reveals the spirit of a born traveller who triumphed over all his physical sufferings.

Erasmus was at the height of his reputation during the years 1518 to 1520. His position as a leading scholar was unchallenged and his books had carried his fame throughout the educated world. One instance of this may be given. Of the books (including almanacs, ballads, etc.) sold by the Oxford bookseller, John Dorne, in 1520, one ninth were by Erasmus. The most popular were *Colloquies*, *Copia*, and *Adages*, his educational books, and also *Enchiridion*, which had not yet been translated into English. As we have seen, some objections had been voiced against *Moria* and the *Novum Instrumentum*, but so far they had not seriously shaken his reputation nor greatly perturbed him. From 1520 onwards he was subject to more persistent attacks; this was largely due to the storm caused by Luther and his followers which compelled men to take sides. Erasmus grew more and more sensitive to criticism as he grew older; at times he allowed himself to become obsessed by the spirit of controversy and imagined himself to be the victim of malevolence; no doubt some of his opponents were moved by unworthy motives, but he found it difficult to believe that anyone could question his conclusions in good faith. They were all barbarians attacking sound literature; all were, in his view, obscurantists. This attitude was to bring him much unhappiness, but, fortunately, this was not his prevailing mood and he could still get completely absorbed in his true work and let the world go by.

Signs of this growing impatience came soon after his return to Louvain, and one may speculate that the after-effects of his serious illness and the continuance of his sufferings from the stone made him more susceptible. The cause of the first disturbance was Edward Lee, who was fifteen or sixteen years younger than Erasmus. He was the brother of Joyce Lee to whom More had presented his *Life of Picus*. Edward had been to Oxford and Cambridge and had been ordained deacon in 1504; he was a good scholar and it was in search of further learning that he went to Louvain in 1517. He was very critical of the *Novum Instrumentum* and made some notes which he submitted to More, Fisher and Latimer, and to his friends at Louvain but not to Erasmus himself. He was also in touch with John Batmanson of the London Charterhouse.[5] He asked for More's support in a letter of April 1519. It was probably in reply to this that More made his first attempt to prevent further trouble. Stapleton preserved the following passage from More's letter,

"You ask me, my dear Lee, not to lessen my affection for you in any way. Trust me, good Lee, I shall not. Although in this case my sympathies are with the party you are attacking, yet I trust you will withdraw your troops from the siege with perfect safety. I shall ever love you, and I am proud to find that my love is so highly valued by you. If ever occasion requires it, my zeal on your behalf shall be no less fervent than it is now on the other side. So that if ever you bring out a book of your own, and Erasmus, casting a critical eye on it, should write a pamphlet in an attempt to refute it (although it would be much more seemly that he should not retaliate), I, although my talents are poor, will yet stand by you to defend you with all the energy of which I am capable. Farewell, my most dear friend."[6]

More was to find it difficult to "stand by" Lee. He wrote again, a long letter this time, urging Lee to refrain from publishing his criticisms. We are reminded of how Erasmus tried to persuade More not to publish his epigrams against De Brie. Erasmus was getting more and more annoyed with Lee's reluctance to come

---

[5] Is there a link here with the letter from the anonymous monk? It suggests that Batmanson may have been prompted by Lee. On 5 May, 1520, Erasmus wrote to Richard Fox a letter in which he accused Lee of getting Batmanson to attack him.

[6] *Rogers*, No. 48. The letter is there dated, conjecturally, 1517, but this seems to me to be too early.

Arch Bᵖ Cantᵇ:

5. WILLIAM WARHAM, Archbishop of Canterbury
Drawing by Hans Holbein, 1527, at Windsor Castle

6. ST JOHN FISH[
By an unknown painte[

7. CUTHBERT
TUNSTALL
By an unknown painter

out into the open with his criticisms; they met on several occasions and had Lee had a little tact, or discussed the points that worried him, the older scholar might have been mollified, but these wrangles between scholars seem to follow a predestined pattern and, sooner or later, after preliminary rumblings, the storm breaks. Lee's *Annotations*, dedicated to the scholars of Louvain, was published in February 1520. In a prefatory letter to Erasmus, Lee said that he would have published his book months earlier but for the restraining hand of Thomas More. Erasmus hurriedly (perhaps too hurriedly) wrote an *Apologia*,[7] followed by a second *Responsio*. In the same month appeared the volume already mentioned entitled *Epistolae Aliquot eruditorum* containing letters against Lee from More, Pace, Lupset and others, a second edition of which, with additional letters, was issued in the following month. All this was crowded into a few months. Erasmus' references to Lee were prejudiced and even unscrupulous; Lee had been unwise in his handling of the dispute, but he was not the "viper"[8] and "monster" of Erasmus' inflamed temper. We have, of course, to make allowances for sixteenth-century manners, or lack of manners, in controversy; More himself could slang an opponent as heartily and coarsely as they could abuse him; some of the epithets recklessly hurled in these paper wars make us wince.

It would be tedious and unrewarding to follow the ins and outs of this Erasmus-Lee argument, but it will be of interest to give one example of the points at issue. This concerns the *Comma Johanneum*. The reference is 1 John v, 7-8, and the text reads (in the Knox translation), "Thus we have a threefold warrant *in heaven, the Father, the Word, and the Holy Ghost, three who are yet one*". Erasmus left out the italicized words from the first and second editions of the *Novum Instrumentum*, and Lee claimed that the text was authentic and, as it established the doctrine of the Trinity, its omission would mean a revival of Arianism. Erasmus explained that he had not found the words in the Greek manuscripts he had examined, but if Lee could tell him of a Greek

[7]Erasmus published two writings entitled *Apologia* in 1520. The first was on "in principio erat verbum" (Basle) and the second "invectivis Eduardi Lee" (Antwerp).
[8]"Viper" seems to have been a favoured term of abuse in those days.

L

manuscript containing them, he would insert them in a new edition. One Greek copy was found to have them; this was the Codex Montfortianus or Britannicus, now at Dublin. It was a fifteenth- or possibly sixteenth-century copy. So Erasmus added the verse to his third edition; textual critics of today would regard with horror such an off-hand decision based on a late manuscript.[9]

While this feud with Edward Lee was raging, an attack came from Spain.[10] It is interesting to note that Erasmus had a strong following in that country during the reign of Charles V. Thus the Spanish translation of the *Enchiridion*, made in 1524, was widely read and admired. The attack in 1520 came from a theologian of Alcalá, Diego Lopez Zuñiga (Stunica). During his lifetime Cardinal Ximenes had forbidden the publication of Stunica's criticisms, but after the Cardinal's death in 1517, Stunica went ahead and launched his first assault. Here again there would be little profit in describing the course of the controversy. It drove Erasmus almost frantic and strengthened his belief that he was the victim of persecution. Eventually he appealed to the Pope (Clement VII) and to the Emperor, and Stunica was silenced.

The circle of English humanists suffered a heavy loss in September 1519 when both John Colet and William Grocyn died. Colet had planned to retire to Shene (Richmond, Surrey) where he had built a lodging in or near the Charterhouse there,[11] but death took him before he was able to withdraw from active life. His last extant letter to Erasmus was written in June 1517. It referred to books by Reuchlin sent by Erasmus to Thomas More to pass on to John Fisher and John Colet. One reached Colet early on, but the other was held up while his two friends read it. The letter is so typical that it deserves quotation.

"I am half angry with you, Erasmus, that you send messages

---

[9]"It is now generally held that this passage, called the *Comma Johanneum*, is a gloss that crept into the text of the Old Latin and Vulgate at an early date, but found its way into the Greek text only in the 15th and 16th century." *Catholic Commentary on Holy Scripture* (1953), p. 1186.

[10]The story of the fame of Erasmus in Spain has been told in M. Bataillon, *Érasme et l'Espagne* (Paris, 1937), a book of wider interest than the title suggests.

[11]It was occupied by Wolsey for a short time after his dismissal.

to me in letters to others, instead of writing direct to myself, for, though I have no distrust of our friendship, yet this round-about way of greeting me through messages in other people's letters makes me jealous lest others should think you love me less than you do. Also, I am half angry with you for another thing—for sending the *Cabalistica* of Reuchlin to Bishop Fisher and not to me. I do not grudge your sending him a copy, but you might have sent me one as well. For I so delight in your love, that I am jealous when I see you more mindful of others than of me. . . .

"O Erasmus, of books and of knowledge there is no end! There is nothing better for us in this short life than to live holily and purely, and to make it our daily care to be purified and enlightened and really to practise what these *Pythagorica* and *Cabalistica* of Reuchlin promise; but, in my opinion, there is no other way for us to attain this than by the earnest love and imitation of Jesus. Wherefore leaving these wandering paths, let us go the short way to work. I long, to the best of my ability, to do so."

On the death of Colet, More said, "For generations we have not had among us any man more learned or holy". Numerous letters from Erasmus expressed his acute distress at the loss of his friend. To Bishop John Fisher he wrote:

"Thus far have I written, grieving for the death of Colet; a death so bitter to me that the loss of no one for the last thirty years has afflicted me more. I know that it is well with him who has been taken from this wicked and troublesome world, and is enjoying the presence of Christ, whom in his lifetime he so dearly loved. In the public interest, I cannot but lament the loss of so rare a pattern of Christian piety, so unique a preacher of Christian doctrine. And on my own private account, I lament so constant a friend, so matchless a patron. For what remains in lieu of funeral obsequies, this duty I will discharge myself; if my writings are of any avail, I will not suffer the memory of such a man to die out among posterity."

Erasmus carried out his intention of commemorating Colet and extracts have been given in these pages from his tribute.

It has already been noted that John Colet did not answer to the accepted conception of a humanist. Indeed none of the English humanists with whom we are here concerned satisfied the conventional idea of the scholar engrossed in classical studies to the exclusion of the outside world. Even William Grocyn and William Latimer left their University to become parish priests. John Colet is best known as the founder of a famous school of which William Lily was the first head; Cuthbert Tunstall was diplomatist, statesman and bishop; Thomas Linacre was a leading physician; Richard Pace served the king in diplomacy and as secretary, and Thomas More was lawyer, councillor, diplomatist and statesman. We may see here the English bias towards the practical. In contrast was Erasmus' steady refusal to get entangled in public affairs.

June 1520 was to see another meeting of Thomas More and Erasmus; it followed that pretentious farce, the Field of Cloth of Gold, which was like a stage representation of medieval pageantry. These meetings of princes might have been designed to illustrate the comments in *Utopia* on the fatuity of leagues and treaties, for, after Henry of England and Francis of France had vowed eternal friendship, the English Court moved on to Gravelines to greet the Emperor Charles V, the declared enemy of France. Among the councillors who accompanied the Emperor was Erasmus who thus had the delight of meeting again such old friends as Thomas More, John Fisher, Warham, Tunstall and Mountjoy. That at least must have compensated them for the wearisomeness of a very royal occasion. In a sermon on his return John Fisher described the colourful and costly scene. "But yet doubtless many were full weary of them at length and had a loathsomeness of them, and some of them had much rather be at home." Erasmus had conversations with Henry VIII and Wolsey, but though they greeted him cordially, it led to nothing to his benefit.

The years 1519-1520 may be regarded as a turning-point in the lives of Erasmus and More. The deaths of Colet and Grocyn broke up a group of friends associated for twenty years. More was being drawn ever more closely into state affairs, while Erasmus was allowing himself to get involved in fruitless controversy. These, however, were relatively unimportant matters compared with the heavy clouds that were storming over from Germany.

CHAPTER XV

Luther

IT WOULD BE TRUE to say that up to 1520, Thomas More was considerably influenced by Erasmus. When Erasmus was criticized, More sprang to his defence. They believed that the serious shortcomings in the Church could be remedied by reason. This was a scholar's dream and it was never entirely shattered. Both continued to appeal to the rational man in the conviction that good-tempered argument based on sound learning must prevail over prejudice and error. With the growing power of Lutheranism, they met a new force, but neither gave up the hope that in the end reason would be effective. After 1520 a divergence of view may be noted between them; not, as has sometimes been said, a cooling of friendship, but rather a difference in the ways in which they had to face the new heresy. It was, in part, the result of circumstances in which they found themselves. More had to deal with what may be described as a localized problem due to the geographical position of England; the influence of heresy was not so widespread nor as explosive as in Germany; Henry VIII remained in control. It has often been remarked that in medieval times England had proved unfruitful soil for heresy; the Lollard movement had been contained; its ideas lingered in a few centres and copies of the Wycliffite Bible were in circulation but most of the copies seem to have lacked the tendentious prologue that had led to episcopal condemnation. Lutheran publications were brought into the country from Germany by traders, but, as they were in Latin or German, their influence was limited. It may be noted that these special conditions in England also determined the special character of the Anglican Church that was eventually established.

By contrast, Erasmus lived most of his time near one of the main trade routes of medieval Europe that conveyed not only goods but books and ideas. He was caught between warring factions of theologians who neither gave nor expected quarter. Yet they all turned to him in the hope of enlisting his support. While set encounters such as those at Augsburg (1518), Leipzig (1519), and Worms (1521) could create widespread excitement on the continent, they made little stir in England. Moreover there was the political complication. Germany was divided into some three hundred principalities and their rulers were more intent on their quarrels among themselves and with the Emperor and with the Pope than on religious doctrines. Added to the confusion of aims, was the policy of the Papacy. Rome was engaged in political manoeuvres; there was the problem of relations with the Empire and with France and the ever-changing complications of the Italian situation. England was not seriously affected by these machinations, and the rather amateurish foreign policy of the King and Wolsey was irrelevant to the European situation.

Thomas More was faced with the problem in his own household. William Roper married Margaret More in 1521, and at that time he was, to quote Harpsfield, "a marvellous zealous Protestant".[1] Harpsfield could have got this information only from Roper himself. The account of this "fall into heresy" may be taken as typical of how others were affected by the teachings of Luther. Roper had been "bewitched" by two pamphlets by Luther, *De Libertate Hominis Christiani* and *De Captivitate Babylonica*, both of which were published in 1520. He became "fully persuaded that faith only did justify, that the works of man did nothing profit, and that if man could once believe that our Saviour Christ shed his precious blood and died on the cross for our sins, the same belief should be sufficient for our salvation. Then thought he that all the ceremonies and sacraments in Christ's Church were very vain, and was at length so far waded into heresy and puffed up with pride that he wished he might be suffered publicly to preach." He studied what Harpsfield called a "Lutheran Bible"; this is a misnomer, unless Roper could read German, which is unlikely, and had managed to get Luther's New

[1]The term "Protestant" is here an anachronism. The *O.E.D.* gives 1539 as the earliest date of its use.

Testament, but that was not published until 1522. Tyndale's New Testament became available in 1526. Roper may therefore have been using a so-called Lollard Bible. Thomas More tried to reason him out of his new notions but failed to convince him. "And therefore, Meg, I will no longer argue and dispute with him, but will clean give him over, and get me another while to God and pray for him." Soon afterwards Roper "perceived his ignorance and turned him again to the Catholic faith". So well-known was his Lutheranism that he was summoned to appear before Wolsey with some merchants of the Steelyard (Germans), who had to abjure their heresy at St Paul's Cross. Roper "for love borne by the Cardinal to Sir Thomas More was with a friendly warning discharged". It is difficult to fix the date for this incident. On 11 February 1526 Robert Barnes and four merchants of the Steelyard made their abjurations at St Paul's Cross. Bishop John Fisher was the preacher. This seems rather late for Roper's discharge, but Harpsfield said that he clung to his heretical opinions "a long time". This close association and argument with a heretic in his own family gave More an understanding of the problems raised by Lutheranism that was to prove of great value when he himself was called to defend the teaching of the Church.

Meanwhile Erasmus, much against his will, inevitably became involved in the Lutheran controversy; inevitably, because of his European eminence as a scholar of the Scriptures; and, as the dispute became more widespread so the contestants hoped to win him over; they knew how influential his word could be and this fact made their subsequent disappointment and anger all the more bitter when he refused to throw the whole weight of his prestige on one side or the other.

We have already noted that in March 1518 Erasmus had sent More, without comment, a copy of the Ninety-five Theses on Indulgences that Luther had posted on the door of the castle church at Wittenberg on 31 October 1517.[2] There was nothing dramatic in Luther's action; he was following the established method of challenging other theologians to dispute with him the propositions he was prepared to sustain. The Theses did not

[2]See for a fuller account, Gordon Rupp's *Luther's Progress to the Diet of Worms* (1951).

constitute a doctrinal statement. The occasion for Luther's action was a particularly flagrant abuse of the granting of an Indulgence. Albert of Brandenburg, already Archbishop of Magdeburg, had become Archbishop of Mainz at the age of twenty-five; he was the third Archbishop within ten years and in consequence the See was impoverished by the heavy payments of annates and fees to Rome. The Pope allowed Albert to retain half the proceeds from an Indulgence that was intended to raise money to rebuild St Peter's in Rome. As the Archbishop had borrowed heavily from the Fuggers, the bankers, one of their clerks accompanied the preacher of the Indulgence. These facts could not have been generally known at the time but the method of raising funds was customary. A Dominican Friar, John Tetzel, was in charge of the campaign, as it may be called, and came within a few miles of Wittenberg. The solemn ceremony with which the Papal Bull was received, and the support of the clergy, made Tetzel's mission unusually impressive to the populace. Luther did not attack the lawfulness of the Indulgences, but he saw that many simple folk, and not-so-simple, thought they were buying a pardon for their sins and were not fully instructed that the efficacy of the Indulgence depended on true contrition. An Indulgence is not a pardon for sin which comes through the sacrament of penance. According to the Catechism, "An Indulgence is a remission, granted by the Church, of the temporal punishment that remains due to sin after its guilt has been forgiven". This merciful provision was undoubtedly abused in the interests of papal finances and some humble folk even got the notion that an Indulgence excused further sin. It would have seemed unlikely that Luther's challenge would be widely noticed. The new University of Wittenberg situated on the eastern fringe of the Empire, had not yet acquired a status in the world of learning, but it so happened that the times, the man, and the means, coincided to carry Luther's challenge far beyond the frontiers of Saxony.

There was much dry tinder lying about that needed only a spark to set it in a blaze. There was growing anger at the demands from Rome for more and more money, and it was known that a good proportion of what was collected did not reach Rome, and what did, was often used for purposes that had little to do with the advancement of true religion. There was much criticism of the worldly conduct of leaders of the Church as well as of clergy and monks and friars; anti-clericism was widespread. There was nothing new about such grievances but they had been growing more and more articulate over the years. A powerful leader was all that was wanted to bring these discontents to a focus; that man was Martin Luther. It would, however, be wrong to regard him as an agitator; he was far more than that. Much as he deplored and denounced the shortcomings of the Church, his main concern was with Christian doctrine and the salvation of souls. His distinctive teaching had evolved over the years in the course of his theological studies, during the preparation of his lectures on the Scriptures, and in his public preaching.

The times—the man—the means. Both Erasmus and Luther owed much to the printing press. Without it, and the organized book trade, their teaching would not have spread so widely nor as speedily. The fate of the work of Lorenzo Valla shows what might have happened; his critical examination of the text of the New Testament was neglected until Erasmus had it printed nearly fifty years after the scholar's death. The lack of property rights for authors meant that any printer was at liberty to publish whatever seemed profitable to him. Luther, for instance, was not responsible for the publication of his Theses in a German translation. So editions, often defective, were multiplied. Erasmus tried to persuade his friend Johann Froben not to print Luther's writings, but Froben had too keen an eye to business to refrain.

In the earlier stages, that of the denunciation of scandals within the Church, Luther had the sympathy of Erasmus. As he wrote to Nicholas Bérault from Louvain in February 1521, "Everybody knew that the Church was oppressed by tyranny and burdened with ceremonies and human decrees invented to make money, and many were already wishing for or devising a remedy, but remedies unskilfully applied are often worse than the disease". To John Colet, as we have seen, he wrote in March 1518, "The court of Rome clearly has lost all sense of shame, for what could be more shameless than these continued Indulgences?" One need only turn the pages of *The Praise of Folly* (published six years before Luther's Theses) to see that Erasmus and Luther were on common ground in condemning existing abuses. It was for this that many expected Erasmus to support Luther. The saying, "Erasmus laid the egg that Luther hatched", expressed the disappointment of Catholics who could not understand why Erasmus refused to come out as a determined opponent of Luther. The truth was that Erasmus and Luther were themselves the heirs of a long line of critics, clerical and lay, who denounced abuses in no uncertain voices. We need go back no further than Chaucer in the fourteenth century to remind ourselves of the stream of censure that was to become a flood. His character sketches of the monk, the friar and the pardoner expressed common opinion.

> "Therefore, in stede of weping and preyeres,
> Men moot yeve silver to povre freres."

> "His walet lay biforn him in his lappe,
> Bret-ful of pardoun come from Rome al hoot."

Yet the ideal was not forgotten. So of the "povre Persoun of a toun",

> "But Cristes lore, and his apostles twelve,
> He taughte, and first he folwed it himselve."

Erasmus with his wit and biting satire put into print the complaints and grumbles that had long been commonplace. He came to regret some of his earlier works; they had been written in days when there seemed to be no serious threat of heresy or schism. In May 1521 he admitted to his old friend Jodocus Jonas that "if I had foreseen that such times as these were coming, I would either have not written some things which I have written, or I would have written in a different spirit. For my desire is to do good to all in such a way as, if possible, to injure no one." The same comment on his earlier writings was repeated in other letters.

Thomas More wrote to Erasmus in June 1532:

"Your opponents cannot be unaware of how you confess

candidly that, before these pestiferous heresies arose, which have since spread everywhere and subverted everything, you dealt with some matters in a way you would not have treated them had you been able to foresee that such enemies of religion and such traitors would ever arise. You would then have expressed what you had to say less provocatively and more moderately. You wrote strongly then because you were indignant at seeing how some cherished their vices as if they were virtues."

About the same date More wrote in his *Confutation*:[3]

"In these days in which men, by their own default, misconstrue and take harm of the very Scripture of God, until men better amend, if any man would now translate *Moria* into English, or some works either that I myself have written ere this, albeit there be none harm therein, folk yet being (as they be) given to take harm of that that is good, I would not only my 'darling's' books,[4] but mine also, help to burn them both with mine own hands, rather than folk should (through their own fault) take any harm of them, seeing that I see them likely in these days so to do."

These regrets for their earlier writings did not imply that they had changed their minds on the defects and abuses of the Church; they had hoped that remedies would be found, or, at least, as Colet had urged, that existing canon laws and the decisions of Councils would be strictly enforced. They knew that they had with them the sympathies of many clerics and laymen in other countries, even in Rome itself. The tragedy was that the Popes, sometimes giving lip-service to the need for reform, failed to act in spite of the pressure of opinion. The outcry of the scandal of the racket in Indulgences brought to a head much of the widespread criticism, but the matter was handled so ineptly that it became the starting point for a movement that threatened the Church itself. Neither More nor Erasmus had criticized received doctrine, but they recognized the new danger; wit and satire were no longer relevant; the very faith was in peril. More, however, saw the way things were moving more quickly than

[3] *English Works*, p. 422.
[4] In his *Answer to Sir Thomas More*, Tyndale had referred to Erasmus as More's "darling".

Erasmus; this was probably, as has been noted, because he was detached from the storm centre.

It was Erasmus who was the first to be involved. His years in Brabant from 1518 had become increasingly irksome. His controversy with Edward Lee had annoyed him and the attacks from the theologians of Louvain and from monks and friars became more bitter and unscrupulous as Luther's influence was extended. Had he joined forces with them against Luther, all would have been well. It was his refusal to do so that exacerbated their hostility. He himself interpreted this animosity as a further example of "barbarism" opposed to "sound learning". It was a short-sighted view. Some were indeed obscurantists but others were convinced that Erasmus was at bottom in sympathy with Luther. So he was up to a point; so indeed were many others who were deeply concerned with the failure of the Church to reform itself. Up to 1520 no decisive doctrinal division had been revealed, nor was the possibility of schism envisaged. Luther had been able to declare early in 1519, "If unfortunately there are such things in Rome as might be improved, there neither is, nor can be, any reason that one should tear oneself away from the Church in schism". But within a brief while he was considering whether "the Pope is Anti-Christ himself".

Luther himself wrote to Erasmus in March 1519:

"Now since I have learned from Fabricius Capito [Archbishop Albert's chaplain] that my name is known to you through my trifles about indulgences and learned also from your most recent preface to the *Enchiridion*, that my notions have not only been seen but have also been accepted by you, I am compelled to acknowledge, even though in barbarous style, your noble spirit, which enriches me and all men. . . . And so, my dear and amiable Erasmus, if you shall see fit, recognize this your little brother (fraterculum) in Christ, indeed a most devoted admirer of yours, but worthy, in his ignorance, only to be buried in his corner and to be unknown to the same sky and sun with you."

Luther was referring to the Epistle to Volz in the 1518 edition of the *Enchiridion*. The passage on indulgences was given by Erasmus as an example of how a writer's words could be distorted by an enemy.

"As if a man did admonish and give us warning, that it is more sure to trust unto good deeds than to trust to the Pope's pardons, yet doth he forsooth condemn the Pope's pardons, but preferreth that which by Christ's learning and doctrine is of more certainty."

Erasmus replied in May from Louvain. He mentioned that he himself was accused of having a hand in some of Luther's writings, but, "I assured them that you were quite a stranger to me, that I have never read your books, and that therefore I neither sanction nor condemn anything you have said". In letters to several correspondents, including Cardinals Campeggio and Wolsey, he repeated that he had only turned over a few pages of Luther's writings. This need not be doubted. Up to the end of 1519, Luther had published some forty pieces, the majority of them being sermons and replies to criticisms, many in German. The only two substantial volumes were his commentaries on Galatians and on the Psalms; on the latter Erasmus wrote in his letter to Luther, "I have skimmed through your commentaries on the Psalms, and I like them exceedingly and hope they will prove useful". He went on in his letter to assert that the root of the trouble was the attack being made on sound learning, "for which they cherish the most deadly hatred because they are afraid it will cloud the majesty of their divinity which many of them prize before Christianity". This must have seemed to Luther a frivolous remark, but it became an *idée fixe* with Erasmus and blinded him to the true issues. The letter went on to question the wisdom of discussing difficult questions "in mixed assemblies"; it was more seemly to confine such matters to academic circles. He urged Luther to avoid "violent wranglings". "More I think is gained by politeness and moderation than by violence. . . . Let us be careful not to do or say anything savouring of arrogance or tending to encourage party feeling; thus only, in my judgment, will our conduct be acceptable to the spirit of Christ."

Erasmus' most elaborate explanation of his attitude was given in a long letter of November 1519 to the Cardinal-Archbishop and Elector of Mainz, the very person whose need for money had occasioned the attack on the trade in Indulgences. The Cardinal had sent Erasmus a present of a gold cup to express his admiration for the great scholar whose friendship he desired. Once more Erasmus blamed those who "are angry that languages and literature flourish . . . and the world returning to the very fountains of truth. They are trembling for their money-boxes!" The last remark must have hit the Cardinal, but Erasmus was probably unaware of the financial crisis that sent Tetzel on the roads. The following extract states the position he maintained as long as he could.

"I am neither Luther's accuser, nor advocate, nor judge; his heart I would not presume to judge, for that is always a matter of extreme difficulty, still less would I condemn. And yet if I were to defend him, as a good man, which even his enemies admit him to be; as one put upon his trial, a duty which the laws permit even to sworn judges; as one persecuted, which would only be in accordance with the dictates of humanity, and trampled on by the bounden enemies of learning, who merely use him as a handle for the accomplishment of their designs, where would be the blame, so long as I abstained from mixing myself up with his cause? In short, I think it is my duty as a Christian to support Luther in this sense, that if he is innocent, I should not wish him to be crushed by a set of malignant villains; if he is in error, I would rather see him put right than destroyed; for thus I should be acting in accordance with the example of Christ, who, as the prophet witnesseth, quencheth not the smoking flax, nor breaketh the bruised reed. I should wish that a mind on which some sparks of evangelical doctrine seem to have fallen, should not be extinguished, but be corrected and taught to preach the glory of Christ. As it is, certain divines with whom I am acquainted neither warn Luther nor teach him; they merely traduce him before the people with insane clamours and tear him to pieces with virulent abuse, while they have not a word on their lips save heresy, heretics, heresiarchs, schism and Anti-Christ."

Much to Erasmus' annoyance, this letter, which he had entrusted to von Hutten, was published, and his letter to Luther was also in circulation. Both were seized upon as evidence that he was a supporter of Luther.

This desire to see fair play for Luther was not an empty gesture. Erasmus wrote to many influential ecclesiastics and statesmen to urge them to do all they could to damp down the fires of controversy and give reason a chance to operate. In August 1519 he took the opportunity of sending a copy of the new edition of his *Novum Testamentum* to Pope Leo X, to write:

"I have no acquaintance with Luther, nor have I ever read his books beyond perhaps ten or twelve pages and that only by snatches. From what I then saw, I judged him to be well qualified to expound the Scriptures in the manner of the Fathers, a work greatly needed in an age like this which is so greatly given to subtleties to the neglect of really important questions. Accordingly I have favoured his good, not his bad qualities, or rather, I have favoured Christ's glory in him."

He then went on to explain why he had not written against Luther. He was so busy with his own studies and plans that he had no time to give Luther's works the careful study they needed. There was certainly substance in this when one considers the amount of work Erasmus accomplished between 1520 and 1530: his *Paraphrases*, new editions of *Novum Testamentum*, the *Adages*, the *Colloquies*, editions of Cyprian, Hilary, Irenaeus, Ambrose and Augustine, and a revision of his edition of Jerome. This was the work he felt was his true vocation and he had no wish to get entangled in controversy unless he himself was attacked. He further declared that he lacked the necessary learning. This was not mock modesty; Erasmus knew his limitations; he never claimed to be a theologian though he had followed the prescribed courses, and indeed he had not the mind of a speculative thinker. Now Luther was a trained theologian and held a professorship as such and he could only be controverted on theological grounds. Yet Erasmus' position as the leading scholar of Europe meant that his opinion was regarded as important. Catholics were irritated by his refusal to come out strongly in support of the Church; Lutherans were equally irritated by his refusal to take what seemed to be the logical step and join them. It has been said

8. ERASMUS
by Albrecht Dürer (1526)

9. ERASMUS
by Hans Holbein (1532)

that he lacked the courage to take sides. It would, on the contrary, have been much more for his peace of mind to have given his whole-hearted support to one side or the other. Had he vehemently attacked Luther, he would have received many favours from the Church; it was hinted, for instance, that a bishopric would be found for him, and had he gone to Rome he could have lived in the greatest comfort. Had he become a Lutheran, he would not have had to leave Basle in 1529 but would have been the most honoured of its citizens. He described himself as between Scylla and Charybdis—on the one hand the Lutherans, and on the other the obscurantist Churchmen. It took courage in such times deliberately to refuse to take either one side or the other. He preferred to maintain that complete independence that he had kept even in his days of penury. But he was not to be left in peace. Events forced the issue.

On 31 October 1517, the day of the posting up of the Theses at Wittenberg, Luther sent a copy with a letter to the Archbishop (later Cardinal) of Mainz; in this he said he was sure the instructions about the Indulgence had been issued "without the knowledge and consent of your Fatherly Reverence", and he begged the Archbishop to withdraw the instructions and "order the indulgence preachers to adopt another style of preaching". Albert sent the Theses to the University of Mainz for an opinion from the theologians and he also sent a copy to Rome. The opinion from Mainz was that the Pope should be asked to withdraw the Bull of Indulgence. Rome, for the present, was silent.

John Eck, professor of theology at Ingolstadt, replied to Luther's Theses in his *Obelisci* in March 1518. Luther was summoned to Rome in July, but the Elector Frederick the Wise of Saxony[5] arranged that instead of going to Rome, Luther should appear at the Diet of Augsburg in October. There he had to face Cardinal Cajetan, general of the Dominicans, who was not

---

[5]The Elector and Luther never met. One of the oddities of history is that Luther owed his immunity, probably his life, to Frederick, the proud possessor of a collection of 17,443 relics, a source of income to him which he did not wish to be reduced by the counter-attraction of the Indulgence. His motives were mixed. Wittenberg University was his foundation and he regarded its professors as under his protection. He was also influenced by his secretary, George Spalatin, who was Luther's firm supporter and adviser. This confusion of motives is a warning against too dogmatic an interpretation of events.

M

prepared to argue but demanded immediate revocation. Luther was unyielding and, for the first time, his powerful personality impressed itself on a wider company than Wittenberg could provide. His friends wisely hurried him away from Augsburg as Cajetan wanted him taken to Rome. The maladroit handling of the situation by the papal legate only served to convince Luther and others that Rome was blind to the gravity of the widespread criticism of the Church. His immediate reaction was to appeal to a General Council.

In June 1519, John Eck had a disputation at Leipzig with Andrew Carlstadt, a senior and more radical colleague of Luther who himself joined in the argument, and for ten days they discussed the Primacy of the Pope, Purgatory, and Indulgences among other subjects. John Eck, cleverly, perhaps too cleverly, drove Luther into advancing opinions that savoured of the heresies for which John Hus had been burned in 1415. One result of these prolonged discussions was that Luther's own ideas were clarified in his own mind. The theologians of Louvain and Cologne combined in February 1520 to condemn a series of propositions drawn from Luther's works, and in June the Pope issued a Bull, *Exsurge Domine*, condemning forty-one propositions and threatening excommunication of anyone who supported them; Luther was not named. A month later Erasmus' old companion of Venetian days, Jerome Aleander, arrived in Brabant to promulgate the Bull but he soon found that public opinion was hostile. When John Eck tried to do the same in Germany, he was shocked at the support shown for Luther. In the pride of what he regarded as his theological victory at Leipzig, he expected to be received like a conquering hero; instead of which, he was glad to escape violence. One more attempt was made to bring Luther to heel. Karl von Miltitz, the Saxon envoy in Rome, met Luther at the suggestion of the Elector Frederick. Miltitz did not use the hectoring manner of Cajetan, nor the cock-a-hoop style of Eck, and he persuaded Luther to write to the Pope, but this was hardly a conciliatory gesture for with it Luther sent a copy of his pamphlet *De Libertate Hominis Christiani*, and in the course of his letter he wrote, "The Evil one is the veritable Pope, for he certainly rules in this

Babylon[6] more truly than you". This was the third of three pamphlets or tracts that Luther produced during 1520, the other two being *An den christlichen Adel deutscher Nation* (August) and *De Captivitate Babylonica Ecclesiae* (October).[7] These three publications are primary documents for an understanding of Luther's position at that date and they therefore call for some examination.

The first, *An Appeal to the Christian Nobility of the German Nation*, was in German and was published in August 1520; a first edition of 4,000 copies was quickly followed by reprints. A Latin version was also published. At the outset Luther declared that "hitherto the popes and Romanists have been able, with the devil's help, to bring kings into conflict with each other. . . . The Romanists have very cleverly surrounded themselves with three walls which have protected them till now in such a way that no one could reform them." These walls are, (1) that no secular power has authority over them, (2) only the Pope is competent to expound the Scriptures, and (3) that only the Pope can summon a Council. There is not space here to show how each of these points is developed, but a few sentences will indicate the tone.

(1) "For all Christians really and truly belong to the religious classes and there is no difference among them except in so far as they do different work. . . . Our baptism consecrates us all without exception and makes us all priests."

(2) "You must acknowledge that there are good Christians among us who have the true faith, spirit, understanding, word, and mind of Christ. Why ever should one reject their opinion and judgment and accept those of the Pope who has neither that faith nor that spirit?"

(3) "When need requires it, and the Pope is acting harmfully to Christian well-being, let anyone who is a true member of the Christian community as a whole take steps as early as possible to bring about a genuinely free council. No one is so able to do this as the secular authorities, especially as

---

[6]In the Apocalypse, "Babylon" stands for Rome. There is also a further reference to the Babylonish Captivity of the Jews, and to the residence of the Popes at Avignon.

[7]These three documents are given in an English translation in Vol. I of *Reformation Writings of Martin Luther*, trans. by B. L. Woolf (1952). The quotations here are from this book.

they are also fellow Christians, fellow priests, similarly religious, and of similar authority in all respects."

Luther then went on to suggest the subjects to be discussed at a Council. These included: the luxury of the papal court, the uselessness of cardinals, pluralism in holding benefices, and "the ecclesiastical market" in jobs. "This wicked régime is not only barefaced robbery, trickery and tyranny appropriate to the nether regions, but also a destruction of the body and soul of Christendom." Then follow twenty-seven proposals for reform, including: the abolition of annates and of appeals to Rome, celibacy not to be enforced, only Sunday to be a feastday, no further canonizations nor indulgences, no more Religious Orders under vows, the abolition of canon law, Aristotle to be banished from the Universities, and so on.

The second publication *Concerning the Babylonish Captivity of the Church* was written in Latin as the author intended it for the educated and not for people in general, but, to his annoyance, it was translated into German and quickly circulated. It was a reasoned statement on the sacraments. Luther argued that only three sacraments were authorized in the Gospels—baptism, penance and the Eucharist; the other four, confirmation, marriage, ordination and extreme unction, he regarded as usages instituted by the Church but not true sacraments. In discussing baptism he argued that the baptismal vows are sufficient; they are "more than we are able to keep. We shall have enough on our hands if we give ourselves to this duty alone." This led him to object again to monastic and other vows demanded by authority; they are contrary to the liberty of Christians. On penance he wrote, "There is no doubt in my mind that a man's secret sins are forgiven him when he makes a voluntary confession before a brother in private, and, on reproof, he asks for pardon and mends his ways. No matter how much any pope may rage against these contentions, the fact is that Christ manifestly gave the power of pronouncing forgiveness to anyone who had faith in Him." In his discussion of the Eucharist, Luther argued that communion in both kinds should be allowed. "To deny both kinds to the laity is impious and oppressive, and it is not in the power of any angel nor of any pope or council whatever to deny them." He dismissed the opinion of St Thomas Aquinas on "the trumpery stuff about transubstantiation" but it is not clear what explanation of the nature of the sacrament Luther wished to substitute. "The only thing I aim at for the present is to banish scruples of conscience so that no one may fear being called a heretic if he believes the bread and wine on the altar are real bread and wine." "It is plainly an impious error to offer or apply a Mass for sins, for satisfaction, for the benefit of the departed, or any necessity of one's own or that of another." He denied that the Mass is a sacrifice; it is a renewal of the promises of Christ "for the remission of sins". Marriage he rejected as a sacrament, and he inveighed against the impediments set up by the "Romanists", "for there is no impediment to marriage nowadays which they cannot legitimize for money". Luther advanced some astonishing opinions on marriage; for instance, if a husband is impotent, he may agree to his wife having coition with another man but ascribing the offspring to the husband; he expressed his hatred of divorce but tentatively put forward bigamy as an alternative. Ordination he considered to be a rite "employed solely to prepare men for certain duties", to be "the rite by which the Church chooses its preacher". On extreme unction he maintained that the passage in the fifth chapter of the Epistle of James (the authorship of which he questioned) had been wrongly interpreted as the institution of a sacrament, "but a piece of James's advice which anyone who wishes may follow". He later reduced the sacraments to two: baptism and the sacrament of the altar.

The third treatise, *On the Liberty of a Christian Man*, which he sent to the Pope, was much shorter than the previous two but it is the most important of the three. The other two have now lost their original significance as they were polemic in intention, and, one may conjecture, somewhat hastily written, but this third one is a primary statement of Luther's belief, and, though he later developed his ideas and gave them greater precision, it retains its importance. One quotation must suffice to give the central teaching.

"Works of merit are not such as to depend on the divine word as in the case of faith, nor can they live in the soul. Only the word and faith exercise sway in the soul. Just as iron becomes red like fire through its union with the fire, so does the soul become the word through its union with the word. Thus we see that a Christian has sufficient in his faith. Works are not needed to make him become acceptable to God. And if such works are no longer a prerequisite, then assuredly all commandments and laws are like broken chains; and if his chains are broken, he is assuredly free. That is Christian freedom, gained by faith alone. It is wrong to think this means that we can either be idle or do evil; rather it means that we have no need to perform works of merit in order to attain godliness and salvation."

Luther did not here make clear what he meant by "faith" and "works", and each of the two terms is used in different senses; they involved problems he had to expound in his later sermons and writings.

This survey of these three crucial documents is not an exposition of Luther's complete thought which deepened during the coming years. It is necessary to know the contents of these three pamphlets in order to appreciate the strength and scope of the attack on the Church and to realize the shock with which they were read. Luther was revealed not only as demanding drastic reform in the governance and institutions of the Church, but as a revolutionary in doctrine. Many who were eager to see long-known corruptions removed, drew back when the very teaching of the Church came under discussion; some followed Luther's lead or adhered to one or other of his rivals as variations developed among his early supporters.

Erasmus had been disturbed when the theologians of Louvain and Cologne had condemned some of Luther's contentions, and he was shocked at the hasty judgment of the Bull *Exsurge Domine*. Both these acts came before the publication of the three pamphlets just described. He still hoped that reason would prevail over passion and during 1520 he did all he could by correspondence and interviews to create a calmer atmosphere. He himself was bitterly attacked and his name was frequently coupled with Luther's; later he was even accused of having written the three pamphlets! After the Bull had been published, but not yet promulgated, Erasmus wrote:

"They who are instigating the Pope to this course give him advice of the piety of which I shall say nothing, but which, in my opinion, is certainly most dangerous. The whole affair sprang first from bad causes and has been pushed on by equally bad methods. The tragedy originated in the stupidity of the monks and their hatred of learning. Then, by means of violent abuse and malicious conspiracies, it proceeded to the height of madness which it has now reached. What this aim is no one can doubt—namely, to suppress the learning of which they are ignorant, and then reign triumphant, they and their barbarism. I am taking no part in this tragedy else I might have a bishopric if I would write against Luther."

A correspondent wrote to Willibald Pirckheimer,[8] "There is no one in Rome who does not know that in many things Martin speaks truly; but all dissemble, the good through fear, the bad through rage at having to hear the truth. Many objected to the issue of the Bull and thought that Martin should have been assailed by reasons rather than by curses, by kindness rather than by tyranny. But rage and fear carried the day."

Erasmus wrote again to Luther in August 1520, telling him that More had defended him (Erasmus) before Henry VIII against the attacks of the Franciscan, Henry Standish, Bishop of St Asaph. Erasmus advised Luther to concentrate on his commentaries on the Scriptures and to avoid controversy. The quotation above and the advice given to Luther show how inadequate was Erasmus' understanding of the issues involved; not that he was alone in that, but it might have been expected that a man of his acute intelligence and wide experience would have seen the radical character of Luther's protest. It suggests that he had become

---

[8]Quoted in *A History of the Papacy*, by Mandell Creighton, Vol. VI, p. 163; this volume gives a useful account, by no means outmoded, of "The German Revolt, 1517-1527". Pirckheimer (1470-1528), the leading scholar of Nuremberg, councillor and ambassador, was a close friend of Erasmus. He supported Luther until the violence of the Reformers disgusted him.

engrossed in his own work and was unable to stretch his mind beyond his own needs. In 1520 he was fifty-four years old; Luther was seventeen years younger, and it is difficult for an elderly man (as Erasmus would be regarded at that period, and as he thought of himself) to sympathize with radical views. There was also a contrast in temperament. Erasmus shrank from violence; to him it seemed that to give way to passion was a surrender of the rational. Luther tended to carry things to the extreme and there was an explosive element in his character that made it difficult for him to keep calm in face of opposition which seemed to him to be the work of the devil. There was an even greater difference between the two men. Luther had gone through a long period of intense spiritual conflict; as an Augustinian friar he had obeyed the rule to which he was vowed, not only meticulously but even beyond need. His profound conviction that he was a sinner and could not get free from his sins in spite of fastings and penance, drove him to the edge of despair. His release from what seemed a spiritual living death came through his fervent study of the Gospels and Epistles, and the words of St Paul struck at his heart, "The just shall live by faith".[9] Erasmus was as silent about his spiritual condition as Luther was informative about his. We know of no religious crisis in Erasmus' life; he may have been like the majority of sincere Christians whose faith grows by its exercise. It would be wrong to interpret his silence as implying a lesser degree of conviction than that proclaimed by Luther. The two types are ever with us. Yet this difference of religious temperament, as it may be called, made it difficult, perhaps impossible, for either to understand the other. Erasmus was more in accord with Philip Melanchthon (1497-1560), who was appointed professor of Greek at Wittenberg on the recommendation of his uncle Johann Reuchlin. Melanchthon was a humanist and his gentle disposition and moderation did something towards restraining Luther's vehemence. He remained one of Erasmus' admirers and deeply regretted that his two friends were at strife.

In spite of the denunciation of Luther by the University theo-

---

[9] Romans, i, 17: a quotation from Hab. ii, 4; "the just shall live by his faith". In his *Liberty of a Christian*, Luther translated St Paul's verse as, "A justified Christian lives only by his faith", the "only" being an interpolation.

logians, and in spite of the Bull, and even in spite of Luther's three incisive pamphlets (had Erasmus read them?), Erasmus continued to do his utmost to create a more favourable frame of mind among the antagonists. Events again overtook him. On 9 December 1520 at Wittenberg, Luther, to the joy of the students who in all ages have loved to see hats in the ring, publicly burned the books of canon law, and, as an after-thought it seems, the Bull *Exsurge Domine*. This act of defiance must have warned Erasmus that there was little hope of reaching an understanding; nevertheless he persevered. His attempts to placate his own critics were not encouraging. An account of one experience was narrated in a letter to Thomas More written from Louvain about November 1520. A Carmelite prior of Louvain, Nicholas of Egmond, a fellow-Dutchman, was among the most bitter of Erasmus' critics and even preached against him. The Rector of the University was distressed at this openly expressed enmity and brought the two together. Erasmus' account of the meeting might be a sketch for another *Colloquy*. No doubt the narrative was coloured; indeed, it is to be hoped it was for the impression that it leaves is that most of the discussion (if it can be termed such) was at a low level of intelligence. A brief specimen, put into the form of a dialogue, will suffice.

> "*Erasmus.* Though it be true that I have written some things in my books not exactly as I ought, nevertheless it was not right for you to abuse the authority implied in a sacred place and a discourse on sacred subjects, as well as the credulity of simple people, to gratify your own vengeance. You might have written against me. As it is you are doing an injury, not so much to me as to this whole University, to the whole people, and to the office of preaching which is dedicated to far other purposes.
> *Egmond.* You and I would like to have the same authority.
> *Erasmus.* What, of preaching? I am a preacher of long standing,[10] and I think I could preach better sermons than I ever hear from you.
> *Egmond.* Why don't you do it then?
> *Erasmus.* Because I think I am doing more good by writing books, though I should find no fault with your employment,

[10]The only reference, I think, to his own preaching.

if you would only teach such things as contribute to good morals."

The exchange ended when Egmond said to the Rector, "As long as he refuses to write against Luther, so long we shall account him a Lutheran". After which he stumped out of the room.

The coronation of Charles V as King of the Romans on 23 October 1520 at Aachen provided an opportunity for Councillor Erasmus to have conversations with a number of leading personages. Before and after the ceremony, the court was at Cologne. Jerome Aleander, the Nuncio, was present and he tried to persuade the Elector Frederick of Saxony to act against Luther. The Elector asked Erasmus to wait on him, and they, with Spalatin, discussed the situation. One of Erasmus' remarks was later recalled by the Elector: "Luther has committed two sins; he has touched the Pope in his crown and the monks in their belly". Afterwards he jotted down for Spalatin some axioms for the guidance of the Elector. These included the following:

"The dispute is carried on with clamour, intrigues, bitter hatred and ambition."
"As Luther is a man void of ambition, he is the less to be suspected."
"The Pope's unmerciful Bull is disapproved by all honest men."

It seems probable that his talk with Erasmus persuaded the Elector to protect Luther; if so, Luther had much for which to thank Erasmus. He also had several meetings with Aleander, his former companion in Venice, but though Erasmus claimed that they had comfortable talks, Aleander was far from being his friend; he seems to have shrunk from denouncing Erasmus to his face, but he later declared that "I have long known Erasmus as the source of this evil . . . he is the corner stone of this heresy". Aleander, like so many others, failed to make a distinction between criticism of abuses and innovations in doctrine.

The Diet of Worms was opened by the new Emperor on 28 January 1521. Cuthbert Tunstall was Henry VIII's envoy to Charles at this period; he was at Aachen and Cologne and went on to Worms; from there he sent to Wolsey two of Luther's pamphlets with the advice that after they had been read they should be burned. Their names are not given but one seems to have been *The Babylonish Captivity*. Tunstall pointed out that the two chief grievances of the Germans were the payment of annates to the Pope and his power to appoint to benefices. Erasmus did not go to Worms, "although I was invited, partly because I did not wish to be involved in the affair of Luther, which was then violently discussed". This absence was a pity as it was the last opportunity for the two men to meet.

The story of Luther at Worms is well known. He arrived there under the safe-conduct of the Emperor on 16 April amid popular acclamation. He was there for ten days engaged in fruitless disputation and was then spirited away by connivance of the Elector Frederick to the Wartburg in Thuringia. A month later Erasmus wrote to Jodocus Jonas:

"What other result, I should like to know, has been produced by so many abusive pamphlets, so much fire and smoke, so many terrific threats, and so much turgid talk, but that what was before debated in the Universities as a probable opinion must hereafter become an article of faith, and even now it is unsafe to teach the Gospel, the passions of men being roused to fury, and calumny laying hold of and perverting every word that may be spoken. Luther might have taught the philosophy of the Gospel with great advantage to the Christian flock, and benefited the world by writing books if he had abstained from what could not but end in disturbance. He has taken from my writings too a great part of the good they might have done. Even the debates in the Universities which used to be perfectly untrammelled, are no longer free. If it were permissible to hate anyone on account of private offences, there is no one who has been more injured by the Lutherans than I have been, yet, if it could be done without taking Luther's life, I should wish that this discussion, which is by far the most dangerous that has ever yet been, might be composed, and composed in such a manner that there might be no fear it would again break out with still more serious danger hereafter as wounds when badly dressed are apt to be."

Here it may be noted that Erasmus at last felt the seriousness of the position—"far the most dangerous that has ever yet been".

For some time he had been finding the atmosphere of Louvain too disturbing for his peace of mind, and with the final collapse of his effort for peace, he decided to go to Basle. He had a big programme of printing for Froben and Basle had the advantage of being an independent city within the Swiss Confederation, and, so far, free from religious strife.

Before he left he wrote to Lord Mountjoy:

"As to your statement that it is in my power to put an end to all this disturbance, I would that what you say were true. Had it been, this tragedy would never even have begun. They say here that I have lost my pen. I have a pen, indeed, but there are a great many reasons which dissuade me from using it in this way. To call Luther a mushroom is very easy, but to defend the cause of the true faith by appropriate arguments, I at least find exceedingly difficult. And so far, others have not succeeded very well. Still, I would gladly gird up my loins for this task if I were assured that certain persons, who, under the pretext of defending the faith, are really pleading the cause of the world, would use their victory for the good of the Christian religion. Nevertheless I will go to Basle with the resolution that, after finishing the work I have in hand, I will undertake something that may tend to allay this strife; or, at any rate, I will give evidence of my own feelings on the subject."

Erasmus left Brabant, never to return, on 28 October 1521 and three weeks later arrived in Basle.

CHAPTER XVI

Against Luther

FROM ANDERLECHT in September 1521 Erasmus wrote to Paul Bombasio in Rome a letter of congratulation on his "good fortune in having relieved yourself of the intolerable burden of poverty". He went on:

"I have as much as enables me to live respectably, and I can sometimes even afford a guinea for a needy friend; so little am I compelled to be a burden to anyone. I do not covet honours, especially when they cost so much, but had they been offered to me gratuitously, or at least at no great expense and had they been offered in time, I should not have been inclined to reject them absolutely."

He then gave news of Thomas More.

"In this, as in everything else, More has shown himself farther-sighted than I, for he has received from his most excellent sovereign the honour of knighthood, and he is now his Privy Councillor and Lord of the Treasury,[1] both of which offices are tolerably independent as well as honourable in the highest degree, so that he is now more beloved of the good and more feared by the bad."

Erasmus next turned to the burning topic of the day.

"I tried to prevent this disturbance arising, then to allay it when it had arisen, and, finally, when the conflagration had spread far and wide, to check it with the least possible interruption of the public tranquillity."

That is a fair account of his conduct during this critical time. In this letter he again excused himself from writing against Luther.

[1]More became *Under*-Treasurer (the one who did the work) on 2 May, 1521, and was probably knighted at the same time.

"For my not having hitherto engaged in a written controversy with Luther, there are a great many reasons, but the main one was that I had no time at all to read what Luther has written. . . . Nor would it suffice to read his books once only. I should be obliged to go through them again and again. . . . It is a task full of danger, and I have had more experience in another field of study. Moreover, after having published so many works, I might fairly expect to be released from labour, and be permitted for the future to pursue my studies in peace."

One's sympathies may well be with Erasmus; he was being badgered by both sides to take an active part in a controversy on problems that were outside his chosen and well-tilled field. He added:

"If however the present mischief can be overcome by pamphlets, swarms of books are appearing every day, so there is no need of Erasmus; or, if vociferations are likely to prove more effectual, Stentors are not wanting."

By the time he wrote that letter, he must have lost heart after his fruitless labours to urge both parties to moderate their anger and discuss matters as reasonable men.

One consolation must have been that the summer of 1521 brought an opportunity of meeting Thomas More again. Wolsey had arrived in Calais at the beginning of August with the ostensible purpose of reconciling the King of France and the Emperor. We can read in Hall and Cavendish of the pomp and all-but-regal ceremony of the occasion. Wolsey even took the Great Seal of England with him. Thomas More was among the councillors who accompanied Wolsey who was informed that "the king signifieth your Grace that, whereas old men do now decay greatly in this realm, his mind is to acquaint other young men with his great affairs, and, therefore, he desireth your Grace to make Sir William Sandys and Sir Thomas More privy to all such matters as your Grace shall treat at Calais".

After a fortnight there, the Cardinal and his vast retinue moved to Bruges to meet the Emperor and, in spite of negotiations with the French, to make a treaty with him. After three weeks at Bruges, they moved back to Calais. More returned in October to report to the King. According to Hall, the outcome of the long discussions with the French was an agreement about fishing rights!

It was during his stay at Bruges in August 1521 that More was able to meet Erasmus, as it proved, for the last time. Erasmus took the opportunity to introduce the young Spanish scholar J. L. Vives[2] who wished to go to England. Erasmus also met Tunstall and Mountjoy. There is unfortunately no account of what must have been a joyous reunion. When Erasmus had a talk —perhaps one should say, an audience—with Wolsey, the Cardinal promised to send him a copy of the book, published in July, that King Henry had written against Luther, *Assertio Septem Sacramentorum*.[3]

Richard Pace, then one of the King's secretaries, apologized to Wolsey in April 1521 for a delay in sending him some newsletters from Germany as the King had only just read them; "he commanded me to write unto your Grace, declaring he was otherwise occupied, i.e. *in scribendo contra Lutherum*, as I do conjecture". A few days later he found the King reading a new book by Luther; this must have been, as subsequent events showed, *De Captivitate Babylonica*. Wolsey was content to encourage the King's interest in theology as it took his mind off politics. It seems that as early as 1518 Henry had begun to write against Luther.[4] Wolsey had raised some criticisms. It may be that his *Assertio* developed from his previous manuscript. He must have worked quickly for on 21 May 1521 he informed the Pope of this evidence of "the resources of his mind". A few days earlier Wolsey had staged at St Paul's Churchyard a solemn burning of Luther's books; this has been called a "holocaust", but it was more likely to have been a solemn committal to the flames of a few copies of Luther's pamphlets. There is no evidence that in such a few months since publication large numbers had

---

[2]Vives was then busy on the commentary he wrote at Erasmus' suggestion, on St Augustine's *De Civitate Dei*; the notes include a tribute to More (see Everyman's Library edition, II, p. 412). He came to England in 1523; his sympathies with Queen Catherine led to a short imprisonment in the Tower, after which he left the country.

[3]During the several weeks More spent at Calais, he must have seen much of Lord Berners who then held the important post of Deputy. Did they discuss Froissart's *Chronicles*, which Berners was translating at the request of Henry VIII? The first volume was published in 1523.

[4]See A. F. Pollard, *Henry VIII*, p. 98.

been brought into the country, nor had there been as yet any English translations.

Bishop John Fisher preached on this occasion before the Cardinal, Archbishop Warham, Tunstall, and probably Thomas More. He spoke of the clouds of heresy that had overshadowed the Church in the past, "and now such another cloud is raised aloft, one Martin Luther, a friar, the which hath stirred a mighty storm and tempest in the Church and had shadowed the clear light of many scriptures of God". The sermon was not, however, a vehement denunciation; it was an exposition of the promise that the spirit of truth would safeguard the faith. One passage is of special interest. The teaching of the Scriptures

> "subverteth one great ground of Martin Luther which is this that faith without works doth justify a sinner. Upon the which ground he buildeth many other erroneous articles and specially that the sacraments of Christ's Church doth not justify but only faith. A perilous article able to subvert all the order of the Church. But touching these sacraments, the King's Grace, our sovereign lord in his own person, hath with his pen substantially foughten against Martin Luther that I doubt not every true Christian man that shall read his book shall see those blessed sacraments cleared and delivered from all the slanderous mouth and cruel teeth that Martin Luther hath set upon them, wherein all England may take great comfort and specially all those that love learning. Plato saith, then shall commonwealths be blessed when either those that be philosophers govern, or else those that govern give them to philosophy."[5]

Doubts were expressed at the time, and have been since, as to Henry's authorship of the *Assertio*. Some said Bishop Fisher had written the book, but the above quotation from his sermon sufficiently meets that suggestion; others hinted that Erasmus himself wrote it, but then he got the blame for so much! The clearest statement was made by Sir Thomas More when he was questioned by the commissioners on his relations with the Nun of Kent in March 1534; they accused him of treachery,

[5] *English Works* (E.E.T.S.), p. 326. This sermon was translated into Latin by Richard Pace and published in 1522. For previous references to Plato's philosopher, see above p. 69 and p. 116.

"for he, by his subtle sinister sleights most unnaturally procuring and provoking him [the King] to set forth a book of the *Assertion of the Seven Sacraments* and maintenance of the Pope's authority, had caused him to his dishonour throughout all Christendom to put a sword to the Pope's hands to fight against himself."

To this astonishing charge, More answered:

"My lords, these terrors be arguments for children and not for me. But to answer that wherewith you do chiefly burden me, I believe the King's Highness of his honour will never lay that to my charge, for none is there that can in that point say in my excuse more than his Highness himself, who right well knoweth that I never was procurer nor counsellor of his Majesty thereunto, but, after it was finished, by his Grace's appointment and consent of the makers of the same, only a sorter out and placer of the principal matters therein contained. Wherein when I found the Pope's authority high advanced, and with strong arguments mightily defended, I said unto his Grace, 'I must put your Highness in remembrance of one thing, and that is this, the Pope, as your Grace knoweth, is a prince as you are, and in league with all other Christian princes. It may hereafter fall out that your Grace and he may vary upon some points of the league, whereupon may grow breach of amity between you both. I think it best therefore that that place be amended, and his authority more slenderly touched.'

'Nay', quoth his Grace, 'that shall it not. We are so much bounden unto the See of Rome that we cannot do too much honour unto it.'

Then did I further put him in remembrance of the Statute of Praemunire, whereby a good part of the Pope's pastoral cure here was pared away.

To that answered his Highness, 'Whatsoever impediment be to the contrary, we will set forth that authority to the uttermost. For we received from that See our Crown Imperial'."

Henry was probably referring here to the Bull (27 March 1487) of Innocent VIII confirming Henry VII as lawful King of England and securing the succession of the crown to the children of Henry and Elizabeth of York.[6]

[6] The existing text of the *Assertio* contains no statement in accordance with More's description. Did Henry, in fact, modify the wording to meet the objection?

How are we to interpret More's statement? The word "makers" presents a difficulty; who were they? Did they write the book? We are still left in some doubt, but perhaps a reasonable construction is this: after the King had drafted his book, his theological advisers scrutinized it and suggested some changes; then Sir Thomas More edited and prepared the manuscript for the printer. Erasmus was satisfied after discussing the matter with Mountjoy that the King was the author. The book is not a profound theological treatise; it sets down clearly the teaching of the Church in a way that was within the scope of a layman, such as Henry, who was well instructed in the tenets of his religion. It was, within its limits, a sound exposition of Catholic doctrine on the sacraments supported by references to the Scriptures and the Fathers.

The book was published by Pynson in July 1521 and a sumptuously bound and autographed copy was presented to Leo X at the beginning of October; on the 11th of that month the Pope conferred on Henry VIII the title of *Fidei Defensor*. When Luther read the book he expressed the opinion that it had been written by Edward Lee who was then attacking Erasmus. A translation into German was made for Luther's opponent, Duke George of Saxony, who thought it must have been written by Erasmus. Luther's reply was published in July 1522 first in German, and was soon followed by a longer Latin version, *Contra Henricum Regem Angliae*, which again was ascribed to Erasmus! The book was notable for the scurrilous abuse poured on the King; among the least indecent epithets were—brigand, ass, king of lies, buffoon, Thomist pig, dolt. Henry laughed at this and declared that the author was only fit to be a fool at the Lord Mayor's banquet. It would have been beneath the dignity of a king to answer such vilification, but Luther's reply contained arguments that could not be ignored. Bishop John Fisher wrote the theologian's reply in his *Defensio Regie Assertionis*,[7] published in Cologne in 1525 in the same year as his other anti-Lutheran book, *Sacri Sacerdoti Defensio*. Presumably it was at the suggestion of the King that More also wrote a reply which certainly showed a

[7] See my *Saint John Fisher*, pp. 101-104.

deeper knowledge of theology than the King could claim to have. This was published by Pynson in 1523 with an involved Latin title attributing the work to William Ross.[8] It must be admitted that while More did not measure down to Luther's scurrility, he went some way towards doing so. A modern comment may be given. "More had certainly for once forgotten his manners, and Luther never had any. We excuse Luther because of the provocation he had received, and we must excuse More for the same reason. Nearly all controversies in the XVI century are in many respects deplorable. More's book, however, is certainly not deficient in reasoning and humour. He wrote in his best forensic style and much of his raillery is inspired by wit."[9] It would be tedious here to attempt to summarize the arguments and counter-arguments; we may note, however, the emphasis More put on Luther's suggestion that princes should free themselves from the yoke of the Papacy.

"The people in their turn will throw off the yoke of the princes, and deprive them of their possessions. And when they shall come to this, dumb with the blood of princes, and exulting in the slaughter of the nobles, they will not submit to plebeian governors, but following the teaching of Luther, and trampling the law under foot, then, at last without government and without law, without rein and without understanding, they will turn their hands against each other."

It was not the first nor the last time that More predicted with surety the outcome of policies of the day, whether those of Luther or of Henry VIII. Erasmus shared More's apprehensions. Writing to Pope Adrian VI in 1522, he said, "I foresee more danger than I could wish, that the end may be slaughter and bloodshed". The extravagances of extremists such as Carlstadt and Münzer and the Peasants' War of 1524 were a grim commentary on these warnings.

Another passage in this book has a bearing on More's view of the Papacy.

[8] A cancelled title-page used the pseudonym of Ferdinand Baravell. There seems no point in the change but apparently there was such a person as William Ross who had fled from England and died abroad.

[9] H. Maynard Smith. *Pre-Reformation England* (1930), p. 514.

"As regards the primacy of the Roman Pontiff, the Bishop of Rochester has made the answer so clear from the Gospels, the Acts of the Apostles, and from the whole of the Old Testament and from the consent of the holy Fathers, not of the Latins only, but of the Greeks also (of whose opposition Luther is wont to boast) and from the definition of a General Council, in which the Armenians and Greeks, who had at that time had been most obstinately resisting, were overcome, and acknowledged themselves overcome, that it would be utterly superfluous for me to write again on the subject."

From this it seems that More had read Fisher's *Defensio* in manuscript and had doubtless discussed the problem with him; this had been written in 1522 but the bishop postponed publication on a rumour that Luther might recant. More referred to this subject in the most important letter he wrote to Thomas Cromwell on 5 March 1534.

"As touching the third point, the primacy of the Pope, I nothing meddle in the matter. Truth it is, that as I told you, when you desired me to show you what I thought therein, I was myself sometime not of the mind that the primacy of that See should be begun by the institution of God, until that I read in that matter those things that the King's Highness had written in his most famous book."

More went on to say that he then studied the question thoroughly and had seen that the primacy was "provided by God", nor during the succeeding decade had he found reason to change his mind.

Cardinal Pole, in the course of a sermon preached during the reign of Mary Tudor, recalled a conversation with Antonio Bonvisi, one of More's oldest friends. The subject of the primacy of the Pope had been raised and More expressed the opinion that the primacy was part of the organization of the Church as a matter of expediency and not of divine origin. Some days later he sought out Bonvisi and said, "Whither was I falling when I made you that answer of the primacy of the Church? I assure you that opinion alone was enough to make me fall from the rest, for that upholdeth all."[10]

[10]Strype, *Memorials*, II, pp. 491-3.

A later passage in the letter to Cromwell from which an extract has just been made, expresses More's view on another aspect of papal authority.

"Albeit that I have for mine own part such opinion of the Pope's supremacy as I have showed you, yet never thought I the Pope above the General Council nor never have in any book of mine put forth among the King's subjects in our vulgar tongue, advanced greatly the Pope's authority."

It may seem surprising to us that Thomas More should even have doubted the divine institution of the papacy and have been uncertain of the relative authority of a General Council. Had we lived at that period we should not have been startled at such opinions for they were widely held. For instance, at the Council of Constance (1414) Jean Gerson (1363-1439), Chancellor of the University of Paris, had declared that "the Church is united in its one Head, Christ, and a General Council, representing the Church, is the authority or rule, guided by the Holy Ghost, ordained by Christ, which all, even the Pope, are bound to obey", a view that was endorsed by some of the bishops at the Council of Basle (1431). The "Babylonish Captivity" of the Popes at Avignon, followed by the Great Schism, together extending over the fourteenth century, and the degradation of the papacy under such a Pope as Alexander VI (1492-1503), had considerably shaken men's confidence; such happenings themselves helped to prepare the ground for the Reformation.

Erasmus never questioned the authority of the Pope, but there were qualifications. In his notes in his *Novum Testamentum*, for instance, on Matt. xvi, 18, "Upon this rock I will build my church", he expressed the view that these words did not apply exclusively to the Pope, "to whom they undoubtedly apply, first of all, seeing that he is head of the Christian Church, but they apply not only to him, but to all Christians". So too on Matt. xvii, 5, "Hear ye him", he commented, "Christ is the only teacher who has been appointed by God himself. Such authority has been committed to no theologian, no Bishop, to no Pope or Prince; not that we ought not to obey them, but we ought to obey Christ first of all." We have seen how bitterly he felt about the warlike activities of Julius II, and he hoped that each succeeding Pope would prove a better pastor of the Church, but the cultured Leo X (1513-1521) was intent on the advancement of his Medici nephews and he failed to see the significance of Luther's revolt. Adrian VI, of Utrecht, had been educated by the Brethren of the Common Life and had been a professor at Louvain; Erasmus had known and respected him, but he died in 1523. His successor, another Medici, Clement VII (1523-1534), rivalled his cousin Leo in nepotism and was too vacillating and irresolute to effect any radical change. When Clement was elected, Erasmus wrote to his friend the Bishop of Basle, "I am waiting for some indication of the spirit of the new Pope. If it shall appear that he is really concerned for the honour of Christ, I mean to give him all the support that can be given by such an insignificant person as myself. . . . I have no desire that the primacy of the Roman See should be abolished, but I could wish that its discipline were such that it might favour every effort making for the religion of the Gospel as for several ages past it has openly taught by its example things plainly averse to the doctrines of Christ." From these quotations it would seem that Erasmus shared More's earlier opinion, that the Primacy was not of divine institution. The test he applied to all priests and monks was, "By their fruits ye shall know them".

In considering the attitudes of More and Erasmus to the Papacy and their views on some of the issues of the day, we need to remind ourselves that there were a number of questions to which the Church had not yet given an authoritative answer. The Council of Trent (1545-1563) and the First Vatican Council (1869-1870) made binding decisions on questions that hitherto had been open. An example of this is provided by the Vulgate text of the Bible. When Erasmus published with his *Novum Instrumentum* a new translation of the Greek text into Latin, he was not controvening the dictates of the Church. There were at that time a number of Latin texts that had suffered from interpolations and mistranslations as well as scribal errors. The Council of Trent decided that a Latin text should be produced that could be declared authentic, a juridical rather than a critical decision. Such decisions do not mean that discussion is ended, but that its purpose is not to question but to elucidate.[11]

Thomas More had been called into the Lutheran controversy before Erasmus had taken part, but he was bombarded by demands that he should speak out. His reasons for refraining have been noted, and they were valid in normal conditions, but the times and the need were exceptional and if Rome could only denounce, then someone must refute Luther on his own ground. And who more influential than Erasmus? We can watch him fighting what was rather like a rearguard action.

He had not planned to settle at Basle, but his health was so precarious that he was unable to travel with comfort. He had several invitations that he refused either on account of his illness or for fear of losing his freedom. In September 1527 Henry VIII invited him to come to England, but he declined as "the journey is too far for my old bones". It may be suspected, however, that he was aware of the troubles that were blowing up as rumours were already circulating that Henry wished to be separated from Catherine of Aragon, the aunt of Charles V. Erasmus seriously thought of going to Rome, but he found that even a short journey to Constance was too much for him. He was in fact very comfortably settled in Basle. John Froben had provided a pleasant lodging, *Zur alten Treue*, and a housekeeper. Erasmus' time was fully occupied with seeing through the press a whole series of publications; his congenial labours were interrupted by penning answers to attacks made on him; unfortunately he was over-sensitive to criticism and had not the philosophic calmness of spirit to ignore his opponents. Nothing was gained by these skirmishes. What is astonishing is the quantity of work he got through during his years at Basle in spite of these distractions. His editorial labours were considerable, but in these he was aided by young scholars such as Beatus Rhenanus; he also produced some of his best and most typical writings in the augmented editions of the *Adages* and of the

[11]The present position is set out in the Encyclical of Pope Pius XII, *Divino Afflante Spiritu* (1943). Pope Pius X in 1907 set in progress the revision of the Vulgate of Clement VIII (1592).

Colloquies. Yet, busy as he was, he could not escape constant appeals to deal with Luther.

In September 1522 he wrote to his fellow-Dutchman, Pope Adrian VI, to congratulate him on his elevation. He begged the Pope not to believe malicious rumours that he favoured the Lutherans and he appealed for every effort to be made to unite all princes in the bonds of Christian charity and to put an end to all the disputes about doctrine. It was not until December that Adrian replied. Meanwhile Erasmus had written again as he thought his letter had gone astray. The Pope reassured Erasmus that he gave no attention to rumours; he pointed out that the best way to kill such rumours would be for Erasmus to take up his pen and write against the new heretics. His great abilities and learning and the prestige he enjoyed could not be better used than in such service to God and Christendom. "Arise, and aid the cause of God, and use in His honour, as you have done hitherto, those splendid talents He has bestowed on you!" The Pope invited Erasmus to come to Rome in the spring; there he would find all the books he needed and be able to have conversations with learned theologians as well as with himself. Adrian replied to Erasmus' second letter in January 1523 and again pressed him to come to Rome. Erasmus waited two months before replying; this delay is eloquent of his reluctance to commit himself. He began by excusing himself from undertaking such a journey on account of "a most cruel tyrant—the stone". He argued that in Rome he would be out of touch with the Lutherans who were on his doorstep at Basle. "As regards their correction, I shall do more good by living near them than if I were removed to a distance. . . . Should I write temperately and civilly against Luther, I shall be thought to be in collusion with him; but if I imitate his style and provoke the Lutherans to war, I shall only succeed in stirring up a hornets' nest." He went on to suggest the wisest way of dealing with the problem. He deprecated the use of violence though he admitted that the Lollards in England had been forcibly suppressed, or, "put down rather than extinguished". This was a fair estimate of the position and it showed that Erasmus had a close knowledge of the position in England gained during his residence there and from his friends. He went on, "And I am not sure that what was possible at that time, and in that kingdom, the whole of which is under one sovereign, would be possible here in so vast a territory, divided among so many princes; certainly if it is decided to stamp out this plague by means of imprisonment, scourging, confiscations, exile, severe sentences and death, there can be no need of my advice". "The first thing will be to discover the sources from which this evil springs up again and again; these must before all else be healed. . . . I would wish, if it were possible, that the licence of publishing pamphlets should be under some restraint. Besides, let hope be given to the world that some grievances of which it justly complains, will be removed." The emphasis placed on the necessity for dealing with grievances will be noted. Finally, Erasmus suggested calling together "from every country men of incorruptible integrity, grave, mild, gracious, unimpassioned, whose opinion . . .". There unfortunately the letter breaks off. It is a matter of conjecture why Erasmus suppressed the rest of it, but the unfinished sentence indicates his line of thought. Erasmus later said, "I sent part, but it displeased".

Pope Adrian died on 14 September 1523. In his brief reign he had shown his desire to correct abuses but, as an Italian prince, he could not avoid political entanglements; so far was he from sympathizing with Erasmus' advice on how to deal with heretics, that when the Diet of Nuremberg met at the end of 1522, he begged the princes to lay aside jealousies and strife among themselves and combine to suppress Luther as the Council of Constance had dealt with Hus.

Erasmus was involved during 1523 in an acrimonious dispute with his former friend, Ulrich von Hutten, who had gone over to the Lutherans. They had known each other when Hutten was in the service of the Archbishop of Mainz. He became more and more violent in his attitude towards the Church, and his physical deterioration was due to his licentious habits. When he arrived in Basle in 1522, Erasmus refused to see him; Hutten then wrote an *Expostulatio* against "Erasmus of Rotterdam, priest and theologian", in which he accused Erasmus of cowardly deserting the ranks of the Reformers and truckling to Rome. This violent attack alarmed Erasmus, who replied with "A Sponge to wipe away Hutten's Aspersions" (1523). It was a brilliant defence of his own position and a barbed attack on Hutten. The dispute does not concern us here save as another indication of the strain imposed on Erasmus by those who wanted him to come down on one side or the other.

Pressure was also coming from his old friend Cuthbert Tunstall, now Bishop of London, who was among the foremost opponents of Lutheranism in England. He wrote to Erasmus in June 1523:

> "All your friends earnestly hope and desire that you should come to grips with this Proteus, this veritable monster. You say you have a bad reputation with Luther and the Lutherans, but no worse than God himself whom Luther makes the author of all evil while he at the same time deprives men of free will and maintains that everything happens by fixed laws of necessity, so that no one is free to do right if he wishes to do so."

This is a travesty of Luther's teaching, but it shows that even a scholar such as Tunstall could misunderstand some of Luther's writings. The passage has a particular interest as it may have suggested to Erasmus a line of argument that would not be purely polemical.

In his reply Erasmus wrote, "There is danger lest in the words of the apostle we should have zeal but not according to knowledge, lest we not merely pluck up the wheat with the tares, but actually pluck up wheat instead of tares".

Some of the reasons advanced by Erasmus for not writing against Luther may seem specious, as if he were searching for excuses from doing something he had no wish to do. He could hardly plead ill-health, for in spite of his genuine debility, he was pouring out works at such a rate that they showed signs of hastiness. He could, for instance, interrupt his "labours of Hercules", as he called them, to answer with vigour and at length the aspersions of Hutten. It was no wonder that his friends were puzzled at his reluctance to write with the same vehemence against Luther. Pages could be filled with their remonstrances and entreaties and more pages with his explanations as he fended them off as long as he could. We must be careful not to fall into their way of interpreting his reluctance to carry out their wishes. Throughout his many letters on the subject, a consistent policy can be seen; he would not add to the turmoil of the times. This is again expressed in the preface addressed to the Cardinal-Archbishop of Mainz to a new edition of the *Method of True Theology* which he brought out in 1523. In it he wrote:

"It is part of my unhappy fate that my old age has fallen in these evil times. We must implore the Lord Jesus that he, who alone has the power to do so by his spirit, will turn the hearts of Christian people to the love of peace and concord. For as long as we permit our spirit to have free play, and to create these disturbances, the more we try to extricate ourselves from our difficulties, the more we shall be entangled in them. Party spirit is so hot that fair criticism is impossible. Quarrels and rioting prevail everywhere.... For my part I would rather be a market-gardener in the possession of Christian tranquillity, and rejoice in evangelical simple-mindedness than the greatest and most renowned theologian in the world, and be involved in these dissensions."

Then follows a passage of importance if we would try to understand the mind of the writer.

"For if the unjust judge in the Gospel of Luke did not entirely refuse to listen to the appeal of the afflicted widow, how much less ought we to neglect the cry of those for whom the Lord Jesus Christ shed his blood? For it was not for the great only that he died, but the humble and the lowly are his peculiar care. These were the first he gathered round him; by their means the kingdom of heaven began to make progress. These things can be done without tumult if kings and princes, in the meanwhile forgoing the satisfaction of their human passions, will devote themselves with all their heart to the public advantage and the glory of Jesus Christ, the Prince of princes, and if all participation in this work be forbidden to those whom the world has already endured too long, who care for nothing but their own glory, their own belly, and their own power, and who think that their kingdom cannot stand if the people are permitted to have either brains or judgment. Wherefore we must besiege with our common prayers almighty and all-merciful Jesus, to put his mind into the leading men of both sides."

This passage shows an aspect of Erasmus that can easily be over-looked. Perhaps it dates back to his formation by the Brethren of the Common Life, for it can be seen here and there throughout his writings. He had a deeply felt concern for the teaching of the Gospel to ordinary folk; their spiritual welfare was more import-ant to him than the fine-spun theological arguments on problems that plain people could not understand; the type of preaching resulting from scholastic training was simply incomprehensible to them. Too much emphasis on ceremonies, on pilgrimages, on indulgences, on relics, on ecclesiastical privileges and on the institutional side of the Church, tended to obscure the teaching of Christ, however justifiable they might be as aids to devotion. In the "Paraclesis" of his *Novum Instrumentum* he had written of the Gospels and Epistles, "I wish the countryman might sing them at his plough, the weaver chant them at his loom, the traveller beguile with them the weariness of his journey".[12] This implied the need for vernacular translations. He came to modify this view after the Peasants' War and when he saw some of the consequences of the unlettered people discussing texts in what Thomas More called "pot-parliaments". He had not realized that Tom, Dick and Harry can get just as disputatious as the theologians. This in no way, however, affected his insistence on the duty of priests preaching the Gospel of Christ to common people in language they could understand.

Erasmus at length felt that he could no longer resist the im-portunities of his friends; perhaps if he did write something against Luther, he would be allowed more peace to carry on with his proper work! It needed care in selecting his ground. He could not, for instance, retain his integrity and defend Rome against Luther if that meant turning his back on his own denunciation of the shortcomings of the Church. It may have been Tunstall's letter, from which an extract has just been made, that prompted

[12]Did William Tyndale have these words in mind when he said to an opponent, "If God spare my life, ere many years I will cause a boy that driveth the plough, shall know more of scripture than thou dost"?

Erasmus to choose the subject of Free Will; a subject that avoided the more contentious and popularly acclaimed opinions of Luther, yet was a fundamental issue.

> "*and reason'd high*
> *Of Providence, Foreknowledge, Will and Fate,*
> *Fixt Fate, free will, foreknowledge absolutely*
> *And found no end, in wandring mazes lost.*"[13]

Erasmus sent a copy of his *Paraphrase of St Luke* to Henry VIII, to whom it was dedicated, in September 1523 and informed him that "I am contemplating an attack on Luther". Two months later he wrote to John Faber, "I have finished the *Paraphrase of Mark*, finished *Our Father*, and, to show that I am in my second childhood, I have finished the *Nux* of Ovid. I am attacking the *Acts of the Apostles* and have begun a treatise on *Confession*. If my powers are equal to it I shall add a work on Free Will."

Evidently the news had spread that Erasmus was at last coming into the field of combat, for Luther wrote to him in April 1524:

"I see that God has not yet granted you the courage and the insight to join freely and confidently with me in fighting these monsters. Nor am I the man to demand of you what goes beyond my own strength and my own limitations. But weakness like your own and the measure of the gift of God in you, I have tolerated. For this plainly the whole world cannot deny; that learning flourishes and prevails whereby men have come to the true understanding of Scripture and this is a great and splendid gift of God in you. In truth I have never wished that you should go beyond your own limitations and mingle in our camp, for though you might help us greatly with your genius and eloquence, yet since your heart is not in it, it would be safer to serve within your own gift. The only thing to be feared was that you would sometime be persuaded by our enemies to publish some attack on our doctrine, and then necessity would compel me to answer you to your face. . . . I could wish that my allies would cease to attack you with such zeal and would permit your old age to fall asleep in the peace of God and this they would do, in my opinion, if they would consider your infirmity and the greatness of our cause, which

[13]Milton, *Paradise Lost*, II, lines 558-561.

has long since passed beyond your limitations; especially now that the matter has now gone so far that there is little fear for our cause, even if Erasmus fight against it with all his might, nay, though sometimes he scatters stings and bites. . . . I beg you meanwhile if you can do no more, to remain a spectator of our conflict and not to join forces with our opponents, especially not to publish books against me, as I will publish nothing against you."

Erasmus described this letter as "polite enough" (*satis humaniter*); indeed, he may have recognized that Luther had sensed the truth, "your heart is not in it", and the advice to keep to his own field, however tactlessly expressed, was in accordance with his own desires. He was probably nettled by Luther's references to his "old age", "limitations", and "infirmity"; true, he wrote of himself in the same way in his own letters but there is a difference between admitting such facts in familiar correspondence and having them pointed out by a younger man. His reply was dated 8 May. He had, he said, the integrity of the Gospel just as much at heart as Luther, but he could not turn a blind eye to the disastrous effect of the dispute on sound learning, and he dreaded lest all should end in trouble and even bloodshed. So far he had not written against Luther as he felt no benefit would accrue to true religion; on the other hand, if Luther wrote against him, from a worldly point of view, nothing more fortunate could befall him as it would silence at least one section of his opponents.

De Libero Arbitrio Diatribe sive Collatio[14] (A Discourse or treatise on Free Will) was ready by the end of August, and early in September Erasmus sent out copies to many important persons as well as to his friends and to the Universities. On the whole, Catholic opinion was favourable; the Pope and Henry VIII, among others, were well satisfied. Melanchthon, ever anxious to keep the peace, wrote to say that the book had been well received

---

[14]The word "Diatribe" was printed in Greek characters. There is a French translation, *Essai sur le Libre Arbitre* (Paris, 1945) with an excellent introduction by Pierre Mesnard. Luther's reply, *On the Bondage of the Will*, translated by J. I. Packer and O. R. Johnston (London, 1957) has an interesting anti-Erasmus introduction containing the astonishing statement that Erasmus professed a "Christianity without Christ". A helpful commentary on the two books will be found in chapter 12 of Gordon Rupp's *The Righteousness of God* (1953).

at Wittenberg and he hoped Luther's reply would be equally moderate in tone.

It is not possible here to go into details of this controversy on a subject on which the Church has not made any final pronouncement. A few points will serve to indicate the general line of argument. Erasmus began by giving two warnings; the first was that some revealed truths must always remain beyond the reach of the human mind, and the second, that texts must not be torn from their contexts; the time, place and circumstances must be taken into account; nor should we force the meaning, for instance of a parable, beyond the intended limits. As Luther based his teaching on his interpretation of the Scriptures, Erasmus built up his argument from the Bible and had less recourse to the early Fathers. His main position was that a man's "spirit is moved by grace alone to *think* of good, and by grace he has the necessary *power* to attain what he has thought, but between these two there is the *consent* by which grace and human will co-operate; all the time grace is the chief *cause*, and the will the important *means*". He pointed out how in place after place in the Scriptures, man is urged and commanded to choose good rather than evil; if there is no freedom of choice, how can he choose?

Luther's reply *De Servo Arbitrio* (On the Bondage of the Will) was published at the end of 1525 and a German translation soon followed. Erasmus had caused Luther to write a major exposition of his doctrine; it reveals the burning conviction of the truth of his message. He recognized that Erasmus had put his finger on a fundamental principle.

"You alone, in contrast to all others, have attacked the real thing, that is the essential issue. You have not wearied me with such peripheral topics as the papacy, purgatory, indulgences, and so on . . . you and you alone, have seen the hinge on which all turns and aimed for the vital spot. . . . By your studies in literature and languages you have rendered me also some service, and I confess myself much indebted to you; certainly, in that regard, I unfeignedly honour and sincerely respect you. But God has not willed nor granted you that you should be equal to the subject of our present debate."

Although Luther allowed himself one or two rude personal remarks,[15] his general attitude was less provocative than usual; perhaps the influence of Melanchthon may be seen here. One quotation indicates Luther's own position.

"Who, you say, will try and reform his life? I reply, Nobody! Nobody can! God has no time for practitioners of self-reformation, for they are hypocrites. The elect, who fear God, will be reformed by the Holy Spirit; the rest will perish unreformed. Who will believe, you say, that God loves him? I reply, Nobody! Nobody can! But the elect shall believe it, and the rest shall perish without believing it, raging and blaspheming."

There have been varying evaluations of this controversy. Here are two contrasting judgments. "A study of the debate reveals that all the incoherence was on Erasmus' side, and that it was Luther who saw things whole, opposing Erasmus' woolly notions with a clear, well-organized system of Biblical truth."[16] "Yet many readers of it as a controversy would, I imagine, give Erasmus a victory on points."[17]

Luther wrote to Erasmus early in 1526 but this letter is not extant; its nature can be gathered from Erasmus' reply, the opening sentence of which reads, "I am not so simple as to be appeased by a few pleasant remarks or soothed by flattery after receiving so many mortal wounds". "Mortal wounds" is an exaggeration, discourteous as some of Luther's remarks had been. So it was that Erasmus had quickly written a reply before getting Luther's letter; it was entitled *Hyperaspistes* (the Champion or Protector), and was printed in February, 1526. He defended himself against Luther's accusation that at bottom he was a sceptic; then he developed his views on how to interpret the Scriptures and his contention that, like St Paul, we must be content to "see through a glass darkly" while we are on earth.

Thomas More wrote to Erasmus in December 1526 to beg him to continue to fight against Luther.

---

[15]E.g. "You ooze Lucian from every pore; you swill Epicurus by the gallon".
[16]J. I. Packer and O. R. Johnston, *op. cit.*, p. 47.
[17]G. Rupp, *op. cit.*, p. 270.

"O my dearest Erasmus, God forbid that, after all your Herculean labours and your dangers, after all the toils and vigils to benefit the world in which you have spent the best years of your life, you should now become so intent on your declining years, that rather than be defeated in controversy, you keep silence. . . . You have answered his [Luther's] calumnies against yourself, and transfixed him with your pen; there now remains only to treat the passages of Holy Scripture; and since in the thousand copies of your first part (i.e. of *Hyperaspistes*) you have promised the world, as by so many bonds, that you would diligently execute that second part, you cannot refuse to pursue the cause of God after having successfully achieved your own, or to perform what you have publicly promised, especially since you can do it so easily."

Did More think that in his first part Erasmus had given too much space to the personal attacks? Was he afraid that Erasmus would not continue the controversy? His reference to "the passages of Holy Scripture" is to the last part of Luther's book in which he took up one by one the quotations from Scripture used by Erasmus and argued that they had been wrongly interpreted in the *Diatribe*. In reply Erasmus wrote, "I am going to complete *Hyperaspistes* since you and Tunstall are so anxious for me to do so".

So the second part of *Hyperaspistes* was published in the autumn of 1527. In it Erasmus took up again his argument on Free Will; he then went on to attack Luther's conception of God as a terrible judge who condemned the "non-elect" however persevering they were in virtuous living. Here he showed a fervour and conviction that rarely found expression in his writing. His opposition to Luther had become absolute.

Luther did not reply, but in his conversation he could refer to "that enraged viper, Erasmus of Rotterdam, the vainest creature in the world", and declare that "to this barefaced scoundrel, God is merely funny".

CHAPTER XVII

Against Tyndale

AFTER JOHN ECK, the theologian of Ingoldstadt, had been in England in 1525, he wrote, "When last summer I passed over to England to visit the King and the Bishop of Rochester, though tumults and seditions were raging in Germany, I never once heard the name of Luther mentioned except in malediction".[1] It may be doubted if a foreign visitor could give a reliable report on the religious attitude of the people, but, even five years later, Bishop Nix of Norwich could write to Archbishop Warham, "for the gentlemen and commonalty be not greatly infect, but merchants and such that hath their abiding not far from the sea". The ordinary folk could not read Luther's Latin or German but ideas derived from him slowly percolated down in distorted forms. This was also the story of the effect of Lollard teaching. We can follow the transition from what may be called popularized Lollardy to popularized Lutheranism[2] in the Rochester registers of Bishop John Fisher. John Mores was accused in May 1525 of expressing "divers doubts concerning Scripture" and in particular that "Christ did not die in perfect charity on Good Friday because he did not die to redeem Lucifer as well as Adam and Eve". This must be a muddled expression of ideas that were floating about. A case that came up in 1532 is more intelligible. Peter Durr was accused of heresy; he declared to the bishop that St Augustine was not in heaven, that the Pope and Archbishops had no authority to make laws, that Luther was not a heretic, and that "my prayer is as good as Our Lady's". Here is a distortion of

[1]Strype, *Cranmer*, i, 695.
[2]The terms "Lollardy" and "Lutheranism" are used loosely in these pages to indicate tendencies rather than specific doctrines. How closely the two were connected, the one absorbed into the other, is a problem that calls for further inquiry. Present knowledge is well set out in the early chapters of A. G. Dickens, *The English Reformation* (1964), an excellent account of the period.

Lutheran ideas. Both these heretics made their public abjurations and were not severely treated.

Lutheran ideas were being discussed in the Universities in the 1520s; the meetings at the White Horse Inn at Cambridge are part of the religious history of England. Not all who met there were "reformers". Some went about preaching and teaching and a few were burned as heretics. Others rose to high position in the Church in its "reformed" state. London was the chief centre from which much of the literature from abroad was disseminated. As Bishop Nix noted, the merchants were the agents; some were Germans of the Steelyard and we have seen how Wolsey dealt with them. All this, however, much as it looks on paper, was restricted in influence. The picture is of the irregular passing on by word of mouth of ill-understood ideas; such notions could link up with the widespread anti-clericism that was becoming more vocal in the early years of the century. The aftermath of Lollardy provided one of the favourable conditions for the reception of Lutheranism and its variations, but it seems safe to say that it was not until William Tyndale's translation of the New Testament became available from 1526, followed by his writings, that the new doctrines began to reach a wider public. In this the reading of the New Testament, privately or aloud to a listening circle, played an important, perhaps decisive part.

As we have seen, when Cuthbert Tunstall was in the Low Countries and at the Diet of Worms, he gained direct impressions of the nature of Lutheranism and he was greatly disturbed lest these heretical ideas should spread to England. As Bishop of London from 1522 he became directly responsible for the suppression of heresy in his diocese, and it was a duty he was little likely to neglect. William Tyndale had applied to Tunstall in 1523 for a post in his household; there is no ground to think that Tunstall's reason for refusing this request was other than the one he gave; his staff, he said, was already greater than he really needed, but Tyndale never forgave Tunstall. It is idle to speculate what might have happened had Tunstall employed Tyndale.

When Tyndale's New Testaments began to circulate, Tunstall issued instructions to his archdeacons to search for and seize copies and on 26 October 1526 he preached at St Paul's Cross at the burning of the confiscated books. His scheme to buy up copies in Antwerp miscarried, for, as the chronicler Hall noted, the Testaments "came thick and threefold into England". Warham had tried the same extravagant method, and More had warned Tunstall that he was throwing his money away. The trade was well-organized by experienced merchants. Reprint followed reprint but there is no record of how many copies were imported; our ancestors had not our mania for counting things. It would, however, be misleading to give the impression that the commonalty was clamouring for English Testaments which most of them could not yet read. The influence of Tyndale's Testament on ordinary folk was the result of having the opportunity to hear it read aloud; its initial impact was on the lettered people, particularly in south-eastern England. Tunstall and others pointed out errors in the translation, but the chief complaint, to quote Tunstall, was in "intermeddling therewith many heretical articles and erroneous opinions" in the form of glosses and prefaces.

Tunstall was determined to prevent this "pestiferous and pernicious poison" from spreading. He soon realized that burning copies of the Testament was an ineffective measure; the heretics had to be answered. So far criticism of Luther's teaching had been made by learned theologians such as John Fisher and had been written in Latin and printed abroad; it was on too high a level to have a direct effect on general opinion. The growing circulation of Tyndale's New Testament and of his writings meant that more and more people could learn the new doctrines. So in March 1528 Tunstall made an official request to Thomas More that he would write in English against the new teaching.[3] It is significant that the bishop linked Wycliffe with Luther.

"Since now of late the Church of God throughout Germany has been infested with heretics there have been found certain children of iniquity who are endeavouring to bring over into our land the old and accursed Wycliffian heresy and along with it the Lutheran heresy, foster-daughter of Wycliffe's. . . . And since you, dearest

[3] C. Sturge, *Cuthbert Tunstal* (1938), Ap. XI. The Latin text is given in *Rogers*, 160.

brother, can play the Demosthenes in our native tongue just as well as in Latin, and are wont in every fight to be a most keen champion of Catholic truth, you could in no wise better occupy your leisure hours—if you can steal any from your duties—than in putting forth some writings in English which will reveal to the simple and uneducated the crafty malice of the heretics, and render such folk better equipped against such impious supplanters of the Church. . . . And lest you should struggle with such spectres, yourself ignorant what you are fighting against, I send you their mad incantations in our tongue as well as some of Luther's books whence these monstrous ideas have sprung. . . . To that end we give and grant you authority and licence to keep and read books of this kind.''[4]

The reference to "your duties" was not just a polite gesture. More had been Chancellor of the Duchy of Lancaster since 1525; he was also High Steward of both Universities; the King was making full use of him in his Council and in embassies abroad, and, in addition, he had his judicial duties to carry out. Few men could have been so fully occupied as he was at that period, yet he cheerfully undertook this additional labour; one can say "cheerfully" because the immediate outcome, *A Dialogue Concerning Heresies*, was clearly the work of a man whose mind and heart were fully engaged. Even while he was at work on this first book of controversy, two new publications of William Tyndale were put in circulation: *The Parable of the Wicked Mammon*, a free translation from Luther's writings, came out in May 1528, to be soon followed by *The Obedience of Christian Man*, based on Luther's *On the Liberty of a Christian Man*.

A Dialogue was published in June 1529 by More's brother-in-law John Rastell. Within a few weeks Tunstall and More were at Calais on their way to the negotiations that resulted in the Peace of Cambrai between Charles V and Francis I; More was also concerned with a new commercial treaty with the Low Countries. Both envoys may well have been content to be out of England while Cardinal Campeggio and Cardinal Wolsey were holding their court at Blackfriars to consider Henry VIII's appeal for the

[4]In 1521 Erasmus had asked permission from Aleander to read heretical books. Aleander would not give it without specific consent from Rome. (*Allen*, 1236.)

annulment of his marriage. Campeggio's adjournment of the court on 30 July undermined Wolsey's position. Tunstall and More were back in England towards the end of August. A few weeks later the second of More's controversial books was published, *The Supplication of Souls*. This was a reply to the anonymous *Supplication of the Beggars* published towards the end of 1528. The author was a lawyer, Simon Fish, who had joined Tyndale abroad. This was not a reasoned discussion but combined a scurrilous outburst of anti-clericism with ridicule of such Catholic beliefs as the doctrine of Purgatory. This fourteen-page pamphlet was reprinted several times and was translated into Latin and German. More's vigorous and lively reply must have been written at speed. He used the device of *The Praise of Folly* by putting his argument in the form of a declamation by souls in Purgatory, praying that they should not be deprived of the prayers of the living.

Tyndale's *Practice of Prelates* was published in 1530; his main attack was on the Papacy but he also denounced Wolsey and the divorce proceedings. A year later, in the summer of 1531 came his *Answer unto Sir Thomas More's Dialogue*; in this he may have been helped by John Frith. More at once set to work on his *Confutation of Tyndale's Answer*; the first three Books were published at the end of 1532, and five more Books in 1533. The eighth Book dealt with Robert Barnes's *What the Church Is*.[5] More next turned his attention to John Frith's writings on the Eucharist. More's *Letter Impugning the Erroneous Writing of John Frith* was ready late in 1532. A fresh challenger wrote *A Treatise Concerning the Division of the Spirituality and the Temporality* which was issued in 1532. The writer was a lawyer, Christopher Saint-Germain, but the book was published anonymously and More was unaware of the author's identity. It prompted him to write his *Apology* which came out about Easter 1533. Saint-Germain, again anonymously, gave his answer in his dialogue *Salem and Bizance*; this led to More's *Debellation of Salem and Bizance* (1533). Finally he wrote his *Answer to the First Part of the Poisoned Book which a Nameless Heretic hath named "The Supper of the Lord"*. This was

---

[5] A ninth Book (unfinished) was added in the *English Works* of 1557.

published before Christmas 1533 but dated 1534.[6] The "Nameless Heretic" was in fact George Joye, a former Fellow of Peterhouse, Cambridge, who had fled abroad about 1528 and joined Tyndale.[7] This was the last of Thomas More's controversial writings. On 17 April 1534 he was taken to the Tower.

June 1529 to January 1534 is a period of four and a half years. The books he wrote during that time fill 930 pages folio of the *English Works* of 1557, something like 900,000 words. It was an output of original writing that even Erasmus could not equal. There is no means of assessing the influence these books had on religious opinion. Only two of them, the *Dialogue* and the *Supplication*, were reprinted during More's lifetime. There are no records of how many copies were printed, but the number was unlikely to have been more than a thousand for each printing, perhaps fewer. After More's execution, no further reprints were possible. Instructions had been sent out that from every pulpit in the land Thomas More and John Fisher should be denounced as seditious traitors. In our times, this would be excellent publicity with a demand for more copies, but in those days people would be intimidated. We can, however, ask why Thomas More should have spent himself so laboriously in controversy. This calls for an examination of his attitude towards heresy and heretics.

The epitaph he composed for his memorial in the chapel he added to his parish church at Chelsea, contained the following statement: "he was severe with thieves, murderers and heretics".[8] He sent a copy of this in his last surviving letter to Erasmus in June (?) 1533, and he underlined the reference to heretics in these words: "As to my declaration that I gave trouble to heretics, I did this deliberately. For I so entirely detest that race of men, that there is none to which I would be more hostile, unless they amend. For every day more and more, I find them to be of such a sort that I greatly dread what they are bringing on the world."

[6]See A. W. Reed, *Early Tudor Drama*, p. 79.
[7]For this identification see W. D. J. C. Thompson in *Harvard Theological Review* (Jan. 1960).
[8]See *Harpsfield*, p. 279: "furibus autem et homicidis haereticisque molestus". The present inscription omits "haereticisque". The history of the tablet is not clear. It was recut in the middle of the XVII century, "being worn by time", and "restored" in 1833. The tablet was moved to the chancel of the church during reconstructions in 1666.

The fullest exposition of his attitude towards heretics will be found in the last six chapters of his *Dialogue against Heresies*. The summary of the thirteenth chapter of Book IV reads:

> "The author sheweth his opinion concerning the burning of heretics and that it is lawful, necessary and well done, and sheweth also that the clergy doth not procure it, but only the good and politic provision of the temporality."

The law of the "temporality" in England was given in the statute of 1401, *De heretico comburendo*, which had been enacted to meet the threat of the Lollard movement. By this the bishop was empowered to arrest and imprison a heretic who had to be tried within three months; if convicted and he abjured, he could be fined and imprisoned. The two cases given at the beginning of this chapter from Rochester show that the bishop could be satisfied if the accused made a public abjuration. If the heretic refused to abjure, or relapsed after abjuration, he was excommunicated and handed over to the sheriff and burned. The statute was strengthened in 1414 by a provision that all magistrates had to take an oath to search out heretics and hand them over to the bishop. When heresy again became a serious problem, Wolsey issued in March 1529 a proclamation reminding magistrates of this obligation. It was under the 1414 statute that Thomas More dealt with heretics; he carried out his duty with diligence. Not all magistrates took this duty seriously; some were themselves critical of Church policy without holding extreme doctrinal views. Their successors in Elizabethan times were equally reluctant to track down Catholic recusants. A suspected heretic would face a preliminary inquiry before the magistrate to establish a *prima facie* case; once that was done, the culprit was handed over to the bishop and the magistrate had nothing further to do with the matter. More had for many years been on the Commission of the Peace for Hampshire and for other counties, but he could not act outside those counties. As Lord Chancellor he had authority to act anywhere. After his resignation he was no longer in a position to apprehend suspected heretics.

The claim that it was not the Church but the civic authorities that condemned the heretic to burning was little better than a quibble, for the bishop knew what the outcome would be when he handed over the man or woman to the sheriff, but no one questioned the justice of the sentence.

It is surely no longer necessary to refute the charges brought against More by John Foxe and others and summarized in J. A. Froude's judgment that he was a "merciless bigot" who "fed the stake with heretics". More himself replied in his *Apology* to contemporary accusations and his statements have not been invalidated.[9] He acted within a law of which he fully approved. The sentence of burning for heresy seems to us harsh and difficult to justify but in the sixteenth century it was accepted as lawful by Catholics and Protestants alike. Heresy was linked in men's minds with civil disorder and insurrection. The abortive Lollard rising had not been forgotten and abroad the more recent Peasants' Revolt was seen as a direct consequence of Lutheranism or of allied religious teachings. The three days' sack of Rome in May 1527 came as a dreadful shock to the Catholic world. While it was not inspired by religious zeal, it was generally blamed on the German Landsknechts who were held to be Lutherans, but among the despoilers there were also Spanish mercenaries who were nominally Catholic. This contemporary interpretation was understandable if partly mistaken. The secular priest, Thomas Münzer (1491-1525), for instance, who was first an admirer of Luther and then his fierce critic, signed his orders "The Sword of the Lord and of Gideon". By Catholics he and other turbulent prophets were all regarded as the spawn of Luther. There would probably have been some kind of Peasants' Revolt against their intolerable conditions had Luther not existed; as it was, in spite of his denunciations, he had to take the blame. This fear that the social fabric was in danger was fed by the outbreaks of church looting that marked the continental movement; so far, England had not been affected by such iconoclasm; when it did come it was under royal patronage.

This contemporary situation must be kept in mind when we

---

[9] See R. W. Chambers, *Thomas More*, pp. 274-282, and A. I. Taft's edition of the *Apology*, pp. 294ff. Cf. S. T. Bindoff, *Tudor England* (1950), p. 104 . . . "the More who committed Protestants to the fire".

read More's denunciations of heretics, who were regarded as bolshevisks and communists are in our century.

Here are some typical statements taken from Book Four of the *Dialogue against Heresies*:

"For here you shall understand that it is not the clergy that laboureth to have them punished by death. Well may it be, that as we be all men and not angels, some of them may have sometime either over fervent mind or indiscreet zeal, or, percase, an angry and cruel heart, by which they may offend God in the selfsame deed whereof they should else greatly merit. But surely the order of the spiritual law therein is both good, reasonable, piteous and charitable, and nothing desiring the death of any man therein. For at the first fault, he is abjured, forsweareth all heresies, doth such penance for his fault as the bishop assigneth him; and is, in such wise, graciously received again into the favour and suffrages of Christ's church. But an if he be taken eftsoons with the same crime again, then is he put out of the Christian flock by excommunication. And because that, being such, his conversation were perilous among Christian men, the Church refuseth him, and thereof the clergy giveth knowledge to the temporalty, not exhorting the prince or any man else either, to kill or punish him, but only in the presence of the temporal officer, the spirituality, not delivereth him, but leaveth him to the secular hand, and forsaketh him as one excommunicate and removed out of the Christian flock." Ch. 13.)

"And surely as the princes are bounden that they shall not suffer their people by infidels to be invaded, so be they as deeply bounded that they shall not suffer their people to be seduced and corrupted by heretics, since the peril shall in short while grow to as great, both with men's souls withdrawen from God, and their goods lost, and their bodies destroyed by common sedition, insurrection and open war, within the bowels of their own land. All which may in the beginning be right easily avoided, by punishment of those few that be the first. Which few well repressed, or if need so require, utterly pulled up, there shall be far fewer have lust to follow." (Ch. 15.)

"From whose [holy doctors and saints] firm faith joined with good works which, as two wings, carried them up to heaven, there shall, but we be more than mad, no fond heretic lead us, seem he never so saintish with any new construction of Christ's holy gospel or other part of holy scripture, which no wise man will doubt but that those holy cunning [learned] men, illumined with the grace of God, much better understood than all the rabble of these lewd heretics. Of all which that ever sprang in Christ's church, the very worst, and the most beastly, be these Lutherans, as their opinions and their lewd living sheweth. And let us never doubt but all that be of that sect, if any seem good as very few do, yet will they in conclusion decline to the like lewd living as their master and their fellows do, if they might once (as by God's grace they never shall) frame the people to their own frantic fantasy. . . . And, finally, that most abominable is of all, of all their own ungracious deeds lay the fault in God (taking away the liberty of man's will, ascribing all our deeds to destiny, with all reward or punishment pursuing upon all our doings) whereby they take away all diligence and good endeavour to virtue, all with-standing and striving against vice, all care of heaven, all fear of hell, all cause of prayer, all desire of devotion." (Ch. 17.)

These extracts show that More's opposition to heresy and heretics was more inflexible than that of Erasmus; not that Erasmus condoned heresy or iconoclasm, but he clung to the hope that sweet reasonableness would prevail. It must be admitted that his more virulent writing was prompted by personal attacks on himself.

It has been objected that More's treatment of heretics was at variance with the toleration shown in Utopia. This view is based on a superficial reading. More narrated, for instance, how a convert to Christianity had been over-zealous (a not uncommon trait in converts) and had been banished "for inflaming the people to sedition". Those who "mixed reproaches or violence" in advocating their religious opinions were "condemned to banish-ment or slavery". Those who were guilty of impiety and did not repent were "seized by the Senate and punished". Those were the notions More ascribed to his imagined island in 1516. The events in Europe during the following decade, and More's practical experience at the centre of government, sharpened his opposition to those who would disrupt both Church and State.

It is not possible here to attempt a detailed examination of the whole corpus of More's controversial writings. His criticisms, for instance of Tyndale's translation, need close study; in his main contention, that Tyndale allowed his bias to colour his choice of terms, he was justified, though to some details scholars today would take exception. Thus he criticized Tyndale for using "congregation" instead of "church" for "ecclesia", but as Tyndale answered, "But how happeth it that Master More hath not contended in like wise against his darling Erasmus all this long while? Doth he not change this word 'ecclesia' into 'congregation', and that not seldom in the New Testament? Peradventure he oweth him favour, because he made *Moria* in his house." It was a shrewd hit, but modern scholars are on the side of More. It will be more to our purpose to note the ways in which More and Erasmus differed in their treatment of heresy.

The most obvious difference was that Thomas More, as a magistrate, had to deal with actual individual cases. He had faced the problem in his own household with his son-in-law, William Roper, and he had questioned suspected heretics before dismissing them or sending them to the bishop. It was surely this first-hand experience that makes his *Dialogue against Heresies* so much alive; he must still have been hoping that heretics would submit to reason. More was too discerning to ignore the strength of the new ideas. He once said to Roper, "I pray God that some of us, as high as we seem to sit upon the mountains, treading heretics under our feet like ants, live not the day that we gladly would wish to be at a league and composition with them, to let them have their churches quietly to themselves, so that they would be content to let us have ours quietly to ourselves". His ex-heretic son-in-law tried to reassure him. " 'Well,' said he, 'I pray God, son Roper, some of us live not till that day'." Roper says that this conversation took place "before the said matter of the matrimony was brought in question". This vague statement at least puts the incident before the writing of the *Dialogue*. It is a true dialogue in the sense that his companion is allowed to state fairly the Lutheran-Tyndale position; the central question of "justification by faith alone" was not dealt with directly but only obliquely as in the last of the extracts give above. The main topics were—invocation of the saints, the use of images, pilgrimages, miracles, the Scriptures, the infallibility of the Church's doctrine, Tyndale's translation, and the treatment of heretics. It will be noted that the first four of these topics had been the butts of the wit and satire of Erasmus; in the *Dialogue* More made a clear distinction between the use and abuse of devotional practices; it was the abuse that he and Erasmus had ridiculed.

This personal contact with heretics and the responsibility for dealing with them, gives an urgency to More's writing that is absent from that of Erasmus; it may also account in some degree for the growing irritability that More revealed as he penned book after book. *The Supplication of Souls* was inevitably more censorious than the *Dialogue* since it was an answer to a calumnious pamphlet that had wide circulation, but it retained some of the mood of the *Dialogue*. There are pages, especially in the *Confutation*, that one wishes More had not written, but he was a child of his age when controversialists did not abstain from gross personal abuse if they thought it would help to discredit an opponent. We have more subtle ways of achieving the same purpose. It calls for perseverance to read through the *Confutation*, but nothing that More wrote is untouched by his humour and humanity, and the reader is well rewarded by witty passages and amusing anecdotes that reveal the true Thomas More. Dullness is not usually associated with his name, but he had two styles of writing. When he wrote dramatically, as in his *Richard III*, or *Utopia*, or in the *Dialogue*, he had no contemporary rival for vigour and lucidity, but even in these books he could occasionally pen an involved sentence that does not yield its meaning at first reading. In the *Confutation* the balance is altered; the dramatic passages come as oases in a toilsome desert. This is all the more noticeable when his later work is compared with that of his chief opponent, William Tyndale. A few figures are of interest to point the contrast. More's *Dialogue* was 162,000 words in length; Tyndale's *Answer* was about half that length. More's *Confutation* of Tyndale's *Answer* ran to 470,000 words. This prolixity must have deterred many a reader. Complaints reached him, and he excused himself in his *Apology* by saying that "the most foolish heretic in a town may write more false heresies in one leaf, than the wisest man in the world can well and conveniently by reason and authority soyle [answer] and confute in forty". The length was in some degree the result of quoting, with meticulous accuracy, his opponent's arguments, but a greater concentration would have been more effective. In this Tyndale had the advantage, and one consequence was that his books were cheaper and so could gain more readers.

This tendency to prolixity might be called the occupational disease of the controversialist. Most of Erasmus' work was published in books of reasonable length; the *Moria*, for instance, was of some 60,000 words and the *Diatribe on Free Will* of about half that number. When, however, he came to answer Luther in the two volumes of *Hyperaspistes* he found it impossible to keep to his usual moderation; the second volume was six times the length of the *Diatribe*. He had, too, the advantage of writing in Latin which is less diffuse than English. The influence of the earlier writings of Erasmus was not unconnected with his ability to express his ideas in a comparatively brief compass.

Thomas More not only had to deal directly with heretics, but from 1529 he had decisions to make that brought him into direct conflict with the King, and he was well aware of the risks he ran. For him, the problems raised by the divorce proceedings, followed by the repudiation of Papal Supremacy, brought a crisis of conscience that he alone could solve. He did not discuss these difficulties with others, nor did he, as far as extant letters show, explain the situation to Erasmus who was probably not aware of the underlying issues; to him the problem may have seemed simply that of the Pope's powers of dispensation in matrimonial affairs. He himself had not to face an acute personal crisis; when difficulties arose, he moved to another town, as he did in 1529 when he left Basle for Freiburg-im-Breisgau. He did his utmost to keep "above the battle", and he succeeded in doing so until he reluctantly gave way to the importunities of others and wrote his

Diatribe. Even in that book, he avoided discussion of doctrines as indeed he had always done. Neither is More's *Dialogue* a doctrinal treatise, but in his later works he dealt with, for instance, the doctrine of purgatory and the nature of the Eucharist, subjects that Erasmus did little more than touch upon.

Did More's controversial writings effect what Tunstall hoped —"reveal to the simple and uneducated the crafty malice of the heretics"? Inasmuch as he wrote in English, More certainly provided the lettered but unlearned with reasoned arguments against current heresies, and even during the period of his active warfare there seems to have been a rapid increase in the numbers of those who could read, one of the contributory factors being the desire to read the New Testament in English. It may be doubted if his later works appealed to a wide public. This is not to say that they were of small value; those who did study them would have a clearer understanding of the Catholic faith and be better equipped for answering its traducers.

CHAPTER XVIII

The Troubled Years

THOMAS MORE'S HOME was in the City of London for more than forty-five years; he left it in 1524 for the new house he had built at Chelsea.[1] We associate his name so closely with Chelsea that we forget that he lived there for only a decade. Erasmus sent to his friend John Faber, Bishop of Vienna, an account of the More family at Chelsea. This was written in December 1532.

"More has built for himself on the banks of the Thames not far from London a country-house which is dignified and adequate without being so magnificent as to excite envy. Here he lives happily with his family, consisting of his wife, his son and daughter-in-law, three daughters with their husbands and already eleven grandchildren. It would be difficult to find a man more fond of children than he. His wife is no longer young, but of so accommodating a disposition is he, or rather of such virtue and prudence, that if any defect appears that cannot be corrected, he sets himself to love it as though it were the happiest thing in the world. You would say that Plato's Academy had come to life again. But I wrong his home in comparing it to Plato's Academy, for in the latter the chief subjects of discussion were arithmetic, geometry and occasionally ethics, but the former rather deserves the name of a school for the knowledge and practice of the Christian faith. No one of either sex there neglects learning or fruitful reading, although the first and chief care is piety."

Erasmus never visited More at Chelsea;[2] he had last been in England in 1517 and the two friends did not meet again after 1521. This in no way impaired their friendship. It is true that few

[1]For plan, etc., see my *Margaret Roper*, p. 45.
[2]Stapleton was responsible for the erroneous statement, even now repeated, that Erasmus had visited More at Chelsea. *Life* (tr. Hallett), p. 94.

letters have survived for the last fourteen years of their lives, only
five from Erasmus and four from More; others may have
perished or gone astray, but there are frequent references to More
in Erasmus' letters to his friends, sometimes sending a message,
sometimes passing on news. As soon, however, as his circumstances allowed, Erasmus used to send from time to time one of
his servants or servant-pupils on tour; he[3] would carry with him
letters and books and make a round of Erasmus' multitude of
friends; he would return with a budget of news, a bundle of
letters, and, no doubt, gifts. It was in this way that Erasmus
learned about the patriarchal household at Chelsea. His friends,
too, would welcome other visitors bearing letters of introduction
from Erasmus. Our knowledge of these comings and goings is
inevitably fragmentary, but it suggests a considerable traffic.

Among those who carried introductions in 1526 was Hans
Holbein, the twenty-nine year old painter who had shown his
genius in portraits of Erasmus,[4] Froben[5] and Amerbach.[6] Erasmus
recommended him to Peter Gilles of Antwerp. "Here the arts",
he wrote from Basle, "are coldly treated, so he makes for England
(Angliam) in the hope of collecting some Angels (Angelatos)."
The English gold coin, the angel-noble, gave the scholar the opening for his little pun. From Antwerp, Holbein went to Chelsea
with letters of introduction from Erasmus and Gilles. More
wrote to Erasmus in December 1526, "Your painter, my dearest
Erasmus, is a wonderful artist, but I fear he will not find England
the rich and fertile field he had hoped; however, lest he find it
quite barren, I shall do what I can". The obvious way of helping
Holbein was to commission him to paint the family portraits.[7]
Of these and the preliminary drawings it is not necessary to
write here, but something must be said of the sketch, now at

---

[3] See "Erasmus' Servant-pupils" in Allen, *Erasmus: Lectures and Wayfaring Sketches*
(1934).
[4] One at Basle; a second in the Louvre (a present to Warham), and a third in the
possession of the Earl of Radnor.
[5] Hampton Court.
[6] Basle.
[7] See Stanley Morison, *The Likeness of Thomas More* (1963). The portraits and drawings
are all reproduced in my *Saint Thomas More* (1953).

P

Basle, for the painting of the family group.[8] This remarkable pen-and-ink drawing was probably taken to Erasmus when Holbein returned to Basle in August 1528. It may have been done as a gift to Erasmus, but he does not seem to have acknowledged it until a year later; this delay may have been because he was planning for one of his scholar-pupils, Quirin Talesius, to go on tour; he reached Chelsea in October 1529. In his letter, dated 5 September, to More he wrote, "Would that it were possible to see once more friends so dear to me—those whom Holbein has presented in his picture, which I have studied with such intense delight". On the following day he wrote to Margaret Roper:

"I cannot find words, Margaret Roper, ornament of Britain, to express the delight I felt when Holbein's picture showed me your whole family almost as faithfully as if I had been among you. I often wish that, before my last day, I could look even once more on that most dear company to whom I owe a great part of whatever little fortune or glory I possess, and to none could I be more willingly indebted. The gifted hand of the painter has given me no small portion of my wish. . . . I am writing in the midst of overwhelming work and in poor health, therefore I must leave it to your skill to convince your sisters that this is a fair letter and is written to each one of them no less than to yourself. Convey my respectful and affectionate salutations to the honoured Lady Alice, your mother; since I cannot kiss her, I kiss her picture. To your brother John I wish every happiness, and you will give a special greeting on my part to your most worthy husband Roper, so rightly dear to you."

Talesius carried back with him to Freiburg letters from the Mores, Tunstall and other friends.

Margaret wrote:

"We freely acknowledge with the greatest gratitude that the arrival of the painter gave you so much pleasure because he brought you the portraits of both my parents and all of us. We pray for nothing more ardently than that we may some

---

[8]The finished painting was in watercolour or tempera on cloth and was probably destroyed in a fire at Kremsier (Moravia) in 1752.

time be able to speak face to face with and see our teacher, by whose learned labours we have received whatever of good letters we have imbibed, and one who is the old and faithful friend of our father.'[9]

More's letter was brief; it was dated 28 October, only three days after he had been appointed Lord Chancellor; he referred to his new responsibilities but without naming his office. "Quirinus", he wrote, "will tell you all the news. Everyone congratulates me; I am sure you will at least pity me." Evidently he had not forgotten Erasmus' regrets when he first entered the service of the King; nor was he mistaken, for Erasmus had not changed his mind. Soon after Talesius had returned, he wrote to Tunstall, "I congratulate England, but not Thomas More". And a year later, to Richard Pace, "I am glad for the sake of the country and the King, but not for More". And to Mountjoy, "The King could not have chosen a first magistrate more just or more incorruptible".

By the time More had become Chancellor in October 1529, Erasmus had for some months been living in Freiburg-im-Breisgau, a delightful university town on the edge of the Black Forest some forty miles north-east of Basle. Life at Basle had become unbearable to him for it was now a centre of reform under the guidance of Œcolampadius who took up a University appointment there in 1523. It was a shock to Erasmus to find that the eager young scholar who had worked with him in 1515-1518 on the New Testament and other publications should have first accepted Luther's teaching and then have followed Zwingli. They managed to keep on reasonably friendly terms for Œcolampadius was not an extremist, but he could not control the fanatics who gathered round him. It had not proved possible for Erasmus to keep friendship with other reformers such as Zwingli who, for instance, had visited Erasmus in 1516 and 1522 and had corresponded with him, but when it was clear that Erasmus would not change his views, Zwingli turned on him and wrote bitterly against him. Then there was Conrad Pellican, a former Franciscan

[9]The wording of these letters suggests that there was more than one portrait in addition to the sketch of the family group; if so, they have been lost.

friar, who put it about in 1526 that Erasmus had accepted
Œcolampadius' view that "there was nothing but bread and wine
in the Eucharist". This made Erasmus really angry and he forced
Pellican to withdraw his statement. "If you are convinced that
in the Eucharist there is nothing but bread and wine, I would
rather be torn limb from limb than profess what you profess, and
would rather suffer anything than depart this life with such a
crime confessed against my conscience." It was indeed rare
for Erasmus to speak out so plainly. He knew that any letter he
wrote would probably be published; already men were so proud
of getting a letter from the famous scholar that, even when they
were at variance with him, they liked to proclaim the association.

A more persistent nuisance was a young German who called
himself Henry von Eppendorf as if he were of noble stock. As a
student at Louvain he had been an admirer of Erasmus but
later on came under the influence of von Hutten and so to regard
Erasmus as a deserter who lacked the courage of his true convictions. He wrote to Zwingli in February 1528, "I am now here
[Basle] to force the great Erasmus to retract". He was referring
to a letter Erasmus had written to Duke George suggesting that
he should recall Eppendorf to Saxony. The pseudo-knight made
the most extravagant demands on Erasmus for an apology. Later
on, Erasmus could see the comic side of the affair, but at the time
it added to his growing uneasiness at Basle. To these local harass-
ments must be added the attacks that came from critics, both
Catholic and Lutheran, in France, Spain, the Low Countries and
even Italy.

His closest tie with Basle was snapped when in September 1527
Johann Froben died. "I bore my brother's death with the greatest
calmness", Erasmus wrote, "but I cannot endure the loss of
Froben." He paid a fine tribute to him. "He was a true friend, so
simple and sincere. To me his kindness was unbounded. What
plots would he lay, what occasions would he not seek, to force
some present on me!" Then comes a glimpse of the true printer-
craftsman. "Sometimes when he showed me and other friends the
first pages of some great author, how he danced for joy, how his
face beamed with triumph!" Erasmus gave his full support to

Froben's son, Jerome, who carried on his father's business in the same spirit.

Two months after Froben's death, Erasmus wrote a long letter to Martin Bucer, a reformer who tried to reconcile Luther's and Zwingli's views on the Eucharist. In this letter Erasmus expressed the feelings he had when the position in Basle was growing more critical. Some sentences from it indicate his point of view.

"I know some who were excellent men before they became followers of your faith. . . . I have learned that several have become worse and none better."

"Not to mention the Prophets and the Anabaptists, what embittered pamphlets have Zwingli, Luther and Osiander written against one another!"

"Above all they should have guarded against sedition. If they had handled the matter with sincerity and moderation, they would have won the support of the princes and bishops."

"It is a long drawn-out tragedy. I have never approved of the abolition of the Mass,[10] even though I have always disliked the money-grubbing mass-priests, There are other things that could have been changed without riots. As things are, some are not satisfied with any of the accepted practices—as if a new world would be built in a moment. There will always be things which the pious must endure. If anyone thinks the Mass ought to be abolished because many misuse it, then the sermon should be abolished also, which is almost the only custom accepted by your party."

The Town Council of Basle tried to stave off the extremists as long as possible; they sought Erasmus' advice. He urged control of the printing press to stop the publication of provocative pamphlets; until disputable subjects had been decided by a General Council, varying opinions should be tolerated; the proposed dispersal of monks should be carried out in an orderly fashion. Admirable as such advice was, public opinion was too

[10]There was an agitation in Basle for the abolition of the Mass. It was abolished in December 1528.

disturbed and became uncontrollable; the mob took charge in an orgy of iconoclasm. Erasmus felt that the time had come for him to leave; there was probably no danger to him personally for all regarded him as a celebrity who added lustre to Basle, but to stay would have meant condoning the very thing he detested— violence and the rule of force. Refuge could have been found in almost any country for he still received invitations to settle elsewhere. He did not want to get too far away from Basle and he found the right place in Freiburg-im-Breisgau, a strongly Catholic town. His friends planned for him to leave quietly, but the citizens of Basle had other views and his departure was made a public occasion. The young Basle printer Boniface Amerbach was his companion. He had friends at Freiburg—indeed, where were they lacking?—the chief of whom was Ulrich Zasius, a distinguished jurisconsult, and an old admirer. The University welcomed him and the town let him live in a house built for the Archduke Maximilian, but there were difficulties with other tenants and about rent, so, for the first time in his life, he bought a house. His subsequent letters were full of his delight in his new property, mingled with grumbles about carpenters and builders and his Xantippe of a housekeeper. He soon settled down to work; there was his ten-volume edition of St Augustine to complete, a projected edition of St Basil in Greek, and a book on preaching that he had promised his friend Bishop John Fisher.

Erasmus made no references to the controversial works of Thomas More; he probably received copies but he could not read English. Although he must have learned enough of the speaking languages in France, England and Italy for ordinary purposes, he did not go further. He once apologized for not being any longer able to write his native Dutch. It would seem that quite early in his life as a scholar, he must have begun thinking in Latin. He had read Henry VIII's book and More's reply, as Guilielmus Rosseus, to Luther's attack. It is probable that he was let into the secret of More's nom de plume; his judgment was that the writer had put Luther in his place.

Tunstall wrote to Erasmus in October 1529 and congratulated

him on getting away from Basle.[11] The letter went on to urge Erasmus to define his belief in the Eucharist and to revise his old writings as St Augustine had done, to remove objectionable opinions. He particularly mentioned the *Colloquies*.

Stapleton wrote:[12]

"Towards the end of his life More realised that many points in the writings of Erasmus needed correction and tried hard to persuade him to follow the example of St Augustine by revising all his works and issuing a book of 'Retractations'. John Fisher, Bishop of Rochester, wrote to the same effect, as is clear from Erasmus' answer. But Erasmus, who was as unlike St Augustine in humility as he was in doctrine, refused and destroyed More's letter so that it should not be inserted in his collected correspondence."

The last extant letter from Fisher to Erasmus is dated 1517, and from Erasmus to him, 4 September 1524. We know that Fisher received a letter while in the Tower[13] from his old friend, but this has not been preserved, and we have noted that Erasmus at Freiburg was writing *Ecclesiastes* at Fisher's suggestion. Other letters may have perished, but there is no evidence to support Stapleton's statement. Nor is there for his reference to a destroyed letter from More. Stapleton may have confused a supposed letter from More with the actual one from Tunstall which was in the terms given. As Erasmus preserved Tunstall's letter, it seems unlikely that he would have destroyed one of the same tenor from More.

Erasmus replied to Tunstall at the end of January 1530. He was not prepared to define more closely his belief in the Eucharist; he would not add to the flames of controversy, neither would he seek peace by giving up his principles, nor would he ever forsake the Church. Tunstall himself, while believing in the Real Presence, as Erasmus did, never committed himself to a belief in

[11]It is interesting to note that this letter was written a week after the fall of Wolsey and the day after More had become Chancellor. Tunstall made no reference to these facts; perhaps an example of the caution with which people wrote of public affairs.

[12]p. 40. It should be remembered that Stapleton and other Catholic apologists of his period looked askance at Erasmus.

[13]Apart from his few letters to Erasmus hardly any of Fisher's personal correspondence has survived.

transubstantiation, and even in the reign of Mary Tudor when examining a suspected heretic, he did not press transubstantiation as essential.[14] For Erasmus it was one of those doctrines that he accepted as part of the teaching of the Church without inquiring too closely into its theology. Nor did More deal with the mystery of how the bread and wine are changed into Christ's body and blood—the change that was termed transubstantiation at the fourth Lateran Council in 1215; he did, however, vigorously defend the dogma of the Real Presence.[15] Far from revising his *Colloquies*, Erasmus added in 1531 such a bitter attack on the Franciscans as that entitled "The Seraphic Funeral", and others that show how little he was disposed to modify his objections to abuses within the Church.

When Henry VIII's matrimonial policy became the talk of Europe, it was inevitable that Erasmus should be asked to give his views. Scholars and councillors would seek his opinions even if, as often happened, they turned round and denounced him. Through Mountjoy, Catherine of Aragon had asked Erasmus in 1524 to write on the subject of marriage, and in response his *Christian Institution of Marriage* was published in the summer of 1526 with a dedication to the Queen. Had Catherine's request been made because she knew Henry's mind as early as 1524?[16] The question cannot be answered; there seem to have been vague rumours of his desire for a divorce some years before he took the first steps; these may have been little more than speculations about the succession as there was no son to follow Henry. Whatever the rumours, the Queen would probably be the last to hear them. In suggesting that Erasmus should write on the subject of marriage, she may have had her young daughter Mary in mind. He had always had a high regard for the Queen and he no doubt recognized that her interest in learning was more genuine than that professed by her husband, whose early enthusiasm waned as he grew older. In his treatise Erasmus stressed that marriage should be regarded as an unbreakable union. He discussed the possible reasons for divorce but made it clear that he regarded

---

[14]Sturge, *Cuthbert Tunstal*, p. 115.
[15]See e.g. *Letter to Frith* (*Rogers*, 190).
[16]For discussion see G. Mattingly, *Catherine of Aragon* (1942).

such a step as disastrous. Two points he made bore on the King's future proceedings; marriage with a brother's widow was permissible under Old Testament law, and, given sufficient grounds, a papal dispensation was valid for the dissolution of a marriage. This short book has been described as "one of the purest and most beneficial moral treatises"[17] that Erasmus wrote, but this did not prevent his detractors objecting that he had not declared marriage to be a sacrament.

As the process went forward, Erasmus could not avoid expressing some opinion to meet questions from his friends. He wrote to Vives in September 1528, "Far be it from me to mix in the affair of Jupiter and Juno, especially as I know little about it. But I should prefer that he should take two Junos rather than put one away." This must not be taken as a considered view in favour of polygamy,[18] but rather the kind of bantering remark that he often dropped in writing to friends, remarks he could not resist making even at the risk of giving a handle to his enemies. He also told Vives that he had written to the Queen and had enclosed the letter, open, in one to "Niger", leaving it to him whether to hand it to her or not. "Niger" here must mean More, using it as an equivalent for "blackamoor". Perhaps the use of a pseudonym indicates again the risks of dealing with public affairs in letters that might be opened. Neither the letter to More nor that to the Queen has been preserved. There are a number of other references to the divorce; thus in July 1533, a month after the crowning of Anne Boleyn, he wrote to Damiano de Gois, "I am not competent to give an opinion on this divorce; I keep off it".

Much is known of Thomas More's attitude towards the divorce problem from his letters and from official records. The letters were either to Thomas Cromwell as the King's Secretary and intended for the eye of the King, or written from the Tower to his daughter Margaret. Apart from the discussion he had at the King's request with theologians and canonists, there is no evidence that he talked the matter over with others. When the greater question of the King's claim to be Supreme Head of the Church of

---

[17]Huizinga, p. 168.
[18]The bigamy of Philip of Hesse in 1539 was approved by Luther, Melanchthon and Bucer.

England arose in January 1531, More kept the problem to himself as it was one of conscience and not of policy. In view of these facts it is most unlikely that he unburdened his mind to Erasmus by correspondence that might be intercepted. Nor do we know how far Erasmus was aware of the facts and circumstances of these contentious and perilous matters. There is just a hint that he may have written to the King himself. In a letter written about March 1535 to John Cochleus, he said that if he had had the wealth of arguments that Cochleus put forward, he would have advised Henry not to seek a divorce; does this suggest that he had had some correspondence with the King on the subject?[19] It could have been in connexion with the missions sent to the Universities to gain their opinions. Simon Gryneus seems to have sounded some of the Reformers at the same time, probably at the suggestion of Henry. This brings us to an interesting episode.

Among the scholars introduced to More by Erasmus was Gryneus, a lecturer in Greek at Basle and a supporter of Œcolampadius. He had earlier been a follower of Luther but had later accepted Zwingli's opinions. He came to England in 1531 to study Greek manuscripts. More welcomed him at Chelsea for the sake of Erasmus, but as he was made aware of his visitor's Zwinglian opinions, he took precautions to prevent any proselytism. They had discussions between themselves, and these no doubt gave More a closer knowledge of how opinion was moving, but he kept an eye on this Zwinglian either personally or by arranging for his secretary John Harris to accompany the visitor. This is shown in the following extract from the Preface to an edition of Plato which Gryneus dedicated to John More in March 1534, only six weeks before his father was imprisoned.

"Your father at that time held the highest rank, but apart from that by his many excellent qualities, he was clearly marked out as the chief man of the realm, whilst I was obscure and unknown. Yet for the love of learning he found time to converse much with me even in the midst of public and private business: he, the Chancellor of the Kingdom, made me sit at his table: going to and from the Court he took me with him and kept

[19] The last extant letter to Henry VIII is dated 1 June 1528.

me ever at his side. He had no difficulty in seeing that my religious opinions were on many points different from his own, but his goodness and courtesy were unchanged. Though he differed so much from my views, yet he helped me in word and deed and carried through my business at his own expense. He gave us a young man, of considerable literary attainments, John Harris, as a companion on my journey, and to the authorities of the University of Oxford he sent a letter couched in such terms that at once not only were the libraries of all the Colleges thrown open to us but the students showed us the greatest favour. . . . Accordingly I returned to my country overjoyed at the treasures I had discovered, laden with your father's generous gifts and almost overwhelmed by his kindness."

Gryneus does not seem to have sensed the full significance of the attention that Thomas More gave to him and his inquiries. The courtesy was part of his nature, but he was not going to allow this visitor to spread his Zwinglism. In a letter dated 14 June 1532 More referred to this visit to Erasmus, "Concerning the person you recommended to me for scholarly not for religious reasons, my friends have prudently put me on my guard so as not to be deceived by him".

When Gryneus later sought the opinions of the Reformers on the divorce problem, he found them divided; Melanchthon thought the marriage valid, and Zwingli that it was invalid.

It has been noted that in this letter of October 1529, Tunstall urged his friend to follow the example of St Augustine and review his writings, "Censuring them", to quote St Augustine, "with a certain judicial severity indicating with a censor's pencil whatever displeases me".[20] Tunstall particularly objected to Erasmus' mockery of ceremonies, fasting, pilgrimages, and prayers to the saints, "which many charge you with railing at mockingly". In his reply Erasmus wrote, "If such men as Augustine were now ruling the Church, I should agree with them excellently. But if Augustine were to write now-a-days as he formerly did, or as our times need, I fear as little heed would be paid to him as to Erasmus." He was quite unrepentant and was not prepared to withdraw his attacks on abuses.

[20]Prologue to the *Retractations*.

We have seen that the first edition of the *Colloquies*[21] of 1519 was a modest affair intended to enliven the learning of Latin. The next edition was published in 1522; ten editions followed, the last during Erasmus' lifetime being that of 1533. To each he added new dialogues and revised old ones. These later ones were less obviously intended for teaching purposes and they contain some of his most typical work. Reference has already been made to two: "The Child's Piety" (1522) and "The Religious Pilgrimage" (1526). It is a temptation to linger over this fascinating book, so attractive for its pictures of the life of those times as well as for its self-portrait of the author, and above all for its ideas. It would lead us too far afield to attempt such a survey, but attention must be drawn to "The Religious Banquet"[22] (1522, but later enlarged) which shows us the Christian humanist in conversation with Johann Froben and two reformers, who may be Zwingli and Œcolampadius, before there had been a complete break with them. It should be supplemented by a reading of "Concerning Faith" which was added in 1524; here an orthodox believer questions a Lutheran.

Through the years Erasmus was also amplifying his *Adages*[23] which began so modestly in 1500 with 818 Adages and finished up in 1536 with 4,139. He dedicated the 1536 volume to Charles Blount, Mountjoy's eldest son. A passage from the dedication is of interest.

"It must be your special care, dear Charles, to be a true son to your accomplished father, the true heir of his excellence, not to degenerate from his culture and to prepare yourself to inherit his virtue even more than his advantages. . . . You have no dull spurs to urge you on: first your father himself: then the example of that noble maid, of almost the same age as yourself, the Princess Mary, daughter of a learned King and a learned and pious Queen, who now writes letters in Latin and of a content showing a nature worthy of her extraction; and finally,

[21]An account of the editions with some identifications is given in Preserved Smith, *A Key to the Colloquies* (1927).

[22]It is examined in detail on pp. 184-197 of Louis Bouyer's *Erasmus and the Humanist Experiment.*

[23]See *The "Adages" of Erasmus*, by M. M. Phillips (1964) for an excellent account with translations from which the quotations are taken.

you have the example of the daughters of the More family, that chorus of Muses, so that I do not see that anything is wanting to stimulate your ambition."

The boy may not have been too incited to learning by having such feminine models held up to him, but he did eventually become a patron of learning like his father.[24]

As edition followed edition of the *Adages*—eleven during his lifetime besides pirated editions—so Erasmus expanded the notes until they became a vehicle for his opinions on a multitude of topics. We should call some of them essays, and, indeed, Erasmus has a claim to be the originator of that literary form. A few, such as *Dulce bellum inexpertis*, were reprinted separately and had a life of their own. A number of themes recur—injustice, tyranny, oppression of the poor, pretentiousness, rapacious priests and, time and time again, his hatred of war and his love of the Gospels. An almost similar list could be made of the topics touched on in *Utopia*. Here is one that might have been written by Thomas More.

"*Simia in purpurea*. A monkey in fine clothes; and how many people in princes' palaces, if they were shorn of their purple, their chains and their jewels, would be found to be no better than labourers."

Erasmus' lifelong dislike of the over-refined arguments of theologians also finds expression.

"*Quot homines, tot sententiae*. If the general run of theologians would listen to this advice, there would not be today such a fierce contention about questions of no moment at all; for there are certainly some things of which one may remain in ignorance without any lack of piety."

As he grew into old age, Erasmus liked to recall his earlier years; sometimes the connexion with the particular Adage is not close, but that is immaterial. Here, for instance, is part of a tribute to Archbishop Warham added in 1526 to the saying *Ne bos quidem pereat*, Not even an ox might perish.

---

[24]Charles Blount's son, also Charles, eighth Lord Mountjoy and Earl of Devonshire (1563-1606), had a notable career under Elizabeth I, and was an associate of the Earl of Essex. He was a successful general in Ireland. His titles became extinct at his death.

"He enticed me, shy as I was, into his net of friendship. . . . And so, much to my own benefit, I was caught, in fact acquiring him as a Maecenas is my one claim to be called lucky. Whether he regrets having such a beneficiary, I do not know, but certainly I have never yet succeeded in returning his kindness in any way satisfactory to myself, nor do I see how ever I could."

It is a matter for wonder that Erasmus should have gone on adding some of the liveliest pages to the *Adages* and *Colloquies* to within the last years of his life in spite of being continually harassed by the attacks of theologians and scholars both Catholic and Lutheran, and in spite of his indifferent health. He never completely lost his poise, and certainly never lost his sense of humour, but he steadily held on his way refusing to change direction whatever the inducements or dangers. It is true that at times he was evasive and even equivocal, and it is not surprising that, considering his vast output, there are occasional inconsistencies. The pen was in his hand for thirty-five years and more and he seems to have written hastily and to have shirked revision, yet there was a persistence in his views that can be traced from beginning to end. To retain his integrity of mind and his independence of action, he needed all his skill and charm to manoeuvre between the two conflicting sides each of which claimed his allegiance at a time when "he who is not with us is against us" was the prevailing sentiment.

He was not called upon to tread the way of the martyr. He wrote to his friend Cardinal Campeggio in December 1520, "Let others affect martydom. I do not think myself worthy of such an honour." When in the following May, Luther disappeared after the Diet of Worms and it was rumoured that he was dead, Albrecht Dürer expressed the hope that Erasmus would take over the leadership. "O Erasmus of Rotterdam", he exclaimed, "where will you be? Hear, you knight of Christ; ride forth beside the Lord Christ, protect the truth, obtain the martyr's Crown." Dürer was, of course, mistaken in casting Erasmus for role of leader. Two months after Dürer's plea, Erasmus wrote to Richard Pace, "All men have not the strength for martyrdom. I fear lest if any tumult should arise, I would emulate Peter. I follow the just decrees of Popes and Emperor because it is right. I endure their evil laws because it is safe; I think this is allowable to good men if they have no hope of successful resistance." To these statements may be added a sentence in *Spongia* (1523), his answer to von Hutten. "I am ready to be a martyr for Christ if he will give me strength to be so, but I have no wish to be a martyr for Luther."

These do not sound like the accents of a hero, but neither are they those of a coward, for a weakling does not proclaim his want of courage, and it should be remembered that the crown of martyrdom is not given to those who deliberately seek that kind of violent end. One may conjecture that had Erasmus been faced with the great decision that the subjects of Henry VIII had to make, he would have followed the example of Cuthbert Tunstall and not that of Thomas More.

CHAPTER XIX

The One Church

WHEN HENRY VIII was declared to be Supreme Head of the Church of England, and all were compelled to accept this unique title, only a handful of men resisted: six Carthusians, a Bridgettine, a secular priest, and Bishop John Fisher and Sir Thomas More. Cuthbert Tunstall, after some discussion with the King, accepted the new order. More did not blame him. He remarked, "No matter, for if he live, he may do more good than to die with us".[1] Fisher and More and their fellow martyrs had seen further into the future than others; they realized that to put the Church of England entirely under the control of King and Parliament meant not only a denial of Papal Supremacy but a cleavage in the Unity of the Church.

Erasmus had written on this subject in 1533 in his *Liber de sarcienda Ecclesiae concordia* (On restoring concord in the Church).[2] It was a meditation on Psalm 84 (Vulgate) containing the verse, "Mercy and truth are met together; righteousness and peace have kissed each other". The critical situation had not yet reached a climax in England and Erasmus was concerned with the furious conflict of the warring sects. A few sentences show his line of thought.

"Simple piety may be accepted, even when it is combined with some degree of error. Christ loves simple souls, and will hear their vows even if the saints do not."

"It is wrong to disturb vexatiously the simple religion of those who attach importance to images. We can all surely agree that

[1] As reported in 1539 by Christopher Chaytor, Tunstall's Registrar. C. Sturge, *Cuthbert Tunstal*, Ap. XVI.
[2] See "Erasmus on Church Unity" in P. S. Allen, *Erasmus: Lectures and Wayfaring Sketches* (1943).

the best way to venerate the saints is to try to emulate their lives."

"Let those who believe that Christ founded confession in its present form, observe it with the utmost care; but they should allow others to retain their own opinions until a Council of the Church has given a definite judgment."

"We have had enough of quarrels; perhaps sheer weariness may bring us together to concord, to dwell in the house of the Lord as friends."

Here again he expressed his concern for "simple souls". His plea was hopeless; men were too embittered and embattled to agree even to a truce during which their differences could be calmly discussed. Each faction claimed a monopoly of righteousness, and neither side would credit the other with integrity of intention.

The problem that Fisher and More had to face was of a different character from doctrinal conflicts. The situation was a blunt Either-Or. Either the Pope was Supreme Head of the Church, or he was not; either the Church was one body, or it was not. There could be no compromise for them. Thomas More would have been content to live quietly and keep silent; he must early have realized that such a position would not for long satisfy the King in spite of royal promises. He had intimate knowledge of Henry's character and knew that he could not rest content with silent disapproval. What he wanted was openly proclaimed partisanship with three cheers added for good measure. So the tragedy moved to its inevitable climax. There is no need here to narrate again the course of the proceedings against Thomas More; it is to our purpose, however, to note how the two friends approached their last days. More had no doubt that his end would come within a matter of months. Erasmus, nearing the age of seventy and suffering debility and frequent pain, knew that death was not far away

More's last controversial work, *Answer to . . . the poisoned book* (1534), ends with this paragraph.

"From which [heresy] our Lord give them grace truly to turn in time, so that we and they together in one Catholic Church,

Q

knit unto God together in one Catholic faith, faith I say, not faith alone as they do, but accompanied with good hope and with her chief sister well-working charity, may so receive Christ's Blessed Sacrament here, and specially that we may so receive himself, his very blessed body, very flesh and blood, in the Blessed Sacrament, our holy blessed housel, that we may here be with him incorporate so by grace, that after the short course of this transitory life, with his tender pity poured upon us in purgatory, at the prayer of good people, and intercession of holy saints, we may be with them in their holy fellowship, incorporate in Christ in his eternal glory. Amen."

At his first interrogation in the Tower, More declared, "that I had fully determined with myself, neither to study nor meddle any matter of this world, but that my whole study should be upon the Passion of Christ and mine own passage out of this world". His writings in the Tower show that this was indeed his course. All controversy was laid aside. For fifteen months he was a prisoner and, after a time, he was allowed writing materials and such books as he needed until 12 June 1535. Stapleton tells us that More then closed the shutters over the window of his cell, and remarked, "Now that the goods and the implements are taken away, the shop must be closed". The fruits of his pen fill nearly four hundred pages folio of the *English Works*. The most substantial was the *Dialogue of Comfort against Tribulation*, first published in 1553. Other writings were his *Treatise upon the Passion of Christ*,[3] and a number of prayers and meditations which became widely known and used by generations of Catholics.

It is impossible to display by quotation the quality of the *Dialogue of Comfort*—its serenity, its quiet humour, its spirit of acceptance, and above all its complete trust in the mercy of God. To say that it lacks the simplicity of Bunyan's *Pilgrim's Progress*, that more famous prison book, is to mark the differences between the two authors. More was writing out of the wealth of his learning and experience; he was writing, too, at a time when his world seemed to be falling to pieces around him; his one sure

---

[3]The English version of this was probably begun before he went to prison; there he continued it in Latin after completing the *Dialogue of Comfort*. The Latin portion was translated into English by his grand-daughter, Mary (Roper) Basset.

foundation was Christ's Universal Catholic Church. Yet he could have echoed Bunyan's proud claim:

> Who would true valour see,
> Let him come hither;
> One here will constant be,
> Come wind, come weather.
> There's no discouragement
> Shall make him once relent
> His first avow'd intent
> To be a pilgrim.

One quotation from the *Dialogue* must serve our purpose; it expresses his resignation and gives one of those "merry tales" of which he was so fond; this one brings in Dame Alice, "my good bedfellow":

"Surely, cousin, in this you say very well. Howbeit, somewhat had your words touched me the nearer if I had said that imprisonment were no displeasure at all. But the thing that I say, cousin, for our comfort therein, is that our fantasy frameth us a false opinion by which we deceive ourself and take it for sorer than it is. And that do we by the reason that we take ourself before for more free than we be, and prisonment for a stranger thing to us than it is indeed. And thus far forth, as I said, have I proved truth in very deed. But now the incommodities that you repeat again, those, I say, that are proper to the imprisonment of their own nature, that is to wit, to have have less room to walk in and to have the door shut upon us, these are, methinketh, so very slender and slight, that in so great a cause as to suffer for God's sake we might be sore ashamed so much as once to think upon them. Many a good man there is, ye wot well, which without any force at all or any necessity wherefore he should so do, suffereth these two things willingly of his own choice with much other hardness more. Holy monks, I mean, of the Charterhouse order such as never pass their cells, but only to the church set fast by their cells, and thence to their cells again. And Saint Bridget's order, and Saint Clare's much like,[4] and in a manner all close religious

---

[4] All three had personal associations; the Charterhouse he had known so intimately in his earlier years; the Bridgettines of Syon Abbey which he visited in later years and of which his friend Richard Reynolds was a member; the Poor Clares (the Minories of today) where Joyce Leigh was a nun. On 4 May 1535 he was to watch three of the Carthusians and Reynolds dragged from the Tower for Tyburn.

houses; and yet anchors and anchoresses most especially, all whose whole room is less than a meetly large chamber. And yet are they there as well content many long years together as are other men, and better too, that walk about the world. And therefore you may see that the loathness of less room and the door shut upon us, while so many folk are so well content therewith, and will for God's love live so to choose, is but an horror enhanced by our own fantasy. And indeed I wist a woman once that came into a prison to visit of her charity a poor prisoner there, whom she found in a chamber, to say the truth, meetly fair, and at the least wise it was strong enough; but with mats of straw the prisoner had made it so warm both under the foot and round about the walls that in these things for the keeping of his health she was on his behalf glad and very well comforted. But among many other displeasures that for his sake she was sorry for, one she lamented much in her mind, that he should have the chamber door upon him by night made fast by the jailer that should shut him in. For, by my troth, quoth she, if the door should be shut upon me I would ween it would stop up my breath. At that word of hers the prisoner laughed in his mind, but he durst not laugh aloud nor say nothing to her, for somewhat indeed he stood in awe of her and had his finding[5] there much part of her charity for alms; but he could not but laugh inwardly, why he wist well enough, that she used on the inside to shut every night full surely her own chamber to her, both door and windows too, and used not to open them of all the long night. And what difference, then, as to stopping of the breath whether they were shut up within or without?"

So he could pray:

"Lord give me patience in tribulation and grace in everything to conform my will to thine, that I may truly say, 'Thy will be done on earth, as it is in heaven'. The things, Lord, that I pray for, give me the grace to labour for. Amen."

Four months before Thomas More was sent to the Tower, Erasmus published a tract entitled *Praeparatio ad mortem* (Preparation for death). Its history has an element of tragedy in it. He had

[5]The fees prisoners had to pay.

been asked to write it by Thomas Boleyn, Lord Rochford, the father of Anne Boleyn and later Earl of Wiltshire; he was to be one of the judges of Thomas More and Bishop John Fisher. His daughter, Queen Anne Boleyn, and his eldest son, George Boleyn, were executed in May 1536.[6] Perhaps Wiltshire was fortunate in surviving to die in his bed in 1539 at the age of sixty-two.

The tone of the tract is quietly devotional, for Erasmus' thoughts must have been turned to his own approaching end.

"Throughout life we must practise meditation on death, and constantly tend the spark of faith so that it burns more brightly, and if charity is there, it will bring hope as well. But none of these come of ourselves; they are the gifts of God; if we lack them we must ceaselessly pray for them; if they are present, we must pray that they should increase."

He goes on to warn against waiting for one's last sickness before seeking the sacraments; each night, before going to sleep, we should examine our consciences and confess our faults to God. A quarter of an hour will suffice; all we need say, if we say it from the heart is, "I have sinned; have mercy on me". It is a great consolation to have a priest with us at that dread hour, but,

"All that is good in the mystical body flows from Christ its head, and all that is good in the body, is shared by all its members, just as in the earthly body, the members, although having varied functions, are animated by the same nature. . . . Therein lies what the Apostles called the Holy Church, the Communion of Saints, for the grace of Christ is not more certainly in the mystical body than natural life is in the earthly body. Those act piously who, at the near approach of death, send to the monks or friars to ask for prayers for the dying; but it is a more effective consolation if the sick man feels that the whole Church suffers with him, its member."

It is an even greater consolation to meditate on the crucified Christ, "the sign of triumph, of victory, of life eternal".

---

[6]Queen Anne and her brother were buried in the Tower chapel of St Peter-ad-Vincula where the bodies of Thomas More and John Fisher had been interred less than a year previously.

Erasmus, like More, could not be over-solemn for long; sooner or later would come the smile that preluded a story. Two men on their death-beds were attacked by the Tempter on the teaching of the Church. One, a philosopher, studied all the arguments and was lost; the other, a decent sort of fellow, replied to all the Tempter's questions that he believed all that the Church believed. "But what does the Church believe?" asked the Tempter. "What I believe", said the man. Or again, "You have", says the Tempter, "prayed much, fasted much, led an austere life and have given much to the poor." "All these things", replies the sinner, "I have in common with the Pharisees. If any good work has come from me, it is the Saviour's, not mine."

So the tract reaches its conclusion.

"We must, with Jesus, climb naked on to the cross, stripped of all earthly affections. . . . Held by three nails, faith, hope and charity, we must persevere steadfastly in our brave fight against the Tempter, until, having conquered, we pass to our eternal rest by the help and grace of Our Saviour Jesus Christ. To Him, to his Father, and to the Holy Spirit, be the praise and glory to all eternity, Amen."

The volume containing this tract included a number of letters, among them two from More, one of June 1532 and the other a year later; the first announced his resignation (16 May) and the second contained his epitaph. Eustace Chapuys, the Emperor's Ambassador in England, wrote to Erasmus in February 1536, a month after the death of Catherine, to say that she had found great consolation in reading *Praeparatio ad Mortem*. She would read too the letters from Thomas More; they must have recalled those happier days when she shared his company with the King and enjoyed his wit and learning. She would appreciate the opening of the first letter.

"From the time I was a boy I have longed, my dearest Desiderius, that what I rejoice you have always enjoyed, I myself might some day enjoy also—that being freed from public business, I might have some time to devote to God and myself, and that by the grace of a great and good God, and by the favour of an indulgent prince, I have at last obtained, though not, it is true, quite as I wished. For I hoped to reach the last stage of my life in a state that, though suitable to my age, might yet enable me to enjoy my remaining years in sound health, free from disease and pain. But it remains in the hand of God whether this wish, perhaps unreasonable, shall be accomplished."

In April 1533 Erasmus had sent Quirinus Hagius to England to see his friends and to gather news. Hagius stayed with Chapuys in London but he may have got misleading impressions of the state of affairs for Chapuys had little real knowledge of public opinion; it is doubtful if More would have told Hagius very much, but he may have given him the Epitaph letter to take back with him to Erasmus. The shape of future events was still hidden.

Vives seems to have sent Erasmus the first news of More's arrest in a letter dated 10 May 1534. From then onwards we can trace Erasmus' anxiety through his letters in which he asked for news or complained that he could get none. There was a rumour in the summer of 1534 that More had been released; Erasmus' comment was, "I dare not think it". He sent off a messenger named Clauthus to England in July, but unfortunately he died at Rochester in September, so this source of information failed.

Erasmus left Freiburg in June 1535 for Basle to see his book *Ecclesiastes* through the press as well as a new edition of the *Adages*. He had a vague intention of then going down the Rhine to Brabant to spend his last days near his native land, but his broken health made that impossible and he was bedridden for much of his time. There were good friends to cheer him and watch over him—Beatus Rhenanus, Boniface Amerbach and Jerome Froben, and he had with him the last of his scholar-pupils, Lambert Coomans.[7] Basle was under the sway of the Reformers, but the old man was left in peace, though, as he wrote in June 1536, "there is so much contention here I wish to end my life elsewhere".

The news of the execution of John Fisher on 22 June 1535

[7]He had been a student at Louvain and then entered the service of Cardinal van Enkevoirt. In 1559 he became Dean of the Collegiate Church of Turnhout. It is not known if he was a priest at the time of his association with Erasmus. See Appendix to W. E. Campbell, *Erasmus, Tyndale and More* (1949).

reached Erasmus before the fate of Thomas More was known. On 24 August Erasmus wrote to Bartholomew Latomus, professor of Latin in the College de France:

"There is a definite and probable rumour here that the Bishop of Rochester's appointment as a Cardinal by Paul III caused the King to hasten his being dragged from prison and beheaded—his method of conferring the red hat. It is only too true that Thomas More has been in prison for a long time and his goods confiscated. It has been said that he too has been executed, but I have as yet no certain information. Would that he had never embroiled himself in this dangerous business and had left theological questions to the theologians. The other friends who used to honour me with letters and gifts, now send and write nothing for fear."

We cannot be sure what Erasmus meant by "theological questions". The dispensing power of the Pope? The Supremacy of the Holy See? It may be that he was not fully aware of the grounds for More's refusal to follow the King's policy.

The first definite news of More's execution came to Erasmus in a letter dated 10 August from Conrad Goclenius of Louvain. "Thomas More was executed in Britain on 6 July showing himself no less steadfast in his trial and execution than did Socrates before his infamous Athenian prosecutors." Erasmus wrote to Peter Tomiczki, Bishop of Cracow, on 31 August, "From the extract I enclose from a letter, you will learn of the fate of the Bishop of Rochester and Thomas More, than whom England never had two men more saintly or more learned. I feel as if I had died with More so closely were our two souls united." The letter also contained the news that the Pope wanted to make Erasmus a Cardinal in preparation for the coming Council, which in fact did not meet until 1545. Erasmus' comment was, "The proverbial cat in court dress!" He wrote in more seemly terms to the Pope, and begged to be excused in view of his age and infirmities.

He probably supervised the preparation of the *Expositio fidelis de morte Thomae Mori* which was published by Jerome Froben in October 1535; it was in part a translation of a newsletter issued in Paris in August;[8] it is the key-document for our knowledge of the trial.

It had been Erasmus' intention to dedicate his *Ecclesiastes* to John Fisher who had suggested the subject of preaching as a desirable theme. The book was already in the press by the time he knew of the executions of his two friends. He added this tribute in the Preface.

"Of how many of my most faithful friends have I not been robbed in these stormy days! Long since by the death of William Warham, Archbishop of Canterbury;[9] recently by that of William Mountjoy,[10] of the Bishop of Rochester and of Thomas More, who was the chief magistrate of his country, whose heart was whiter than snow, a genius such as England never had before, nor ever will have again, a country by no means lacking genius."

Damiano de Gois wrote to Erasmus in January 1536, "Your friends are surprised that you have not undertaken to vindicate the memory of More at greater length than in *Ecclesiastes*". He may have had it in mind to do so, but he was in feeble health and was perhaps too grief-stricken to undertake such a task. Indeed, what more could he add to the tributes he had paid while they were both living in those letters to Hutten and Faber and in numerous references in his correspondence?

The last edition of the *Adages* for which he was responsible was ready for the printers in February 1536; it was, as we have seen, appropriately dedicated to Charles Blount,[11] the eldest son of Mountjoy, and his thoughts must have gone back over the forty years that separated him from his early struggles in Paris.

He gradually became weaker and there were periods of sharp suffering, but his mind and spirit were undimmed. When his three friends Boniface Amerbach, Jerome Froben and Nicholas Episcopius visited him he pointed out that unlike Job's comforters they had forgotten to put on sackcloth. They and Lambert

---

[8]For a discussion of the problems of the *Expositio*, see my *Trial of St Thomas More* (1964), pp. 4ff.
[9]d. 22 August 1532.
[10]d. 8 November 1534.
[11]See above.

Coomans and others gave him all the care they could, but they, and he, knew that the end was near. His last recorded words were spoken in the native tongue he had long ceased to use, "Lieve God!" He died during the night of 11 and 12 July 1536; members of the University were the bearers at the funeral on 18 July when he was buried, with every mark of honour, in the Cathedral.

CHAPTER XX

The Two Friends

SOON AFTER the death of Erasmus, one of the Presidents of the Collegium Trilingue at Louvain, Peter Nannius, wrote some verses on More and Erasmus. In translation they read: "Erasmus, the glory of our times, lived in the heart of More. More, the sole light of Britain, his country, lived in the heart of Erasmus. The one exchanged life with the other; each lived a life not his own. It is no marvel that, with the death of More, Erasmus wished for death, unwilling to live longer."[1]

The tribute came from a fitting place. The Collegium Trilingue had been founded by Jerome Busleyden. A year before his death he had contributed the letter printed in *Utopia*. It ended, "Farewell, most learned and most genial More, the glory of Britain and of this world of ours". When Busleyden died there was some opposition from the Louvain theologians to the setting up of a new College where Hebrew, as well as Latin and Greek, was to be taught. Fortunately Erasmus was at hand and he did all he could to foster an enterprise that soon proved a success. His death was mourned by the College and it was inevitable that his name should be joined with that of Thomas More, the friend of their founder.

It would be possible to fill many pages with tributes linking the two friends, but the London folk-tale given at the beginning of this book is as conclusive evidence as can be desired, that the two

---

[1] *De Moro et Erasmo*
Vivebat in pectusculo Mori sui
Erasmus ille seculi nostri decus.
Vivebat in praecordis Erasmicis
Morus, Britanniae unicum lumen suae
Vitamque mutuabat alter alteri,
Aliena uterque non sua vixit anima.
Mirum nihil si mortuo Moro, mori
Voluit Erasmus, nequit ultra vivere.

names became inseparable in men's minds. The basis of such a close friendship is elusive; it is essentially a harmony of spirit and mind though not always of concordance of ideas, but such concepts as "mind" and "spirit" defy analysis. If we say that they were of similar temperaments we do not say much; we exchange one imprecise term for another. All one can do is to indicate some common characteristics, and even here one is dealing with imponderables; an approximation is all that can be expected.

Three tributes to Thomas More will provide a starting-point. The first was written in 1521 by an Oxford grammarian, Robert Whittinton; he was probably about the same age as More; he had an acrimonious dispute on grammar with William Lily and Robert Aldrich.

"More is a man of an angel's wit and singular learning. I know not his fellow. For where is the man of that gentleness, lowliness and affability? And, as time requireth, a man of marvellous mirth and pastimes, and sometime of a sad gravity. A man for all seasons."[2]

The second tribute is from a younger contemporary, Edward Hall, who was an Under-Sheriff of London at the time of More's execution and may have been present.

". . . a man well learned in the tongues, and also in the Common Law, whose wit was fine and full of imaginations; by reason whereof, he was also too much given to mocking, which was to his gravity a great blemish . . . he was Lord Chancellor of England, and in that time a great persecutor of such as detested the Supremacy of the Pope of Rome, which he himself so highly favoured that he stood to it till he was brought to the scaffold on the Tower Hill where on a block his head was stricken from his shoulders and had no more harm. I cannot tell whether I should call him a foolish wiseman, or a wise foolish man, for undoubtedly he, beside his learning, had a great wit, but it was so mingled with taunting and mocking, that it seemed to them that best knew him, that he thought nothing to be well spoken except he had ministered some mock in the communication . . . thus with a mock he ended his life.'[3]

[2]*Vulgaria.* (E.E.T.S.), p. 64. The last phrase gave the title to Robert Bolt's play of 1960.
[3]*Henry VIII* (ed. Whibley), II, p. 158 and p. 265.

The third tribute comes from Ralph Robinson's epistle to William Cecil in his translation of *Utopia*. Robinson had entered Corpus Christi College, Oxford, the year after More's execution.

"This only I say, that it is much to be lamented of all, and not only of us Englishmen, that a man of such incomparable wit, of so profound knowledge, of so absolute learning, and of so fine eloquence, was yet nevertheless so much blinded, rather with obstinacy than with ignorance, that he could not, or rather would not, see the shining light of God's holy truth in certain principal points of Christian religion."[4]

Hall was a hostile witness as he was an uncompromising admirer of Henry VIII; Robinson wrote apologetically as he feared, no doubt, that a work by Thomas More might have an uncertain welcome under the rule of the Protestant Protector Somerset. Of the three, Hall probably knew More personally, though not intimately, and Whittinton may have had some acquaintance-ship.

Both Hall and Robinson were baffled by what seemed to them the paradox of such a sensible person refusing to follow the King's lead. They were not the last to be bewildered. In his *Great Englishmen of the Sixteenth Century* (1904), Sir Sidney Lee expressed his surprise that an enlightened scholar died "for what seems, in the dry light of reason, to be superstition". This perplexity, going back to More's own day, and shown by some historians today, is a failure to understand that his religious faith was the beginning and the end for him; it informed his whole life and gave meaning to the great decision he had to make. For us, the problem is why only he and John Fisher, among the leading men of the country, "stood against all the realm in their opinion", to quote Hall. A consideration of this is outside our present purpose, though it stands in the background like a gigantic question mark.

Robert Whittinton noted More's "gentleness, lowliness, affability". These were well-chosen terms for which the records supply ample justification. One testimony may be given as it came within the personal experience of William Roper.

"This Sir Thomas More, among all other his virtues, was of

4Lupton's *Utopia*, p. 17.

such meekness that if it had fortuned him with any learned men resorting to him from Oxford, Cambridge or elsewhere, as there did divers, some for desire of his acquaintance, some for the famous report of his wisdom and learning, and some for suits of the universities, to have entered into argument, wherein few were comparable unto him, and so far to have discoursed with them therein that he might perceive they could not without some inconvenience hold out much further disputation against him; then, least he should discomfort them, as he that sought not his own glory, but rather would seem conquered than to discourage students in their studies, ever shewing himself more desirous to learn than to teach, then would he by some witty device courteously break off into some other matter, and give over."

Beatus Rhenanus used almost the same terms in describing Erasmus: "in society polite and genial, without any air of superiority, always truly amiable". Neither of them was always "gentle" in controversy, but it was a rough age and we must not import into it the manners of ours, though even today a paper-controversy can be astonishingly scant of courtesy.

Each of these three witnesses mentioned wit and learning as characteristics of Thomas More. So also were they of Erasmus, but distinctions can be made. Many instances of their wit have been given in these pages and it would be possible to compile a large More-Erasmus anthology of their wit. The point need not be laboured. It is, however, interesting to see how each used his wit and sense of humour. More was noted for his jests and merry-making; "merry" was a favourite word; he even seems to have enjoyed that lower form of humour, the practical joke. It was this irresistible impulse that Hall probably had in mind when he chided More for his "mocks". He felt that a Lord Chancellor should take life very seriously at all times and not risk his dignity by making jokes. When More took up his pen, his humour was expressed in the tales he loved to tell and also in the irony that found expression in his earlier work but less frequently in his later work. The irony, for instance, in the Second Book of *Utopia* often escapes those solemn readers who search it for a coherent political philosophy. In reading More one has to be intellectually on the alert. The love of Lucian he shared with Erasmus in their earlier years was in part their enjoyment of the satire and irony of the dialogues, and this influenced their own writing. It was shown in More's *Epigrams* where his words were sometimes more biting than in anything he wrote in after years. It was the mood of that early letter to John Colet[5] which was written at a time when More and Lily were competing in translations from the Greek Anthology; it was a young man's mood and he outgrew it.

Erasmus went on to give his genius full play and it can be seen in the last *Colloquy* he wrote just as it found its first full expression in *Praise of Folly*. Some of the indiscretions of which he was accused were outcomes of an impulse he found it difficult to curb. He had his bugbears such as the monks and friars, but he used his talent mainly in ridiculing, or mocking, as Hall would say, the shortcomings and abuses of the Church; in that he followed a long line of predecessors but he did it with such mastery that he surpassed them all in effectiveness. More did not follow him in this; he was content to leave it to such an incomparable performer. It was probably from Colet that More learned to denounce the abuses of the day, but when the time came for him to enter controversy, he found that the defence of the clergy, however culpable they were, had become the more urgent duty. He grew with the times and changed his tactics to meet new situations. Erasmus, to some extent, failed to realise the full seriousness of the Lutheran challenge to the Church when it passed from denouncing abuses to framing new doctrines; he deplored the tumult of discordant and conflicting voices, but to him it was all a nuisance that could soon be corrected if only men would talk it all over quietly, which was the last thing they were likely to do.

This difference of approach was in some measure due to the circumstances of their lives. From the age of forty, Thomas More was fully engaged in public affairs—as councillor and magistrate, on embassies and in Parliament, and as the holder of important

[5] See above, p. 37.

offices of state. Reluctant as he was to enter such a career, there must have been in his nature the urge to be active in the world of men; it was his own recognition of this fact that made him forgo the cloister. His reluctance to enter the King's service was also due to a pull in another direction, the life of the scholar. His learning was gained largely in his earlier years; it was considerable as all acknowledged, but it inevitably lacked the depth that was possible to Erasmus. More's close contact with practical needs and with government policy may explain why he so quickly saw the true danger of Lutheranism, the danger of schism. Erasmus was far from being the proverbial scholar whose world is bounded by the book-lined walls of his study. He was constantly on the move; as he travelled up and down the Rhine, or across the Channel, or over the Alps, he met men of all ranks of society, and his *Colloquies* show how closely he observed them. He had not, however, been called upon to take part in practical politics, for his Imperial councillorship was all-but nominal; nor had he experience of administration; nor had he ever had to handle men. He lacked too one of Thomas More's outstanding characteristics, his percipience, which even the most experienced office-holder may lack.

Erasmus had taken his positions quite early in life; we can find the roots of his later opinions in his first writings. These ideas developed, so to speak, within themselves, or, it would be more correct to say, they deepened, but he did not venture outside or beyond them. One statement of his will illustrate this point. It was made in a letter written in 1519. Luther had just begun to disturb men's minds, but he had not yet published his three explosive pamphlets.

"In my opinion", Erasmus wrote, "many might be reconciled to the Church of Rome if, instead of everything being defined, we were content with what is evidently set forth in the Scriptures or is necessary to salvation. And these things are few in number, and the fewer the easier for many to accept. Nowadays out of one article we make six hundred, some of which are such that men might be ignorant of them or doubt them without injury to piety. It is in human nature to cling

tooth and nail to what has once been defined. The sum of the
philosophy of Christ lies in this—that we should know that all
our hope is placed in God, who freely gives us all things through
his son Jesus; that by his death we are redeemed; that we are
united to his body in baptism in order that, dead to the desires
of the world, we may so follow his teaching and example as
not only not to admit of evil, but also to deserve well of good;
that if adversity comes upon us we should bear it in the hope
of the future reward which is in store for all good men at the
coming of Christ. Thus we should always be progressing from
virtue to virtue, and whilst assuming nothing to ourselves,
ascribe all that is good to God. If there should be any who would
inquire into the Divine nature, or the nature of Christ, or
abstruse points about the sacraments, let him do so; only let
him not try to force his views upon others. Many definitions
lead to differences. Nor should we be ashamed to reply to
some questions, 'God knows how this should be so, it is enough
for me to believe it is'. I know that the pure blood and body of
Christ are to be taken purely by the pure, and that he wished
it to be a sacred sign and pledge both of his love to us and of
fellowship of Christians among themselves. Let me therefore
examine myself to see whether there be anything in me
inconsistent with Christ, whether there be any difference
between me and my neighbour. As to the rest, how the same
body can exist in so small a form and in so many places at once,
such questions, in my opinion, can hardly tend to the increase of
piety. I know that I shall rise again, for this was promised to
all by Christ, who was the first who rose from the dead. As to
the questions, with what body, and how it can be the same
after having gone through so many changes, though I do not
disapprove of these matters being inquired into in moderation
on suitable occasions, yet it conduces very little to piety to
spend too much labour upon them. Nowadays men's minds are
diverted by these and innumerable other subtleties, from things
of vital importance. Lastly it would tend greatly to the estab-
lishment of concord, if secular princes, and especially the
Roman Pontiff, would abstain from all tyranny and avarice.
For men easily revolt when they see preparations for enslaving
them, when they see that they are not to be invited to piety
but caught for plunder. If they saw that we were innocent

R

and desirous to do them good, they would very readily accept our faith."

That rather long passage states the position from which Erasmus never moved in spite of the rapid spread of Lutheranism and its progeny. The message he had to give was sharply relevant to the times. The teaching of Christ had become veiled by the over-refinements of dialectics, and by the undue emphasis put on popular devotions, on the veneration of relics, on pilgrimages, on indulgences, and other adventitious aids; added to this was the weakening in the spiritual fervour and discipline of some monks and friars and seculars. "Back to the sources" was a salutary precept. The teaching of Erasmus can be seen as one effect of his training by the Brethren of the Common Life; it was to be strengthened under the influence of John Colet and shared with such friends as Thomas More.

We can admire Erasmus' consistency in this mission—for such it was to him—and, indeed, the courage with which he kept to his chosen path, but there must always be a lingering regret that he failed to answer to the changing needs of what was a revolutionary era. Yet, when he gave the world so much, it is ungracious to complain that he did not do something else. Towards the end of his life he said, "There is nothing I congratulate myself on more heartily than on never having joined a sect". Perhaps that is the best comment.

Thomas More had to meet a specific situation. His own religious experience meant an inexorable opposition to Lutheranism in all its forms, and when his bishop called upon him to counteract the spread of its English expression by William Tyndale, he took up his pen in the conviction that he was defending eternal truth. It was this immediate need that compelled him to take a definite stand against heresy. We cannot know whether he would have embarked on the sea of controversy had it not been for Tunstall's request; his letters to Dorp and to a monk suggest that he could not have kept silent when the full impact of Tyndale's propaganda was experienced. Erasmus was not faced with such an imperative need. Round him were several factions in internecine conflict. Luther had withdrawn to his own fortress; the enemy now had several names, each a leader of a sect as bitterly opposed to the other sects as all were to Rome. Erasmus tried to calm them down, but it was a hopeless task. His protest was to remove himself from Basle, an action that proclaimed his unshakeable loyalty to the Catholic Church.

One characteristic of More noted by Whittinton shows true perception: "sometime of a sad gravity". That is the Thomas More of Holbein's portrait. There is nothing contradictory in the union of a cheerful, laughing disposition with a deep seriousness; indeed, it is the man who is not sure of the meaning of life who is apt to be moody and capricious. The portraits of Erasmus by Holbein give a hint of his quizzical spirit, but here, too, is revealed the earnestness that was at the basis of his work. Dürer's drawing and engraving emphasize the seriousness, while the early portrait by Metsys reveals a gentler disposition. It is fitting that the three artists should have stressed different aspects of a man of such complex nature.

John Colet, Thomas More and Erasmus are usually called Christian Humanists. How one wishes such terms had never been invented! This kind of convenient shorthand can mislead; it is simpler to study the individual cases and discard labels. John Colet went to Italy but he did not study Greek there. Erasmus was forty years old when he went to Italy, and he later declared that he took almost as much Greek to Italy as he brought away. His gain was in seeing something of a civilization very different from that in which he had matured, and in meeting leading scholars and ecclesiastics; above all he had the opportunity to read manuscripts hitherto out of his reach; to this should be added, and it is by no means the least important, the first-hand knowledge he gained of the craft of printing. Thomas More did not go to Italy, and Erasmus regretted this fact. In his *Utopia* letter of 1517 to Froben he wrote,

> "What would not such marvellous natural gifts have accomplished, if his intellect had been trained in Italy; if it were wholly devoted to literature; if it had had time to ripen to its proper harvest, its own autumn? While quite young, he amused

himself with composing epigrams, many of them written when he was a mere boy. He has never gone out of his native Britain, save once or twice, when acting as ambassador for his sovereign in the Netherlands.[6] He is married, and has the cares of a family; he has the duties of a public office to discharge, and is immersed in the business of the law-courts; with so many important affairs of state distracting him besides, that you would wonder at his having leisure even to think of books."[7]

Erasmus often pointed out that in some classical authors was to be found an emphasis on moral virtues from which Christians could profit. It should be repeated that for the three friends the writings of the Early Fathers were more important than those of the classical authors. Apart from his early translations the signs of his classical learning are not prominent in More's writings, but his knowledge of the Fathers is impressive. In his letter to William Gonnell, he stipulated that his children should read the works of St Augustine and St Jerome. Colet, as we have seen, had some doubts about the classical authors, but Erasmus all his life drew upon them to point his arguments.

When we attempt to estimate the after-influence of the two friends, we are again dealing in imponderables, and all that can be done is to give some indications.

Erasmus' two books, the *Adages* and the *Colloquies*, continued to be printed for more than a century after his death and his ideas therefore continued to influence several generations of students and readers even if they used the books solely for instructional purposes. The *Colloquies* had the longer life; thus Roger L'Estrange made a translation of twenty dialogues in 1680 and these have frequently been reprinted. Nathan Bailey's translation of the whole, first published in 1733, has also been reprinted several times.[8] This is not to say that the rest of Erasmus' work has

---

[6]Erasmus may not have known of More's flying visit to Paris and Louvain about 1507.
[7]Lupton's *Utopia*, p. lxxviii. Lupton suggested that Erasmus was thinking that More's Latin style would have profited by Italian experience. Of this style, he remarks, "As a rule, it is fluent and vigorous, with a great command of vocabulary. But it has not the elegance of Erasmus, and it shows the same tendency as appears in the author's English writings, to run off into inordinately long sentences."
[8]See also *Ten Colloquies of Erasmus*, trans. by C. R. Thompson (1957).

dropped into oblivion.[9] His *Complaint of Peace*, the *Praise of Folly*, and the *Enchiridion* have all been reprinted during this century. The monumental edition of the correspondence to which P. S. Allen devoted himself made available to scholars a mass of information that revealed new aspects of Erasmus' life and character. His letters have never been neglected, but they had previously to be read in the third volume of the collected edition of 1703. Nothing, however, that Erasmus wrote has stood the test of time as *Utopia* has done; yet, if influence could be assessed, it would surely be found that Erasmian ideas have had a greater effect on men's way of thinking than even *Utopia* has had. This influence was in spite of the disfavour of the authorities of the Roman Catholic Church. All the works of Erasmus were put on the Index in 1559, though they have since been removed. The attitude of Thomas Stapleton (1535-1598) was typical of his generation of apologists. In his *Tres Thomae* the nearest he came to a criticism of Thomas More was to regret that his friendship with Erasmus had not been broken. Nor has this mistrust died out.

It is difficult to trace the influence of More's controversial works. The public denunciation of him and of John Fisher must have hindered their circulation, and while Henry VIII was alive it was dangerous even to mention his two victims. The *Dialogue Concerning Heresies*, published six years before More's death and of which a revised edition was printed, had the best chance of affecting opinion during his lifetime especially as it was such a readable book and came nearer than his later writings to the need that Tunstall expressed, for something that ordinary folk would read. It may have rescued some who were being drawn towards the teaching of Tyndale. With the accession of Edward VI in 1547, men felt at liberty to mention Thomas More. The publication of Robinson's translation of *Utopia* is an indication of this. A more interesting example is to be found in a sermon by Hugh Latimer, the same Dr Latimer who was "very merry" at Lambeth

---

[9]One finds references to Erasmus' books in unlikely places, as, for example: "27th (Lord's day) January 1667 . . . reading Erasmus *De Scribendis Epistolis*, a very good book, especially one letter of advice to a courtier most true and good, which made me once resolve to tear out the two leaves that it was writ on, but I forbore it". *Diary of Samuel Pepys*.

when More refused the oath. In a sermon preached on 10 March 1550 before the King and the court, Latimer said, "And here by the way I will tell you a merry tale. Master More was once sent in commission into Kent." He then related the story of Sandwich Haven and Tenterden church steeple from the *Dialogue against Heresies*.[10]

During the reign of Mary Tudor it was possible to print the *Dialogue of Comfort* (1553) and the *English Works* (1557). When Elizabeth came to the throne More's Latin works were printed abroad (Basle, 1563; Louvain, 1565), and the *Dialogue of Comfort* was reprinted in Antwerp (1573). More's prayers, written in the Tower, were included in Fr Robert Person's *Manual of Prayers* (Rouen, 1583) which quickly gained popularity; these prayers became part of the devotions of English Catholics, though few may have known their origin. All this time *Richard III* could be read in the Chronicles.

Thomas Stapleton's *Tres Thomae* came out in 1588. A Spanish life of More was published in Seville in 1592. Roper's life was published in 1626 with the false imprint of Paris; it was in fact printed at the English College, St Omer, where Roper was regarded as one of their benefactors. Cresacre More's well-known biography came out soon afterwards.

We have seen how a group of Elizabethan playwrights wrote a play which was not acted; the manuscript has the superscription, *The Booke of Sir Thomas Moore*; the legend was being built up. It would be possible to trace how the fame of Thomas More was cherished through the centuries, not only in this country, but in Europe, and culminated in the canonization of 1935. One example of the European legend must suffice. It was recorded by William Blundell during the Civil Wars of the seventeenth century. He was a staunch Catholic and Royalist who had to suffer much as a recusant.

"A Colonel of Parliament", he wrote, "told me that beyond the seas it is reported of England that it produceth but one wise man in an age, and that people gaze on him awhile as a monster and then cut his off his head. 'So', said he, 'did they ;with Sir Thomas More and the Earl of Strafford.' "[11]

[10]Book IV, ch. 14. More did not say that it was his own experience. I have not been able to find that he was appointed to such a commission. The story presents one difficulty: Tenterden is about forty miles west of Sandwich.

[11]*Cavalier*, by Margaret Blundell (1933), p. 7. The date of the entry is not given.

This fame was not the prerogative of Catholics. Such a firm Protestant as Dean Swift could declare that "More was the person of the greatest virtue these islands ever produced". Probably few could have given the reasons for the execution of Thomas More. Why then has he captured such universal admiration? The answer is not *Utopia*; the perennial attraction of that book keeps his name in men's minds, but the authorship of a classic does not always mean that the author himself wins a place in popular regard. The fact that More dared to defy a King, and accepted death rather than betray his conscience, gave him a high place in history, but he was not the first nor the last to sacrifice all for a principle. Without ranging over the centuries, we can note the example of John Fisher who died for the same cause. Yet Fisher's name is all but unknown in popular esteem. Here we come to the heart of the matter. Fisher remains, as a person, a shadowy figure; we know a great deal about his public life; we know that he was a friend of More and Erasmus; but it is difficult to imagine oneself in his company. By contrast Thomas More has always been a real person, a companionable man. Anecdotes about him and his sayings were in circulation during his lifetime and they entered the common memory of folk. Until the publication of Roper's little book in 1626, nearly a century after his death, there was no printed record in English to keep his name alive; it was, and the word must be repeated, a popular,[12] verbal tradition, and the more one thinks about it, the more extraordinary it seems. Roper followed by Cresacre More turned the folk-tales into fact. The emphasis throughout the years was on Thomas More, the man; the laughter-loving father of a close-knit family; the upright judge—that was always part of the portrait—, a man of learning and wisdom; a good man. All that has been revealed since by the State Papers, by the renewed study of his works and by the devoted labours of scholars, has continued to add to his stature and renown. And with his name will always be linked that of Erasmus Roterodamus.

---

[12]One might almost say, canonization by popular acclamation, as in early centuries. About 1660, the Protestant John Aubrey wrote, "Methinks 'tis strange that all this time he is not canonized, for he merited highly of the church".

See page 63

Index

E = Erasmus. M = More.

DATE DUE

NOV 1 '66	DEC 10 '68	OC 27 '79	
NOV 19 '66	MAR 12 '69	NO 12 '79	
NOV 22 '66	MAR 26 '69	NO 20 '80	
DEC 12 '66	APR 9 '69	AP 19 '83	
DEC 14 '66	OCT 7 '69	NO 9 '83	
SEP 28 '67	OCT 21 '69	APR 15 '85	
OCT 14 '67	NOV 3 '69	DEC 3 '86	
NOV 7 '67	NOV 19 '69		
NOV 13 '67	DEC 2 '69		
NOV 21 '67	NOV 16 '70		
	NOV 17 '71		
MAR 4 '68	FEB 16 '72		
MAR 18 '68	OCT 26 '72		
APR 6 '68	NOV 14 '72		
OCT 10 '68	MAR 12 '73		
OCT 29 '68	SEP 24 '73		
NOV 25 '68	NOV 14 '73		
DEC 4 '68	NOV 27 '73		